Kiss

of

Death

Kiss
of
Death

True Cases of
Fatal Attraction

Jean Ritchie

Michael O'Mara Books Limited

First published in Great Britain in 2020 by
Michael O'Mara Books Limited
9 Lion Yard
Tremadoc Road
London SW4 7NQ

A CIP catalogue record for this book is available from the British Library.

Papers used by Michael O'Mara Books Limited are natural, recyclable products made from wood grown in sustainable forests. The manufacturing processes conform to the environmental regulations of the country of origin.

ISBN: 978-1-78929-229-9 in paperback print format
ISBN: 978-1-78929-230-5 in ebook format

1 2 3 4 5 6 7 8 9 10

Cover design by Natasha Le Coultre
Designed and typeset by Design23
Printed and bound by CPI Group (UK) Ltd, Croydon, CR0 4YY

www.mombooks.com

MIX
Paper from
responsible sources
FSC® C020471
FSC
www.fsc.org

Contents

Introduction

EVERYONE FEARS DEATH AT THE HAND OF A STRANGER, THE FLASH of a knife in a dark alley, the deranged killer, the sadistic rapist who murders to conceal his crimes. But the truth is women are far more likely to be killed by their husbands, partners, lovers or ex-lovers than by a stranger. It is the person you know intimately who is the one who administers the lethal blow, the staged accident, the poison in the favourite meal or even hires a hitman. Murder is not only very rare, for women the most common form is domestic.

Men, too, are killed by their spouses, but for young men in particular death is more likely in a fight outside a pub or club than at the hands of a vengeful lover. That does not mean women don't kill: they do, and when they do it is most likely to be someone they have been involved with, romantically and sexually.

Jealousy, possessiveness, feelings of rejection, the need to get an ex-partner out of the way for financial reasons or to free the killer for a new life are the motives that impel crimes of passion. Love spawns some of the greatest higher feelings, but it also leads to the most debased acts of vengeance.

There's nothing new about fatal attraction: history is full of murders primed by tortured jealousy. This book is a compilation of some of the most intriguing and shocking cases.

1

The Giggling Blonde

WHEN THE SMALL BLONDE WITH THE WIDE SMILE AND TWINKLING eyes walked into the pub, heads turned. More than one man who met her described the flirtatious Dena as a dead ringer for the *Carry On* star Barbara Windsor: cuddly, sexy, with a great sense of fun. She found it easy to attract men, and once hooked they were devoted to her. She in turn seemed to be devoted to them, giggling at their jokes, deferring, keeping her blue eyes fixed only on them. They walked out of the bar with their arms protectively round her shoulder, instantly head over heels in love with a woman who appeared to feel the same. They could not believe their luck.

But the really lucky ones were those who did not fall under the spell of Dena Thompson. The men who succumbed to her charms believed her string of implausible lies, blind to the fact she was defrauding them and would leave their lives in ruins. And when one of them began to suspect her unravelling fantasies, she killed him.

So did Dena have a bad start in life? Not at all. Life started uneventfully. She was raised in Hendon, north London, by her father, Michael, a former prison officer, and her mother, Margaret. She was good at gymnastics, left school with ten GCSEs and started work at the Halifax Building Society. She met her first husband, Lee Wyatt, an electrician, when she was twenty-two, on a blind date arranged by Lee's cousin, Bob. They set up home in a modern three-bedroom house in Lancing, a seaside town in West Sussex, married in a register office on 12 October 1984, and their son Darren was born in 1987.

So far so normal, but Dena had dreams of making a fortune. She and Lee set up a business, Denalee Crafts, which made and distributed soft toys. Lee was the salesman while Dena, now at the Woolwich Building Society, doubled as a seamstress in the evenings and at weekends. Dena's plan was to create a toy that would become a character in cartoon films, attracting lucrative franchising deals. The problem was as soon as she thought of something it became a reality to her, so when she and Lee dreamed up a cuddly, little leprechaun with a bushy, white beard, which they named Sean the Leprechaun, she was immediately telling everyone stories of the immense wealth their lucky leprechaun was providing.

Dena had a vivid imagination and the ability to convince those around her. She claimed to have had an approach from the Irish airline Aer Lingus, which wanted to give a Sean toy to every first-class passenger. There was no such approach. She claimed to have a multi-million-pound contract with the Disney Corporation in America, which wanted exclusive rights. There was no such contract. But Lee, who was completely in thrall to his wife, believed her. He also believed her when she said that the mafia were after him, as the front man of the business, because they wanted a substantial cut of the huge Disney contract. They had, she told him, set hired assassins on him. Her imagination fleshed out her lies: the assassins, she said, were a group known as The G-Men.

When the business went bust, Lee briefly worked at a hotel in nearby Brighton, but all the time living in fear of his life. It was at this time, when Dena's dreams of a fortune were dashed, that she started defrauding her employers, the Woolwich Building Society. She set up an account under the name of Christina Duke and siphoned more than £26,000 into it from other accounts.

Before this came to light, the family moved in 1991 to Yapton village, 16 miles away, and closer to Dena's job. With Lee still terrified and convinced that his wife and son were also in peril, Dena persuaded him that the safest thing for them all was for him to disappear. Amazingly, so in thrall to her was he that he did. He also believed her when she said they'd be even safer if they divorced, in order to confuse The G-Men, and she served papers on him just before he left home. He went on the run for the next three years, living as a vagrant, sometimes sleeping rough on park benches and even a bowling green. He changed his name and created a new identity, using the same method outlined in Frederick Forsyth's bestselling novel *The Day of the Jackal*, and under the new persona of Colin Mitchell he found a job in an amusement arcade 300 miles away in Newquay, Cornwall.

The distance did not lessen the hold she had over him, and although colleagues at the arcade found him easy to get on with and sociable, he was phoning Dena when he could, and every time she strengthened his fears with stories of sinister encounters with The G-Men. Dena also hatched a plot to cover her fraud at the Woolwich; she dictated a series of letters to Lee, which he dutifully wrote and sent to her, worded as if he was threatening her and telling her he was on the run with the mythical Christina Duke, and demanding that Dena get them money. He also made phone calls, which she recorded, in which he threatened her. These calls, carefully scripted by Dena, were, she told him, to deflect heat from the assassins away from her and their son.

Lee was living very frugally in a flat above the amusement arcade, paying his wages directly into Dena's bank account to help support her and Darren. What Lee did not realize, as he struggled with his lonely new life, still afraid that The G-Men would catch up with him, was that Dena, too, had a new life. He later said: 'She lives a life of lies and fantasy and I was the mug who went along with her lies.' But he was far from the only mug.

With her husband conveniently out of the way, Dena's love life took off. A succession of different men passed through her clutches in the next few years, all of them victims who lost money to her, but by far the most tragic was Julian Webb, who lost a lot more than money. After making him her second, bigamous, husband, Dena killed him.

She met Julian Webb in 1991. He was an advertising executive for a local newspaper, popular with colleagues, had a loving family and friends through his hobbies of body-building and sea angling. The pretty, vivacious new lover soon put paid to much of his previous life and friendships, and like Lee before him, he became slavishly devoted to her. He even put her forward to model for a makeover that the paper was running with local companies, and she loved every minute of the attention.

Within six months of meeting, they were married. Although Dena had served divorce papers on Lee she had never gone through with it, and was legally still married, a small matter she chose to forget. Julian's mother, Rosemary, a school teacher, was shocked by the speed by which her son's new relationship was progressing.

'The first time I met her, she and Julian told me they were getting married. I was taken aback at the speed. He only met her in May, and this was August,' Rosemary said. They married that November and went to Florida on honeymoon, Dena falling in love with the sunshine and the lifestyle. Florida would provide a regular backdrop for her life of cruel deception.

Back home, the neighbours in Yapton were confused: Pete and

Jackie Howells, who lived next door, had met Lee briefly before he disappeared, and yet now here was Dena getting married to Julian. Their window ledge was covered with wedding cards. And they soon realized that Julian was not the only man in her life, as they saw other men coming and going. Dena had to move quickly on more than one occasion if Julian arrived home for lunch unexpectedly.

Her fraud at the Woolwich had now been discovered and was being investigated, and Dena knew she would be sacked. She covered this up by telling Julian she was terminally ill, and that she was losing her job for having to have so much time off work. He was devastated and told colleagues he believed her employers were behaving appallingly. Terminal illness became a recurring ruse Dena perfected over the years to tie her lovers to her side.

Meanwhile, Dena used the fictional threatening letters and calls from Lee to make Julian believe there was a dangerous ex-husband stalking her. She even told her neighbours that once, when Lee re-appeared, desperate to see her and his son again, he had attacked and raped her. The police were called and she repeated the allegations; now Lee really *was* a wanted man – not by the fictitious G-Men but by the police.

Like others who would come after him, Julian believed in Dena's plans that they would start a new life together in Florida, but at some point detectives think he was beginning to see through her layers of compulsive lies. Their idyllic life was starting to unravel, and then Julian discovered the truth, including the fact that she had married him bigamously. Dena had a problem. She could not dispose of Julian quite as easily as Lee. So she took more drastic action.

On Julian's thirty-first birthday, in June 1994, his mother rang to wish him many happy returns. Dena answered the phone and told Rosemary her son was ill, and had been ill for two days, too poorly to open his birthday cards or presents. She said he had had 'too much sun', which Rosemary thought odd because Julian, who spent hours by the sea angling, was careful about exposure. She also said he had been drinking heavily, which again was quite out of character. Rosemary rang her three times during the course of the day, hoping to speak to her son and begging Dena to call a doctor.

At 1.20 a.m. the next morning Pete and Jackie Howells were woken by frantic hammering on their door. Dena told them Julian had stopped breathing and that she had called an ambulance. When the ambulance arrived they confirmed Julian was dead, and had been dead for a couple of hours, despite Dena saying she had been speaking with him just minutes earlier. Jackie, concerned for Dena, put an arm around her and asked what had happened, and Dena told her Julian had taken some pills. She was already telling different stories about his death, and the stories would proliferate the more people she talked to.

'I knew, when I saw the police, I just knew Julian had died before I spoke to them,' said Rosemary, who was convinced that Dena was in some way responsible.

Despite losing her husband in the early hours of the morning, Dena wasted no time going to see his boss at the newspaper office to claim his £36,000 death-in-service benefit, turning up the same day. She was described as 'cold and unemotional' when she inquired about the money, and was later furious when it all went to Rosemary who had been able to prove that Dena's marriage to Julian was bigamous. Julian's mother, having established herself as next of kin, insisted that Julian was buried near her home on Hayling Island, among the family graves: Dena had wanted to have him cremated. The relationship between the two women was acrimonious, with little sign that Dena was grieving for the husband she had lost.

At the funeral Dena wore a black leather mini-skirt and a black blouse, and waved cheerfully to the Howells as she set off for the church. The atmosphere was fraught, with Dena sitting on her own while Julian's friends, family and colleagues packed the other side of the aisle. According to one of Julian's work colleagues, 'There were some lovely wreaths, but Dena's flowers looked as if they had been gathered from round the cemetery, and were wrapped in brown paper. The note said: "To Julian, because you loved me so much." Which struck me as odd.'

At the inquest into his death, the coroner commented there was no evidence that Julian had taken an accidental overdose of the anti-depressant dothiepin and aspirin found in his body, and recorded an open verdict, which means there is simply not enough evidence to give a cause of death. Outside the court, the police said they had no evidence to suggest the death was suspicious. But Julian's mother, Rosemary, was not the only one to feel that there was definitely something suspicious about her son's sudden death, just over four years after he had first met Dena.

Dena was now single again, and touting for business, i.e. innocent dupes who would fund her lifestyle with their credit cards. She put ads in Lonely Hearts columns, and neighbours again saw a procession of men going in and out of her house. Her next 'serious' lover was an old colleague, Robert Waite, who had worked with her back in the early eighties when she was at the Halifax in north London. He received a message from her inviting him to a reunion, and when he rang she invited him round for dinner.

At first, he said, he was shocked to find she had lost her sparkle, but when she told him that her first husband beat her up and stalked her, and her second husband had died (this time she said from an overdose of steroids), he felt sorry for her. This, compounded by the fact that she said she was being treated for terminal cancer of the kidney, and had just weeks to live, convinced Robert he should look after her, and he agreed they would travel to Florida, her favourite place, where she wanted to be when she died, being cared for by him.

But, after a few days in the sunshine, she abandoned him, using the pretext that she had to fly to New York to be a witness in a court case involving the mafia. Robert discovered she had cleaned out every penny that he had, and, after waiting for her to reappear, he was eventually, and humiliatingly, arrested for not paying bills at the motel and deported back to Britain.

There was no prospect of Dena returning to him in Florida because she was now back in Britain, facing a court charge for the theft of £26,000 from the Woolwich. Her efforts to shift the blame on to her first husband, Lee, using the letters she dictated and the scripted phone calls she recorded, came unstuck when Lee was tracked down by the police. He was initially charged, but he had an alibi: he had been working at the amusement arcade. Dena was convicted and sentenced to eighteen months in prison.

While she was inside, Robert went straight to her house in Yapton, angry and confused by what she had done, and wanting an explanation of what had happened to his money and possessions. The neighbour, Jackie Howells, broke the news that Dena was in jail for theft and was not terminally ill or involved in a court case in New York. Yes, Robert had lost out financially and was left penniless, and he had endured the trauma of being treated like a criminal in the States, but at least he had escaped with his life.

To the surprise of many of the neighbours, when Dena was released after serving half of her sentence, she returned to the house in Yapton, and resumed her previous 'career': meeting men, entrancing them, then relieving them of all their money. Police later identified at least a dozen men who had had encounters with her, and they believe there are probably many more too embarrassed to come forward.

Graham Binks' story was typical. They met through a lonely hearts ad, and she moved in with him a week later. She told him she was dying of cancer and took him on an all-expenses-paid trip to Orlando, Florida, claiming she was a successful businesswoman. But guess what? Graham paid for the trip himself: she had stolen his credit card and ran up a debt of £4,400 on it.

Phil Trott was another victim. A landscape gardener, he was thrilled when the new sexy lady in his life also offered him a fantastic career break: she claimed to have a wealthy friend in Florida who would give him a lucrative contract to redesign her garden. In preparation for going out there, the couple toured stately homes, looking for garden ideas and indulging in Dena's taste for sex in the fresh air. For Phil it was a 'fun, carefree relationship'.

Then one night she appeared to be coughing up blood – there was blood in her hand – and she told Phil she had cancer of the throat. She used this as an excuse to postpone the trip to Florida. But when Phil found his credit cards in her bag, and money missing from his account, it dawned on him that things she had said did not add up. He accused her of being a fake, and he changed the locks on his home, breaking off contact with her. Again, he is one of the lucky ones because his time with Dena only cost him money.

Shortly afterwards Richard Thompson, a divorced telecoms manager, spotted a lonely hearts ad by a 'bubbly blonde'. Soon he was under her spell. She told him she was a college teacher and an antiques dealer, and that she had terminal breast and ovarian cancer. Again, like previous lovers she duped, he wanted to stand by her and look after her, and the couple arranged to get married at a Holiday Inn in Florida. For Richard it was a happy day, although the friends whom Dena said would join them as witnesses failed to show up, and hotel staff had to step in.

Back home from their honeymoon, Dena persuaded Richard to take early retirement to start a new life in Florida, convincing him he could fulfil a dream running a charter boat company with her in the Florida Keys. She used the £36,000 from his pension payout to spruce up his cottage near Littlehampton, West Sussex, telling him that they could rent it out while they were abroad. She also persuaded him to take out a building society loan for more work on the property, to be paid off, she said, with a £300,000 National Lottery win she claimed to have. She said there was a delay in accessing the money because it was in a Jersey bank.

Richard gave her £3000 for the deposit on a house in Florida, but she instead used the money to pay off a bill on a credit card she had set up in his name. Furthermore, she promised that a contact would get Richard a job when they arrived in Florida, but then explained that the contact was temporarily unavailable because – never settling for a routine excuse – he was now working undercover for the FBI.

When the move to Florida grew closer, Richard took a course in deep-sea fishing to prepare for their new business venture, and Dena told him his green card (the documentation needed to work in the States) would be delivered the next day. She then offered him, by way of celebration, a surprise. After first shutting their German Shepherd dog away in another room, Richard allowed himself to be tied up naked and a towel placed over his face as he lay on the floor of the bathroom, anticipating a sex game. But Richard heard rustling noises coming from the bedroom and a sixth sense told him something was not right. He had just wriggled his hands free when Dena returned …

As he lay there she clubbed him hard on his head, twice, with a metal baseball bat, and plunged a carving knife into his shoulder. But when she slipped on the blood on the floor, he overpowered her, sticking his fingers in her eyes until she gave in. Dena broke down and admitted everything she had told him was a lie. Then she packed her bags and left.

Unable to take it all in, and reeling from the physical attack, it was not until the next day that Richard called the police, after an estate agent called round to take down the particulars of the house. This was the first that Richard knew that Dena had put his home up for sale. The estate agent was surprised to find Richard there because Dena had told him her husband had left to live in Florida. Richard suddenly understood. 'She was going to kill me, tell everyone I was in Florida, then live on the proceeds of selling my house,' he said. Then he discovered that she had been making inquiries about cashing in his £89,000 insurance policy.

Dena was arrested and charged with attempted murder. The charge, and Richard's allegations that she had stolen his money, coupled with her previous fraud conviction, prompted the police to start unravelling Dena's life, and they uncovered many more examples of her obtaining money by deception, fifteen of which they charged her with (seven involving Richard, and the others relating to former lovers), alongside the attempted murder charge.

When the case came up at Lewes Crown Court in August 2000, Dena pleaded that she had acted in self-defence when she hit and stabbed Richard, stating he had attacked her first when he discovered the truth about the money she had taken from him. She blackened his character and tried to make him out to be a violent man. She said she had not tried to kill him because 'I was going to leave him in America like I did with Robert Waite.'

Her version of events was that a row broke out over the move to America. In her defence in court she said: 'He was concerned about lack of money and when my lottery money was coming through. I admitted there was none, it was a lie and there was no America. He turned round and I realized he had a knife in his hand and he said he was going to kill me and came towards me. I picked up a baseball bat and hit him.'

She worked her charm on the jury and, to the disgust of everyone who knew her, was found not guilty of attempted murder. Richard called it 'a miscarriage of justice'. He added: 'Her skill was honing in on people's hopes and ambitions … It can make you blind to what was happening.' However, she couldn't wriggle out of the other charges though she tried to justify her behaviour, claiming she told Richard about the non-existent lottery money 'to get him to spend money on me, and lied about my health to make him like me more.'

Dena was sentenced to three years and nine months in prison for the fraud charges. Julian's mother was just one of those who felt justice had not been done in Richard's case, and even less so for her much-loved son. She began demanding that the police re-open the case against Dena over her son's death and, with the evidence of Dena's ruthless behaviour mounting, a re-investigation was announced. Julian's body was exhumed, but the new examination showed nothing more than was already known: he had a lethal amount of prescription drugs in his body.

Even so, circumstantial evidence against Dena was mounting. The more people the police interviewed, the more different stories they heard Dena had told about her husband's death: there were nine different versions of his last day. The most telling one contradicted others that he had not eaten for four days because she described how she had served him his favourite hot curry the night he died, the night of his thirty-first birthday. It was true that Julian liked hot curries, and it's easy to disguise the taste of a large number of the bitter-tasting anti-depressants in a very spicy vindaloo.

The witness who came forward with this crucial evidence was a fellow angler, American Don Hutson, who got to know Dena and Julian when they were out in Florida, talking about their 'new life' out there. After Julian's death, Dena told him her husband had taken sea sickness pills, anti-histamines and aspirin, and had a lot to drink, coupled with a hot curry. Always up for embellishing a story, she told Don her husband was taking steroids and was so overweight it took four paramedics to carry him downstairs to the ambulance. Don described his suspicions that Dena had killed Julian as 'off the scale'.

Coupled with evidence from neighbours that Dena and Julian had been heard rowing about money the day before he died, the police realized that, even if the evidence was circumstantial, there was enough to charge her with murder.

Dena was brought from prison for questioning, but insisted she could not remember much about her second husband's last day on earth. She stonewalled any attempt to get her to say more. She was charged, and came up at the Old Bailey in 2003. Her defence was that Julian was depressed and had killed himself.

Found guilty by a majority verdict, she was sentenced to life imprisonment with a recommendation that she serve a minimum of sixteen years. In the public gallery, stifled sobs were heard from Julian's family.

The devastation caused by Dena Thompson, dubbed The Black Widow, was summed up by the judge, who described her as 'one of the most fluent liars I have ever come across'. He said: 'You no doubt thought you would benefit financially from Mr Webb's death. What you did was utterly ruthless and without pity. Nothing can excuse you for the wickedness of what you did.'

After the case was over Rosemary Webb, Julian's mother, made a dignified statement:

> The circumstances surrounding his death have been a source of great pain to me and my family. Even now, only one person knows what really happened, and she is not saying. Those of us who knew Julian well know that he would never have committed suicide.
>
> There is never a day when he is not the first thought that I have when I awake. He was my only, much loved child but he was also a good friend … I cannot get out of my mind thoughts of what Julian might have gone through when he was denied access to all friends and family who tried to contact him. The woman who insisted he was ill refused to call a doctor. One thing is clear, his last day was very unpleasant.
>
> He will never come back but there are a lot of us for whom his memory will remain alive. Julian was a much loved, kind, loyal and friendly young man.

Rosemary described her son as a happy, straightforward man.

One of the policemen who finally brought Dena to justice, Detective Inspector Martin Underhill, said: 'This woman is every man's worst nightmare. For a decade she has degraded men sexually, financially and physically. Men across southern England can sleep safe knowing that she is off the streets. I for one am very glad that she is behind bars.'

Following her conviction, she was investigated over the disappearance of another man, Stoyan Kostov, a Bulgarian boyfriend she was involved with in her late teens, before she met her first husband, Lee. Stoyan vanished without trace, but despite suspicions the British police and Interpol found no evidence to link Dena to his unexplained disappearance.

In 2005, Dena's appeal against her sentence was rejected, and she was told she had to serve a minimum of sixteen years. She may now be starting on the preparation for her release within the next year or two.

2

Smiley Kylie

SHE WAS THE YOUNG WOMAN WHOSE WIDE SMILE EARNED HER THE nickname Smiley Kylie. To family, friends, her nursing colleagues and the patients whose lives she cheered with her broad grin, she was a tonic who lifted their spirits: always happy, always ready to have fun, brightening the day with her laughter. Then something happened that changed everything for Kylie, caught her up in a trail of bizarre and horrific fantasies, that ultimately cost her life. That something was a man called Paul Wilkinson.

Kylie Labouchardiere did not have the best start in life. Her parents divorced when she was five and her mother Carol married again, but her new husband was, according to Carol, 'very violent'. Kylie, the youngest of the three children, moved to live with her grandmother, Louisa Windeyer, who lived in Erina, in the Central Coast Region of New South Wales, about an hour's drive outside Sydney. Kylie lived with Louisa from the age of five until she left home at sixteen to train as a nurse, and she and her grandmother had a very close bond. She never lost contact with her mother, her sister Leanne and brother Michael, but her gran was her touchstone.

When Kylie was twenty-one she met Sean Labouchardiere in a restaurant in Melbourne, where Kylie was studying midwifery, and the pair clicked on that first night and swiftly fell in love. Like everyone else who knew Kylie in those days, Sean, who was in the Australian navy, recognized her as a caring and understanding person who wanted to help people through her job, who had a great sense of humour and was always smiling. They married within a year. 'I have never seen her looking more beautiful or happier than on the day she married,' her grandmother said, recalling a radiant bride with a smile on her face that never faded all day.

Sean had a good job, a regular income and he and Kylie shared dreams of a stable family life with children. They decided to move back to Sydney at the end of 2003, two years after they met, but from that moment things started to go wrong for them. Kylie was working at Sutherland Hospital, and it was there that she met a dark, handsome charmer, Paul Wilkinson, an Aboriginal Community Liaison Officer with the New South Wales police. He and Kylie had met before, socially, but it was when he was admitted as a patient that they first talked and got to know each other. Kylie was smitten, and in less than five months she would lose everything to him, including her life and the life of her unborn baby.

Paul was four years older than Kylie and was also married. He met his wife, Julie Thurecht, when she was studying at the Police Academy and he came to give a lecture on his work with the aboriginal community. Like Kylie, Julie was struck by his wit, charm and great sense of humour. He was a real ladies' man: another police cadet remembers being similarly bowled over by him, describing him as 'funny, witty, charming, attractive, intelligent'. She said he sent her a large number of explicit text messages, but she broke with him when she found out he was married and had no intention of leaving his pregnant wife.

Julie said that her relationship with him started well. 'We'd go out, we'd have fun. But I think once he had reeled me in, that's when his claws came out and things started to change. He became controlling and abusive. He'd say things to put me down and to make me feel worthless, and then it gradually escalated into physical abuse.'

Paul controlled what Julie wore, banning anything short or low-cut because, he claimed, other men would look at her. He badgered her to give up the police, arguing that all male police officers are 'sleazebags', and he wore her down so much that she agreed to abandon her dream career. She believes that he feared she'd have a better job than his. On their wedding day, Julie knew she had made a mistake. And after their son was born, Paul became even more controlling about where she went and what she wore. 'He had a shocking temper and hit me at times. I wasn't allowed to have any male friends and he tried to alienate me from a lot of my female friends.'

Paul found out that before he met her, Julie had had a very brief relationship with Geoff Lowe, another police officer. It was an unimportant, casual affair, and Geoff had also moved on and was now happily married, but for Paul his very existence became an obsession. To the astonishment and ultimate anguish of Geoff and his wife, Sue, it was an obsession that would threaten their lives and destroy almost everything they had.

In 2002, Geoff, by this time a sergeant, began to receive late night phone calls from a drunken and abusive male who called him a dog, threatened to cut his throat and accused him of being a rapist. At first Geoff put it down to his job: police officers can make enemies easily enough, and they get used to people disliking them. But one night the drunkard mentioned Julie's name, and for the first time Geoff put two and two together. He knew Paul Wilkinson was Julie's husband, and although he had never met him, he knew Paul worked as a liaison officer with the Force and had a reputation as a trouble-maker, getting thrown out of pubs and clubs for drunken behaviour.

'I think he wanted to be a cop and when that didn't happen, he basically went anti-cop,' Geoff said. He did not worry too much about the calls, and when he changed his mobile number the calls stopped and he never thought about them again.

Julie became pregnant soon after their marriage and in November 2003 gave birth to a little boy. At the time Paul seemed excited and proud, but to Julie's annoyance when he collected her from hospital instead of taking her home he took her to her parents' house, on the pretext that he wanted her to have a couple of weeks of being looked after as she settled in to new motherhood. Julie would have preferred to spend those precious days as a family unit, but Paul stayed in their home while she and the baby lived with her mum and dad.

Julie's parents noticed how in thrall to Paul she was – as her father said later: 'When Paul said "Jump", Julie said "How far?"' It seemed Julie was not allowed to do anything without Paul telling her, and it was at this stage that he started to ask Julie for money. She always gave in to his threats and gave him whatever she had, not knowing until much later that he was feeding a gambling habit, spending all the money he could get on poker games and running up big debts.

Julie's 'exile' coincided with Paul meeting Kylie, and in the end Julie spent five months living with her parents, during which time Paul kept up a sustained campaign to keep her away from her family home, where he was conducting a passionate affair with Kylie. He was creating a fantasy world that he was feeding to both women at the same time, with slight variations. Their stars had aligned in a terrible confluence that would have awful consequences for Julie, and a much worse fate for Kylie.

He told them both wild stories about his life being in danger from the police because he was a whistleblower. He was a convincing liar, and claimed he knew the truth behind the death of an aboriginal man that had sparked riots, and this made him a marked man. Both women were reeled in by the tales he embroidered.

For Kylie's husband, Sean, things started to go wrong with their marriage very soon after they arrived in Sydney. 'She started becoming very secretive,' he said. 'She became paranoid that someone was following her, people were after her. She cut her hair, she started smoking – and Kylie was very against smoking all the way through our courtship and marriage up to this point. Within a few weeks she was literally chain smoking.'

Sean watched her whole personality change, and she mysteriously claimed she was involved in something she could not get out of. When he offered to help, because at this stage he was desperate to get the marriage back on track, she said there was nothing he could do. She had told him about meeting Paul, whom she said was an undercover policeman, working for a specialist unit of the New South Wales Police. 'She said: "I can't tell you any more but he is working on special operations type things that may require my assistance from time to time." And I just thought that this couldn't be right. Surely the police aren't going to use civilians to do their operations.'

Sean decided that Paul was telling Kylie stories to win her over, and that she was getting caught up in his lies. But he could not reason with her. She and Paul were constantly texting one another, with Kylie sleeping with her phone next to her on the pillow. Throughout the night Sean would hear it beeping, and neither he nor Kylie were getting much sleep. In the five-month period that Kylie knew Paul, they exchanged 23,836 texts, which works out at one every ten minutes, night and day. She still denied she was having an affair with Paul, but her behaviour was becoming more and more erratic and her temper was constantly frayed. She was no longer Smiley Kylie; she was losing weight and looking ill.

On one occasion Sean remembered the phone ringing at about 2.30 a.m., and he heard Kylie say: 'I'll be there in five minutes.' He challenged his wife, as she hurried into her clothes, telling her that it was not safe for her rushing out at that time. Her only reply was: 'He's picking me up.' When Sean, in desperation, rang her phone after she had been out for two hours she yelled at him: 'Don't ever ring me on this number.' When she came home she told him in fury: 'You nearly got me shot. As soon as the phone rang he jumped and went for his gun.'

She did not need to say who 'he' was because Sean knew it was Paul Wilkinson, and he also knew that his marriage was over. He could not continue to live with Kylie and in March 2004, just four months after she met Paul, Kylie moved back to live with her grandmother in Erina. 'In the last weeks it was constant bickering, stress, anger, yelling, slamming doors, storming out of the room,' Sean said.

Kylie did struggle to make sense of her conflicting emotions. On Valentine's Day she put two adverts in a local newspaper, one for Sean – 'I love you with all my heart' – and one for Paul – 'I know there is a future for us and I cannot wait to spend it with you.' She also saw a psychiatrist to talk about feeling 'helpless and trapped', torn between two men. But it was soon clear that Paul, with his exciting fantasies that she bought into, was going to be the winner in the battle for Kylie.

Her family were shocked when she split with Sean, after just over a year of marriage. 'He was a fantastic gentleman. We all adored him,' said her mother, Carol, who was very concerned about Kylie. 'She had left her job as a nurse. She was smoking and drinking, which she absolutely detested. She'd lost a lot of weight, she was very thin and gaunt.' The family's first thought was that she had become involved in drugs because she was very nervous and on edge all the time. But they excused it as part of the breakdown of her marriage.

Just as Julie was dragged into Paul's financial mess, Kylie was also unwittingly raising money to pay off his debts, although he did not tell her what the money was for, almost certainly spinning her convincing yarns about 'protection money'.

Before she split from Sean, Kylie turned up at her husband's workplace and asked him for $4000 (Australian), without giving him any explanation. She also asked her father, John, for $1500, and after her disappearance, going through her things for clues as to where she had gone, he found records of borrowing from other family members and friends, as well as from loan companies.

'I found a flip-top notebook she had. It had my name and the $1500, and lots of other names with amounts, 200, 500, and so on, and documents from loan companies,' he said. Altogether, in the short time she knew Paul, Kylie borrowed a massive $30,000. And at the time of her disappearance, police estimated from bank withdrawal records that she was carrying $25,000 in cash.

Like his ex-wife, John also suspected Kylie must be involved in drugs. It was only later, when he heard about Paul Wilkinson's gambling debts, that he realized where the money was going. 'I think Kylie was completely gullible. She was looking for love and happiness, and I think she was blind to some of the things that were happening.'

At the same time that Paul had Kylie running around raising money, spending all her time either with him or texting him night and day, he was also managing to keep Julie on side. He told her that she needed to stay away from home for her own safety. When Julie demanded to return home, within hours a handwritten letter, threatening death to the entire family, arrived. There were more letters to come, more threats and, on one occasion when Julie insisted on going back to the marital home, she found one of her son's teddy bears pinned to the wall by a sharp knife with the message 'Bye bye baby' attached to it, with the name of their baby son scrawled on the wall in red paint.

Then, quite suddenly, Julie's banishment from the home ended. The death threats stopped and Paul began to act like a normal husband and father. Julie later recalled he was the nicest he had been to her for months. It seemed to Julie that something in his life had changed. And it had. To Kylie.

A week before she went missing, Kylie excitedly invited all her family to a meal. She said she wanted to tell them some big news about her plans for the future, and she was going to introduce them to someone special. They all assembled, but before they could sit down to eat Kylie's phone rang. Then she told them the 'special' person could not attend and the dinner was called off. Her mother and sister Leanne could not understand why they could not go ahead with the meal, but Kylie was adamant.

The following day she told her grandmother, Louisa, that she was pregnant and the father was to have been the special dinner guest. She did not reveal his name, but was apparently very excited. Her phone records showed on the day the pregnancy was confirmed she sent 119 text messages to Paul, and he replied ninety-one times. Her pregnancy had convinced her that Paul would now leave his wife for her.

On 28 April 2004, she packed some of her belongings into two duffel bags and took the train to Sydney, promising her grandmother that she would be away for a week at the most, returning in time for a planned family party. She was wearing jeans, trainers and a blue jacket with the emblem of a local football team. At 8.30 p.m. she rang her grandmother from Sydney Central Station to say she had arrived safely, and that she would be back the following Tuesday or

Thursday. That conversation with her beloved gran was the last time Kylie spoke to anyone – apart from Paul Wilkinson. She was never heard or seen again.

Louisa had another phone call the following day, one that mystified her and the rest of the family. It was from a firm of furniture removers, wanting to know why Kylie had not met them as arranged in Dubbo, a small city 190 miles from Sydney. Apparently they had taken her furniture (from the split with Sean) to Dubbo as instructed, and she was supposed to meet them to tell them where to deliver it.

Numerous calls to Kylie's mobile were going unanswered, and eventually Carol and Leanne searched Kylie's room at her grand-mother's house. They found a phone bill with one number listed repeatedly. Both Leanne and Kylie's brother Michael rang it; Paul Wilkinson answered, the first time they had heard his name. He told them he was a policeman and he had not seen Kylie for a while, but had been involved in a case where she alleged she had been sexually assaulted. Her family were astonished that Kylie, who until she met Paul was always open and honest, had not mentioned the assault to anyone. Just over a week later Paul rang Michael to say he had had a text from Kylie explaining that she had moved to Adelaide to live with a man she had met.

After Kylie was reported to the police as missing, they, too, found Paul's number, and one of the investigating officers rang him to see if he could help. The first time Julie heard the name of the woman who had been her love rival was when Paul took the phone call, and she could hear him saying: 'Is everything OK?' When she asked him what the call was about, he explained that a young woman called Kylie Labouchardiere had disappeared, and as he had met her on one of his cases the officer was checking if she had been in contact.

Kylie's estranged husband Sean received a text – 'See you soon, I love you' – two days after she disappeared, and a few days later her mobile phone was briefly switched on. The detectives on the case believe this was Paul trying to divert them.

As the investigation progressed, Paul was asked to go to the police station to be formally interviewed. The evening before the interview, more bizarre events occurred. Julie, Paul and the baby were due to go to dinner at Julie's parents' home, but at the last minute Paul said he could not go, for work reasons. He insisted Julie take with her the album of photographs of the baby that they had been compiling. Julie resisted because her parents had already seen all the pictures, but Paul was adamant that she should take them.

Halfway through dinner Julie received a phone call from the police to say that her family home was on fire, and that Paul had been taken to hospital. Four separate fires had been started in the house, and Paul told police he had been ambushed there by Kylie and an aboriginal man, that they had tied him up and started the fires, but that he had escaped by diving through a window. The police immediately went to Kylie's last known address, her grandmother's, and woke Louisa to ask if Kylie had returned. The old lady was very disturbed and upset, and the whole family were shocked by the implication that Kylie was involved in crime.

When Paul turned up at Julie's parents later the same evening, having been discharged from hospital, he seemed remarkably un-scathed but he enacted a great dramatic scene, crying: 'Oh, if my son had been in the house, he would have been killed . . .' Although her parents were cynical, Julie still completely believed Paul, and once again was terrified that her family were under threat.

The police went ahead with their planned interview with Paul the following day, and he gave more allegations about Kylie: she was dealing drugs and having an affair with a police officer. He knew the police would be able to correlate his phone records with hers, and even the location where the calls were made from, so he admitted he had arranged to meet her at Sutherland railway station, but that she had not turned up. The phone details showed they were both in that area at 9.11 p.m. that night, and that the two had been in frequent contact throughout that day. But from then on, neither had contacted the other.

Having got rid of his problem with the pregnant Kylie, Paul now allowed his obsession with Geoff Lowe to return to the centre of his tortured mind. It was in October, six months after Kylie's disappearance, that Geoff was called with colleagues to a disturbance outside a club, where a drunken, abusive Paul was being restrained by the police. As he walked up to the scene, one of the other cops greeted Geoff by name and, according to Geoff, Paul instantly became calm and turned to him: 'Are you Geoff Lowe? You raped my wife, you dog.'

He tried to attack Geoff but was restrained, wrestled to the ground, handcuffed and taken to the police station to be charged with assaulting policemen and resisting arrest. It was the first time that Geoff and Paul had clapped eyes on each other. When Paul came up in court on the charges, he was found guilty, and this cost him his job, something that he blamed on Geoff.

'It seems incredible now that one five-minute job turned my life upside down in ways that I just did not see coming,' Geoff said. 'It was like being in *The Twilight Zone*.'

Paul's behaviour was now so erratic and violent that Julie called time on the marriage and moved in to live with her parents. Paul was angry and threatened to kill her if she tried to divorce him. Julie was relieved to be away from him but, aware that he posed a real danger to her and their son, she tried to maintain friendly terms with him. But when, a few weeks later, the police visited her and told her about the texts between Paul and Kylie, and that Kylie was pregnant when she disappeared and that, after ten months of her being missing they believed she had been murdered, Julie had absolutely no doubt – Paul was involved.

The police agreed, but unfortunately there was no evidence. As Senior Constable Glenn Smith, who headed the investigation, said later: 'We had no crime scene, no body, no witness, no forensic evidence.' Add on the fact that Paul had worked with the police for years and knew all about police procedure, he was able to play cat and mouse with them for four years.

So Julie began to play a dangerous game, staying friendly with Paul but feeding information back to the police. She was now even more convinced he was the murderer, but while he was at large she was genuinely worried for herself and her family. On one occasion Paul tried to persuade her to ring the police pretending to be Kylie, saying that she did not want to be found, but Julie refused.

It was time for Geoff Lowe's nightmare to unfold. Fifteen months after Kylie disappeared, Geoff was called by a detective to say that a very serious complaint had been made against him. He was not told what it was, other than that he was accused of being a major drug dealer, and that he had held a gun to someone's head. It was only by chance he found out the substance of the allegations, when his wife, Sue, found herself in conversation with Julie, Paul's estranged wife. The two women did not know each other, but the connection gradually emerged, and Julie was able to give Geoff and Sue a copy of the nine pages of allegations that Paul had made to the police against Geoff.

The main accusation was that Geoff had murdered Kylie, and Paul went into gruesome details of how he had done it, claiming to have witnessed it. He claimed he had been threatened at gunpoint, and that Geoff was a major drug dealer and rapist. Julie also told them that Paul had tried to force her to change diary entries and register a complaint that Geoff had raped her during their brief affair, but Julie refused.

The police had to follow protocol and interview Geoff about the allegations. Geoff also discovered that Paul had been stalking his wife, Sue, following her to the station when she went to work, and that he not only had details of their home address but also their car number plates. Sue was terrified, especially when Geoff was working night shifts and she was at home on her own. So they sold their house and their cars, changed their phone numbers again and never travelled by regular routes. Their whole lives had been turned upside down.

In August 2005 Senior Constable Glenn Smith took over the case. The police were monitoring Paul's movements, and he seemed aware that they were intercepting his texts, taunting them with pieces of false information about the location of the body. He even appeared to suss out an undercover cop who pretended to be a film director making a programme about police corruption in a bid to get him to talk, and he gave nothing away.

Julie was still playing along with Paul. She even persuaded him to take her to one of the possible places where Kylie was buried, before worrying that she was herself in danger. When she heard his wild allegations against Geoff, she suggested that he take police to the body so that 'they can get Geoff's DNA'. In response Julie received an astonishing text, one which confirmed everyone's fears about Paul, and which became perhaps the most notorious piece of evidence at his trial. It read: 'Everybody has reasons 4 hiding a crime. Mine is the family can live not knowing where and why. Call me cruel, call me nasty and YES I'd agree, howeva my knowledge ISNT goin 2 b theres … Her family can live their lives in misery 4 all I care

F … THEM … Weapon they can have. Her, no.'

Paul was effectively admitting the crime, two years after Kylie disappeared. But he still refused to tell Julie where the body was. 'It indicated he knew the weapon and where the body was,' Constable Smith said, 'but that was not enough.'

Several searches were mounted to try and locate Kylie after anonymous tip-offs to the police. But they all failed to yield anything. 'It was a mother's worst nightmare,' Carol said. At first the family were hoping that no body was found because they were clinging to the belief that Kylie was alive somewhere, but after three years they were reconciled to the fact that she would never come back, and they were also despairing of her killer, whose identity they knew, ever being brought to justice.

Glenn Smith worked with small resources, as the case was now old and seemed legally impossible to pin on Paul, even though all involved in the investigation believed he was at the heart of it. Finally, all his hard work paid off and there was a major breakthrough.Trawling through the huge file of paperwork on the case he discovered some exhibits that had been misfiled at the very beginning of the investigation, before he was on the case, and which he had never seen. Among them was a second phone of Kylie's, found in her bedroom at her grandmother's house after she disappeared. When the techie experts cracked it, they found, among other messages, a text sent to Paul that said: '2day and Wednesday and then its DB u and I are 2getha 4eva'.

'DB' stood for Dubbo, and the message confirmed what Paul had always denied in interviews: the couple had planned to go away together. It was the final bit of evidence the detective needed, and four years after she disappeared Kylie's murderer was finally arrested. It was almost another two years before he was finally brought to trial.

Sifting through all the lies he told took hours of police time, and he constantly played games with his interrogators, refusing to talk or giving them false leads. He eventually gave three different versions of how Kylie died, even inventing an entirely new one during the court case. Realizing that his wife, Julie, had been helping the police, he even tried to implicate her in the murder.

He gave another five sites where he claimed her body was, but all the searches found nothing. Altogether the police spent more than $200,000 trying to find the young nurse's remains. Eventually he signed a statement admitting the murder, but the admission was self-serving, accusing Kylie of threatening to kill Julie and that, in fear for the life of his wife and son, he put his hands around her throat and throttled her, without intending to do so.

Even at his trial, Paul was playing games with the police and the court authorities, pleading guilty and then, at the last minute, changing his plea to not guilty. Days were spent deliberating which plea could stand until an eventual decision was made that the original guilty plea could not be overturned. The court also rejected his claims of accidentally killing Kylie in a fit of temper, and Paul was sentenced to twenty-eight years for the murder and a further six for arson. He will not be eligible for parole until 2031.

The judge was scathing in his attack on the killer: 'The offender appears to have a particularly cold-blooded approach to the locating of Ms Labouchardiere's body. His denigration of the victim and his heartless lies and pretences point to a complete absence of remorse.'

In his wake he has left a trail of devastated lives. John Edwards, Kylie's father, had promised his children when he and Carol split up that he would always be there for them and protect them. He felt the burden of Kylie's disappearance acutely, missing her but also feeling he had in some way failed her. He collapsed during the court case, and has now moved from Australia to live in a village in South East Asia, which he got to know during his twenty-five years' service with the Australian army. He said it was impossible to live on Australian soil 'knowing that my daughter lies callously discarded somewhere'.

The rest of Julie's family feel they live in a state of suspended animation, with some closure after his conviction but no comfort from knowing that she has been properly buried. 'I doubt very much that he will ever come forward and tell us and give us peace,' Carol said.

For Julie, Paul's ex-wife, the whole affair left her needing treatment for post-traumatic stress disorder. She suffered anxiety attacks and migraines, and she faces the prospect of having to tell her son, when he is older, about his father.

For Geoff and Sue Lowe, Paul's involvement in their lives has been catastrophic. The couple have split because of the stress and pressure they were under. Sue says: 'Geoff is a very different person. He used to be positive, happy-go-lucky, and he's just not that person anymore.' He has left the police force, a career he loved for twenty-five years, feeling that his career has been tainted and that he was passed over for promotion, and that the police did not offer enough support to him and Sue when Paul was making their lives hell. 'I've lost my job, I've lost my wife, I've lost everything.'

Different explanations have been put forward about why Paul Wilkinson won't reveal the location of Kylie's remains. One is that he had an accomplice and does not want to implicate them. If this is the case, it is the only finer feeling he has ever shown. Another reason is that her death was so horrific that the evidence of her remains could have landed him with an even longer sentence.

But the most likely explanation is that, in his warped mind, he still possesses power.

3

One Go was Not Enough

JILL CAHILL'S DEATH AT THE HANDS OF HER JEALOUS AND VIOLENT husband was a long drawn-out and horribly painful affair, a terrible end to a life that her friends remembered as full of laughter and love, especially for her two young children.

Jill, known as Jilly to her family, was working as an air stewardess when she first met James 'Jeff' Cahill, then a stockbroker with Merrill Lynch. Jill had been briefly married before, but was not ready to settle down again until she met Jeff. He was good-looking, bright and shared her enthusiasm for life; she could see herself spending the rest of her life with him, having his children. There was one stumbling block, but Jill closed her eyes to it: Jeff had a deeply devout mother who dominated the lives of all her family, and kept them all firmly on track with their Roman Catholic religion, even expecting her four grown-up sons to attend daily mass. Jeff's mother, Patty, did not approve of Jill, who was not a Catholic.

When Jill became pregnant a few months into the relationship, the couple married, ignoring Patty's protestations, and settled down together in Skaneateles, a small town in Onondago County, New York State. Jill was heartened that Jeff seemed to be standing up to his mother, even though they were living close to his parents' home. Their son, Timothy, was born in 1988, when Jill was thirty-one and Jeff twenty-eight. She became a full-time mother, giving birth to

Mary less than two years later. Neither of the births was easy, and she was advised against having more babies, which was a great sadness to her. She was consoled by her two children, and once they were in nursery school was able to turn her attention to her favourite pastime: gardening. After high school she studied at agricultural college, and was able to use her green fingers to help bring some money into the family, doing a job that fitted around the children's timetable.

At least, that was the intention. By the time the children were born Jeff had set up his own construction company because he was a good carpenter, and said he preferred to work with his hands than in an office. He had not been successful in the cut-throat financial world of Merrill Lynch, a job he had taken following in his father's footsteps, and his departure was welcomed on both sides.

He did not take on large carpentry jobs, and worked mainly as an odd job man, replacing windows and steps, and repairing decks. In the early days Jill sometimes worked with him. But Jeff became increasingly reluctant to work, and the family finances became more and more Jill's responsibility. She worked hard, with some friends, in a landscape gardening business that was going from strength to strength, often having to turn down work because they could not cope with the growing demand.

Jeff, although he made little effort to find more work himself, resented Jill's success, and was not prepared to hand over control of the purse strings to her. He still pretended to be handling all their bills, but unknown to her he was hiding final demands, and the first she knew about it was when their electricity was cut off. In 1996, Jeff was arrested for bouncing cheques. Jill realized she had no future with this man. She began to make plans to leave, encouraged by her close friends and family, but she was determined to do it in a way that would cause her children the least distress. Also, she had met another man, Tom Tulloch, and although they were developing deep feelings for each other, they were determined to behave well until Jill could free herself from her marriage.

Outside the home Jeff had a few friends. He volunteered as a Little League soccer coach and was popular with the parents whose children he taught, one of them even describing him as a calming influence on the kids. But by Hallowe'en 1997, was he already harbouring plans to murder his wife? The couple had been invited to a fancy dress party, and Jeff suggested they go as O.J. Simpson and his murdered wife, Nicole. Did Jill shudder with premonition? Or was she simply horrified by the tastelessness of the suggestion? Whatever prompted her reaction, she swiftly vetoed the idea.

Soon after this she bit the bullet and told Jeff she wanted a legal separation and divorce, and after some heated rows Jeff reluctantly signed the separation papers. Unable to afford two homes, and burdened by the debts Jeff had run up, they were forced to stay in the same house, where the atmosphere became increasingly acrimonious as Jeff tried to persuade her to stay. He promised to change, but there was no sign of him making any effort to do so. The matriarch of the Cahill family, Patty, had opposed their marriage but was even more opposed to divorce for religious reasons.

Jeff, who was not working at all now, was showing signs of being increasingly disturbed. More debts were racking up. Friends were worried about Jill's safety, and at Christmas a good friend gave her some cash so that she could buy presents and nice food for her children. Shortly afterwards Jeff was arrested for shoplifting steak and lobster from a supermarket. The arresting officer noticed his truck had no insurance and impounded it. Writing a letter to the court, Jeff blamed Jill, saying she had run up credit card debts and was being unfaithful to him.

Jill did everything she could to appease Jeff in the divorce settlement. She signed the house over to him, agreed to share custody of Tim and Mary and only took $400 a month in child support. And then she had to find herself and the children a new home but, without a large income, that was hard.

A few months later Jill, worn out by the tense atmosphere, took the children – Tim was now ten and Mary nine – for a week's holiday with her sister, Debra, in Tonowanda, 130 miles away, close to where her parents lived. Debra and her husband welcomed her, and they were relieved to see her visibly relax when she was with her own family. But when Jill left to go back to Skaneateles she prophetically told her sister: 'If Jeff kills me, you can have all my things.' She did not make it sound as if she was under serious threat, but her family were worried. And with very good reason. The next time her parents and sister saw Jill she was on life support in intensive care.

On returning to the home she shared with Jeff, Jill had discovered that the place had been bugged with secret recording devices. After the children were safely in bed on Tuesday, 21 April 1998, a fierce row broke out, and Jill tried to escape through the mudroom (a boot room, or secondary porch where dirty shoes and outer clothes are stored) at the back of the house when the first blow from an aluminium baseball bat crashed down on her skull. She was dragged by the hair into the kitchen. Jeff frenziedly hammered more blows against her skull. At the height of the screams and violence, Mary appeared on the stairs and Jill cried out to her frightened children to get help. Jeff ordered them back to bed.

As Jill lay on the kitchen floor, clinging to life by a thread, her blood spattered up the walls and on the ceiling, Jeff did not call for an ambulance. He went to the garage where he attached a garden hose to the exhaust of his car. He may have genuinely intended to kill himself, but he did not go through with his suicide, saying later that he saw a rosary in the car and was reminded that suicide was a crime in the eyes of God. Then he went out to the front porch and calmly rang his family, waiting for his parents and brother, Kevin, who turned up within minutes. Still no call was made to the emergency services to help Jill. Instead, Jeff's father rang a doctor, who was a family friend, and it was this doctor who saved Jill's life by immediately calling for emergency care. The first policeman on the scene described how the huge amount of blood meant he could not even see that Jill had blonde hair.

She was rushed to Upstate University Hospital in Syracuse, 20 miles away. Her injuries were devastating. It was estimated that she had been hit at least four times on her skull, her eye sockets were fractured, her right arm was broken where she had tried to fend off the attack, there was bruising on her neck and left breast, and the skin was scraped off her right shoulder, right elbow, right forearm and wrist where she had been dragged. Her right hand was badly bruised and swollen, and the nail on her middle right finger ripped off. There was minor bruising on her left hand.

At the hospital it took a surgical team an hour to sew up her cuts and staunch the heavy bleeding. She was given 10 pints of blood, and the operation lasted several hours, when a blood clot was removed from her brain. By the time Debra and her parents reached her bedside, she was in an induced coma and her head was 'swollen to the size of a pumpkin'.

'It was devastating,' said her father, Fred. 'We couldn't see any of her face and her head was swollen to twice the size it should have been. She had things over her eyes. Her arm was broken and it was strapped down and there were tubes coming out of everywhere. It didn't look like her. She was almost completely drained of blood.'

Jeff had minor injuries, was taken to a different hospital for treatment, and then arrested and charged with assault. He told the police that Jill had attacked him with a knife, but the small knife wound he had was later proved to be self-inflicted, and when challenged about this by the police he admitted it, saying he wanted to 'make it look like more of a struggle than it was'. He also made a statement alleging that Jill had attacked him on previous occasions, and that his parents knew about these attacks.

In the aftermath, the children were taken to live with Jeff's parents: in those early days Jill's mother, Joan, father and sister were spending all their time at her bedside, and they were happy initially for the children to be cared for by the Cahills. Meanwhile, a protective order was issued against Jeff, which banned him from entering the University Hospital where Jill was being treated and from having any contact with his children. The hospital made sure that his photograph was posted at every nurses' station.

After one night in custody, Jeff was released on bail of $100,000, which was posted by his family. His family lawyer made him out to be a pillar of the community, but the District Attorney refuted this by reading out a list of his convictions. So the only consideration for bail was whether he was likely to turn up at the next hearing, and whether he was a danger. In court his lawyer said: 'There is no reason to believe that Cahill is a threat to Mrs Cahill. He has been examined by psychiatrists who determined he is not dangerous.'

To the despair of Jill's devoted family, who were now living miles away from their own homes, staying at first in a hotel and then with friends of Jill, Jeff was freed by the court. He could walk around town and was driving a jeep belonging to his wealthy stockbroker brother, Mark. He even moved back into the family home. The Cahills closed ranks and, with the exception of a couple of the brothers, never expressed any concern or asked any questions about Jill. Moreover, Jill's parents were very worried that the Cahills were colluding with Jeff to get round the order prohibiting him seeing the children.

Neighbours reported seeing him parked outside stores in the town while his mother was inside with the children. They were also very concerned that Tim and Mary were being fed a different version of events from what actually happened. When, after persistence from Jill's family, a counsellor was brought in to help the children, she reported that they told her that God wanted their father to do what he did because their mother had attacked him with a knife. Tim gave an extra reason for the fight, adding that his mother loved another man who was 'very, very bad'. And, he added, he was going to see his dad in a couple of weeks.

The Cahills were under a court order not to discuss the case with Tim and Mary, but Jill's family knew they were disobeying it. To make matters worse, when Jill's parents were looking after the children one weekend, the Cahills demanded the right to take them to church, and on one occasion when Joan turned up at school to collect them she was told: 'You can't take them, Mrs Cahill is in charge of the children.'

When the children's custody came to court, it looked as if it would be split fifty-fifty between the two families, until the children's counsellor gave evidence and the Cahills were granted only every other weekend and one evening after school until 7 p.m. Furthermore, one of their sons was banned from ever seeing the children, and another was given permission only if his parents were present.

While Jill's family were battered by everything that had happened and exhausted from weeks spent at her bedside, they were also having to find legal representation to fight for custody of the children. And Jill? Hospital staff were amazed and in awe of her determination to survive. She had more brain surgery to relieve the swelling, making a total of fifteen operations. She fought off several serious infections including meningitis and was slowly, gradually, inching her way towards recovery.

'Every time you gave this woman a chance to get better, she did,' said the lead surgeon who cared for her. Six months after the attack she was out of acute care and beginning a programme of rehabilitation. She could speak a few words, remembered the names of her children and on Mother's Day was able to see them for the first time. She also, in moments of complete lucidity, showed that she was aware what had happened: 'Can you believe what that son of a bitch did to me?' Her next words were chillingly prophetic: 'He's going to finish me.' She repeated the unsettling prophesy to other visitors later the same day. On another occasion she said, 'Jeff is lurking around the corners,' but it was difficult to know if she had actually seen him, as she also babbled nonsense at times.

Sometimes her recovery seemed to go backwards after she was then felled by an infection. Her devoted family knew that, realistically, she would never regain all her old faculties and may for the rest of her life have some brain impairment, but they were hopeful that with sustained care and a programme of exercise, she would have a good life again with her beloved Tim and Mary.

Jeff Cahill had other ideas.

He searched the internet for cyanide several times, and worked out a devious way of acquiring it. To buy cyanide it was necessary to have a government licence, so he forged a letter heading for General Super Plating, a company based in Dewitt, just a few miles away. The company had a licence to purchase potassium cyanide, which they used in the electroplating process. With his fake letterhead, Jeff ordered a shipment of cyanide for $30 from a laboratory in

California, arranging for it to be delivered overnight by UPS (United Parcel Service) to the General Super Plating address. The following day he tracked the UPS delivery van, following it at a discreet distance. When it arrived at the plating company he intercepted the driver, telling him he worked there and would deliver the package. The driver handed it over but was sufficiently suspicious to make a note of the licence plate of Jeff's car, and also to make a report to the company, who immediately called the police.

Astonishingly, although the number plate checked out as belonging to one of Jeff's family, and although the plating company made it clear to the police that they had not ordered or received the highly toxic cyanide, the connection was not made so Jeff was not rearrested. He went ahead with his plan.

A couple of weeks before he carried it out, his mother visited Jill in hospital for the first time, and was present as nurses attended and talked to her. Jill was able to respond to them, and it is more than possible that when his mother told Jeff that Jill was talking, he decided now was the time to act. Quickly. To silence her forever so that she could not give evidence against him.

He began watching the hospital, particularly in the evenings, noting when the nurses and janitors changed shifts. Then he gradually acquired his disguise, buying a wig, boots, glasses and a uniform of blue shirt and white pants that resembled (though not exactly) the outfit worn by the hospital maintenance workers and cleaning staff. Then he faked a hospital ID tag.

A week before he murdered Jill, he got into the hospital using a mop and bucket to complete his disguise, and was actually in Jill's room when a nurse came in and demanded to know what he was doing there. 'I just came to say hi to Jill,' he replied, and left. But on 27 October he went back. He administered a fatal dose of potassium cyanide, either by forcing it down her throat or by using a feeding tube. Moments later he was seen by several hospital employees as he lurked in the hallway.

One of them reported 'he didn't look right', partly because his wig was obvious and because he was wearing outdoor boots instead of the rubber-soled ones worn by cleaners. Another said: 'It looked like he was having a bad hair day. He didn't blend in. He was wearing the wrong boots and while his shirt and pants were close to those worn by hospital staff, they weren't right.' And a nurse said: 'I noticed that the identification card he was wearing was just a slip of white paper inside a plastic holder.'

Two nurses went straight into Jill's room. 'I found her gasping for air,' Tyrone Hunter said. 'She couldn't catch her breath. There was an unusual odour in the room.' His colleague Julie Labayewski said: 'Her face was blue. There was a white, waxy substance on her chest. She lost consciousness within two to three minutes. She had been fine when I checked on her ten to fifteen minutes earlier.'

Jill swiftly went into cardiac arrest, and staff noticed that there was bruising, scrapes and cuts around her mouth, consistent with her having been force-fed. One of the nurses who tried to save her life quickly felt a burning sensation on her hands after touching the bedclothes. The forensic scientist who examined the bedding said: 'The sheets had such a strong odour they had to be treated carefully to remove toxic fumes.'

In the early hours of the next morning, Jill died.

Tests identified cyanide as the cause of death. It is a rapid action poison that can, if administered in small doses, be successfully treated with an antidote, but the amount forced into Jill's mouth made it impossible to save her. She had 15 micrograms per millilitre in her blood, with 1 mg being a fatal dose. A vial containing a crystalline substance wrapped in the blankets from Jill's bed was found to contain cyanide. It did not take great detective work to know who was the suspect, and Jeff was arrested and charged with murder that night. A partly burned wig and an opened bottle of cyanide were found in his house.

Four hundred mourners were at Jill's funeral, including the man she had fallen in love with, Tom Tulloch, who had been a faithful visitor throughout her long hospital stay. Jeff's parents and family were then banned by a Family Court judge from 'any and all contact, direct or indirect, with Tim and Mary Cahill' or Jill's parents. And another court hearing gave Jill's parents full custody of the children. Consumed with grief, they and Debbie finally left the small town where Jill had lived, and took Tim and Mary back with them, to be brought up with Debbie's children. And Jeff?

The court ruled that his murder charge would be heard alongside the previous charge, which also now became one of murder. At his trial the prosecution demanded the death penalty for Jeff. The prosecutor dramatically shocked the court by showing the jury photographs of Jill's horrendous injuries after the baseball bat attack. Picking up the dented metal bat he walloped it hard into his other, outstretched hand. 'Did he snap during the first blow? Did he snap during the second blow? Or did he snap during the multiple, multiple blows to her head?' Each time, he slammed the bat into his hand. The jurors flinched; half of them were in tears. Jeff Cahill showed no emotion.

The defence presented a string of character witnesses to demonstrate that Jeff was not such a bad man after all. Astonishingly, they were even allowed to put a twelve-year-old girl on the witness stand, who tearfully told the court that Jeff was 'a great dad' to his two children. A mother talked about 'the calming effect' Jeff had on her ten-year-old son. There was evidence from his brothers, John and Mark ('he loves his children, enjoys fishing, playing soccer and was raised as a devout Catholic'), and from the family doctor, the one who had the sense to call the emergency services after the horrendous attack, who testified that Jeff had been suffering from anxiety and insomnia because of the marriage break-up. Despite all this, at the end of the seven-day trial, the five women and seven men of the jury took only three hours to find him guilty; he was sentenced to death by lethal injection.

On appeal, the death sentence was overturned and he was given thirty-seven-and-a-half years in jail, meaning he will be seventy-five when he is eligible for parole in 2036. At the sentencing Jill's mother, Joan, came face-to-face with Jeff Cahill, and delivered a moving victim impact address. Speaking directly to him she said:

Just hearing your name sickens us. What does God think of you now? Thou shalt not kill, that's one of ten command-ments, isn't it? So much for your holier-than-thou upbringing … You do not deserve to ever see Tim and Mary. I wish we could keep you from writing to them, especially after your last birthday card to Mary. It was sick and pretty raunchy and totally inappropriate for a fourteen-year-old girl.

She also condemned his family because none of them had gone with Jill in the ambulance after her savage beating.

Passing sentence the judge said: 'Mr Cahill, when I look at you I see a coward. You are an evil man, one who has committed a series of evil and unimaginable acts. You deserve no mercy and you de-serve never to be paroled.'

Jill's sister, Debbie, followed this up by becoming a vigorous campaigner for justice for women in abusive relationships. She fought to introduce Jilly's Law into New York legislature, which would prevent abusers being able to get bail so easily. Although she failed, in 2012 the Comprehensive Domestic Violence bill was enacted, and this encompasses much of Jilly's Law.

On the tenth anniversary of Jill's death, Debbie gave a moving tribute to her:

> What happened to Jill should not define her. She was a beautiful person inside and out. She was so creative and brought much beauty to our world through her art and her perennial gardens. She was a great sister, daughter, friend and mother who loved her children more than anything on earth. We were the classic example of a family who thought 'This could never happen to us'. But it did.

She added that the children, Tim and Mary, were doing well, partly because they'd had good counselling before they left Skaneateles to live with her family, and this continued when they settled in Tonowanda. Debbie revealed that Mary had been corresponding with her father, but Tim had not.

Meanwhile, in Jill's hometown of Skaneateles, families are carefully nurturing her lasting legacy: the gardens she designed and planted for them.

4

Lover in the Wardrobe

BEHIND THE DOORS OF HER EXPENSIVE, DETACHED HOME IN THE upmarket Nashville suburb of Brentwood, one of the most affluent areas of America, bored housewife Martha Freeman was concealing an astonishing secret. While her husband Jeffrey slept in a separate bedroom, Martha's lover, an illegal Mexican immigrant, Rafael Rocha-Perez, was living in her walk-in, wardrobe, with a floor space of 2 ft × 8 ft. During the day, when Jeffrey – a short, stocky man with a full head of hair who was described as 'a teddy bear' – went to work, Rafael lounged around the house watching videos, playing on his Nintendo Gameboy and making love to Martha. The two could only communicate with a Spanish–English electronic translator, as neither spoke the other's language, although they shared a pet name for each other: Snookums.

In the evening and overnight, when Jeffrey was home, Rafael was confined to the wardrobe. He had a thin foam mattress, some bedding, his Gameboy, a radio, cans of drink, a selection of adult magazines including the Spanish language *Maxim* and, when his hideout was discovered, three loaves of bread. Bizarrely, the couple lived like this for a month, without Jeffrey or the neighbours having a clue.

It was only when Jeffrey heard Rafael snoring loudly one Sunday evening in April 2005, and burst into the room and yanked him out of the wardrobe, that things turned very nasty. Martha and Rafael murdered Jeffrey by clubbing him, tying him up and strangling him, but it was an astonishing sixteen hours before the emergency services were called, a whole day in which Martha walked the dog twice and went shopping as if nothing had happened. In a macabre development, she and Rafael made love on a beach towel spread on the living-room floor, while her husband lay dead upstairs.

The Freemans' marriage had been deteriorating for more than a year. At the time of the murder, forty-year-old Martha and Jeffrey, forty-four, had been married for ten years. The couple had set up their own business, Resi-Fax Inc., which provided companies and estate agents with background checks on future employees or clients. At first Jeffrey worked on the new venture in his spare time, from home in the evenings. The couple had no children, and for a time Martha, who had studied business at college for two years, also worked in the company, which she jointly owned. When her ailing mother moved in with them before her death, much of Martha's time was spent looking after the old lady.

As the demand for the business grew, Jeffrey was still holding down another job so their neighbour, Raegene Beverly, helped Martha with the admin. Eventually, Jeffrey decided to commit full-time to their business and rented offices just a ten-minute drive away and employed an office manager, Tara Cantrell. Tara was married to Tony, the odd job man who cleaned the Freemans' windows and helped in their home and garden, occasionally looking after Martha's mother if the couple went away. When he knew Jeffrey was looking for office staff, Tony suggested his wife.

Jeffrey worked long hours, starting at 8 a.m. and often not getting home until after 7 p.m., and he regularly went into his office at weekends. He was understandably keen to make a success of his fledgling business. Tara said after his death that he was always first in, last to leave, but she also stressed that he was a good employer and she was happy working for him.

After her mother died, Martha was bored and frustrated, and not seeing a great deal of her workaholic husband. The TV series *Desperate Housewives* first hit the screens around this time, and Martha later said she identified with the fictional characters of Wisteria Lane who had tangled love lives and were bored with their affluent lifestyles.

Aware that they were facing marital difficulties, the couple decided to splash out on a hotel room in Nashville for the night of the big Independence Day celebrations on 4 July, an event that the town claims is the second biggest firework display in the whole country. They probably hoped they'd reignite their marriage. They didn't.

They had a row and Jeffrey decided to go home, on his own, while Martha stayed partying with the crowds. She had the use of the hotel room, and she certainly used it … That night she teamed up with three construction workers, all South American illegal immigrants, none of them speaking English. But language was no barrier for Martha, who took them back to the hotel room and had sex with each of them. It was Rafael, whom she knew as 'Christian' (they were all using assumed names to confuse immigration officials) and with whom she struck up a real sexual rapport, and their affair, a physical passion that overcame the language barrier, started that night.

At first it was just a clandestine affair, on and off, but after a few months Martha could no longer stand living in the same house as Jeffrey, and she moved into a hotel in Brentwood, the Candlewood Suites, in October 2004, where guests can make long-term reservations and suites are provided with small kitchens. Rafael, who shared an apartment with friends in Murfreesboro, a city 30 miles from Nashville, moved in with her, and until her money ran out at the end of January they enjoyed the honeymoon of their relationship. According to the male housekeeper at the hotel, Rafael was always there when he serviced the room, but he kept away from Martha because she was 'over friendly' and made him feel uncomfortable.

Martha used Tony, the odd job man, to run errands for her. She rang him to get money from an ATM and collect prescriptions for the many drugs she took: it was reported at her trial that in the three months before her husband's murder she cashed prescriptions at Walgreens, a huge chain of pharmacies, for anti-histamines, an anti-anxiety drug, two different anti-depressants, cholesterol-reducing drugs, blood pressure medication, two different types of sleeping tablets, pain killers, birth control pills, a drug to prevent seizures, and antibiotics. Most of the drugs were prescribed by a psychiatrist. Tony never told Jeffrey about his work for Martha, which included driving Rafael back to Murfreesboro, at which point he assumed the relationship with Martha was over. When Martha told him to give Rafael $100 from an ATM, Tony assumed this was a pay-off.

Jeffrey came to see her at the hotel a couple of times, perhaps to plead with her to give the marriage another go or sort out other arrangements. According to hotel staff she never allowed him into her room but talked to him in the lobby. They were not angry or confrontational meetings, the staff reported. In December, Jeffrey consulted a divorce lawyer about his legal rights, but never went any further with a divorce case. He never took off his wedding ring.

In January 2005, Raegene saw Martha on Superbowl Sunday and the two women chatted. Martha seemed depressed, and Raegene offered to meet up with her to go for walks. The arrangement never happened, but a couple of weeks later Martha explained that she was on medication, implying that she wasn't up to exercising. Tara also noticed that Martha's moods included 'severe ups and downs', and on one occasion she picked up a prescription for her.

When Martha moved back into the family home in January, as far as the neighbours could see, everything had returned to normal. They reckoned the marriage had suffered a glitch: these things happen, Jeffrey had forgiven her. And yes, perhaps Martha was making a big effort to stay away from Rafael because it was another six weeks or so before he secretly moved into the house and her wardrobe. But she had not moved back into the master bedroom to sleep beside Jeffrey: she was sleeping in the second bedroom, with its walk-in wardrobe.

Martha and Jeffrey were seen together and outwardly life appeared to go on as normal, with Tony continuing to do odd jobs for them. On Thursday, 7 April he was meant to wash their deck, but when it started to rain he had to postpone finishing the job. He explained to Martha that he was leaving early the following morning for a motorbike rally, and that he would finish the job on Monday.

He saw no sign that anything was wrong, and he had no suspicion that Martha had restarted her affair with Rafael, even though Rafael had been secretly living in the house for the past month, keeping out of sight during the day if anyone was around, and hiding in the wardrobe whenever Jeffrey was at home. It must have been very stressful for both lovers, and it is small wonder that she needed such massive amounts of medication.

Did they plan to live like this indefinitely? They did not seem to have any plans for a permanent future together, but clearly the sexual attraction was so strong that they were prepared to take huge risks. Did they plan to move out together? Was the murder of Jeffrey something they discussed? Any discussion was difficult because they still needed the electronic translator to communicate. Emails between them, in which they used the pet name Snookums, were always run through an online translation service.

On the night Jeffrey died, Martha later told the court, Jeffrey heard the sound of snoring coming from the wardrobe and discovered Rafael asleep. He was, she said, angry. 'He ordered me to get up and take this man home. I was getting up and getting ready, and he told me he was going outside to walk the dog and when he got back the man had better be out of his house.'

When he returned, according to Martha, Rafael confronted Jeffrey with the shotgun and Jeffrey started to pray. That upset Christian, she told the court, 'and that is when he pulled Jeffrey into the bathroom and shut the door. I heard water running, I heard a lot of thumping, a lot of noise. I was absolutely terrified of what was going on and also, if he could do this to my husband, I wasn't sure what he was going to do to me.'

Martha's story was not consistent with the evidence from the pathologist who later examined Jeffrey's body. He suffered a horrifying catalogue of injuries. He had 'multiple haemorrhages on the scalp', a black eye, a swollen, cut lip, ligature marks around his wrist where he had been tied up, bruises on his shoulder and chest, and scratches on his face and inside his mouth. He had suffered between four and seven blows to his head. The cause of death was strangulation; the blows to the head would not have killed him, but could have knocked him unconscious. The pathologist was not able to say whether he was strangled with hands or a ligature. And while the body was wet when it was found on the floor of the bathroom, he almost certainly did not drown, although this could not be completely ruled out.

In fact there was clear evidence that Jeffrey was conscious when his wrists were tied because he struggled against the ligatures, and it almost certainly required one person to be holding him while another fastened the ties. Moreover, the time of death was estimated as between approximately 10 p.m. and 2 a.m. on the night he died, and from the evidence of what happened next, it was most likely to have been closer to 10 p.m., which meant it was eighteen hours before Martha summoned help, a terrible delay which she was never able to explain, other than to suggest that her medication left her spaced out.

At 10 p.m. that night Martha had picked up a prescription for painkillers from the local pharmacy. An hour later she coolly rang Jeffrey's mother, Hazel. Jeffrey rang his mother every Sunday evening at around 11 p.m., so Hazel was waiting for the call. Martha stalled suspicion by saying he was unwell, and that she had given him some Nyquil, a cough suppressant that allows sufferers to get some sleep. She said she did not want to wake him for the regular call, and Hazel did not detect anything unusual in her voice. He must have been dead by then.

The next morning Karen Neal, a neighbour who lived across the way in Incline Drive, was getting ready for work when she saw Martha standing in the front porch of her home at about 7.45 a.m., with an unlit cigarette in her hand, 'staring down'. She said Martha was 'very still' and she did wonder if something was wrong and she needed help. She was not obviously in distress or panicky but, in Karen's words, 'she looked emotionless and zoned out'.

Between 8 a.m. and 8.30 a.m. Martha rang Jeffrey's office and spoke to Tara Cantrell, telling her that Jeffrey was unwell and would not be coming in. It was unusual: in the three years she had worked for the business Tara had never known him be off sick before, but she did not notice anything unusual in the way Martha spoke.

Over the next few hours Martha was seen walking the dog twice. Then at about 4 p.m. Raegene heard someone pounding at her front door. Martha rushed in and baldly said: 'A man has killed my husband.' She wasn't crying but shaking and looked anxious, then she quickly calmed down, a pattern of mood swings repeated over the following few hours.

Raegene was aware that Martha didn't look her in the eye. She asked if she had called the police, and when she said she hadn't, Raegene rang 911. While Raegene spoke to the call handler, Martha 'just stood there'. The handler asked Raegene a few questions, and then she handed the phone to Martha. Martha appeared catatonic and did not speak, so Raegene took the phone back and relayed the questions to Martha. Martha said she knew the man who killed her husband, that her husband had 'found him', and she did not know if the man was still in the house. Raegene described her manner as 'somewhat stern'; she was not crying or emotional and after a few minutes she sat on the bottom stair. Raegene assumed the murder had just happened: nothing Martha said suggested it had actually happened hours earlier.

Fifteen minutes or so earlier another neighbour, Karen Kirby, saw a Hispanic-looking man running from a wooded area nearby and going into a partly built new home. She described him as having shoulder-length hair, wearing a maroon T-shirt and knee-length shorts, and later in court she identified him as Rafael.

When the emergency services got to the house in Incline Drive, Martha ran across the street from Raegene's home, now crying and hysterical according to the first responder, fireman Brian Hampton. He'd been sent to investigate 'a potentially expired person', and when he questioned Martha about it she nodded when he asked if it had happened 'twenty to thirty minutes ago'. But she was incoherent, her arms flailing about and she was 'in a highly excitable state'. Again, she calmed down within minutes.

The fireman and medical personnel, who were next on the scene, found Jeffrey's body on the tiled floor of the master bathroom, soaking wet, in a sleeping bag with a plastic rubbish bag over his head, which was taped to secure it. It was immediately clear that he had been dead for some hours because lividity had set in (the body changes colour as blood pools with gravity when it is no longer being pumped around by the heart), and rigor mortis had begun.

When police arrived they found a black plastic bin bag on the kitchen floor containing a telephone cord and latex gloves, another white bin bag containing a silver ring and, upstairs on the landing, another black bin bag with a wet bath mat and a blood-stained pillowcase inside. There was also a paper sack containing six *Playboy*, *Penthouse* and *Maxim* magazines, a book of sexual positions, lingerie including panties and a bustier, and a Polaroid picture of Rafael, naked and showing his genitalia. More nude pictures of Rafael were found on a computer, and in a camera at the house there was a picture of Jeffrey, wearing the silver ring that had been found in the rubbish bag. In a third, unoccupied bedroom, there was a shotgun, unloaded, although no shells were found in the house. Rafael's fingerprints were found on the magazines. A beach towel was spread on the floor of the living room, and on it there were traces of Rafael's sperm and Martha's DNA, recent enough for them to have had sex there in the aftermath of the murder.

The detective in charge of the inquiry concluded that the plastic bags were part of a clean-up operation after the murder, but Martha and Rafael had, despite all the time that elapsed, not made any effort to get rid of them. They would have known that Tony was due at any moment to carry on washing the deck, and it was this that probably spurred Rafael to run away and Martha to go to Raegene's house to report the murder.

Karen Kirby's husband, seeing the flurry of activity at the Freemans' home, flagged down one of the police cars on its way to the scene and Karen told the officer what she had seen. It was nearly two hours later that the police went into the partly built house. Two men from the construction company examining the site told the police they had heard a noise from upstairs. Rafael was found hiding in the roof timbers.

At his trial, his lawyer made a point of stating that his client was an illegal immigrant, and that was why Rafael ran away. The lawyer also made sure when the jurors were sworn in that they did not appear to be prejudiced against Rafael because of his illegal status. (His defence team was paid by money raised in a collection from other bricklayers and construction workers in the area, a testament to his being a well-liked member of their community.)

While Rafael was being arrested, Martha was helping the police at her home, willingly showing them everything they asked to see. They described her as co-operative, and in a pattern already established, at first she was very upset and then she quickly became calm. She was taken to the police station to make a statement, and there was, at this stage, no suggestion that she was involved in the murder.

She was taken into the same interview room that had held her lover Rafael just minutes earlier, but while he was handcuffed with his hands in front of him, being interviewed as a murder suspect, Martha was interviewed as a witness. As she walked into the room she spotted a gold ring on the floor, which she claimed was Jeffrey's wedding ring. After her interview was over, Rafael was asked about the ring and said he 'found it'.

Martha was not arrested, and she was able to carry on with her life, closing down the business straightaway. On the paperwork she recorded the date of Jeffrey's death as the Sunday, suggesting she knew he died that day rather than the early hours of the following morning (the official date of his death was the date when the body was found). A week after the murder, she paid Tara to clean the bathroom where the body was found.

Martha was the main witness at the preliminary hearing into the murder charge against Rafael, nine days after Jeffrey's death, and she told in detail what happened on the night of the murder, while Rafael, sitting only a few feet from her, kept his head cocked to one side to hear the Spanish-language court interpreter. She admitted the affair and said that Rafael moved into the wardrobe in March, a month before the murder.

She said the reason she did not raise the alarm for so many hours was because of the medication she was taking for her bipolar disorder, although in the huge amounts of her medication there was none normally used for treating this. She went on to describe how she picked up a prescription, made the phone call to her mother-in-law and walked the dog. But before she could go any further, the judge abruptly stopped the proceedings, less than an hour into her testimony. 'I've got a problem with allowing this to go any further without allowing her some representation because I can see her being charged in this case,' said Judge Casey Moreland. 'This is so bizarre, it's hard to believe.'

After a brief adjournment, Martha came back into court and on the advice of her lawyer refused to answer any more questions, invoking the Fifth Amendment not to incriminate herself. It was the judge's words that finally alerted the police and prosecutors to the fact they had another suspect. They reopened the investigation into Martha's role in the killing and, four months later, in August 2005, she was indicted on a charge of first-degree murder and released on $75,000 bail.

During the time she was on bail, and living in the house on Incline Drive where the murder happened, she tried to kill herself by swallowing sixty anti-depressants and some of her other medication. She was taken to hospital in an ambulance but recovered quickly. Her mental state so worried her neighbour Raegene that she alerted Martha's defence lawyers.

When the case came to court in September 2006, eighteen months after Jeffrey's death, it took the jury less than two hours to come back with guilty verdicts against the lovers, a speedy result in contrast with the eighteen hours it took Martha and Rafael to report the death. The speed of the verdict, according to the prosecutors, reaffirmed the strength of the case against them.

As the verdict was read out, Martha held her face in her hands and her eyes filled with tears, but her one-time lover Rafael showed no emotion. Technically they will both serve fifty-one years in prison before they are eligible for parole: Martha will be in her nineties.

'Now Jeffrey can rest,' said the lawyer representing Jeffrey's elderly parents, who clutched hands and smiled when the verdicts came in, but hurried away afterwards. 'This is a new day for the Freeman family. The jury's verdict is a validation of Jeffrey Freeman's life.' And Don Aaron, spokesman for Nashville Police, said: 'From time to time you come across a case with very unique, even bizarre, circumstances. This one rates right up there with them.'

Three years after the conviction Martha and Rafael appealed against their sentences, both claiming their cases should have been heard separately, not as co-defendants. Martha also claimed that including the naked picture of Rafael in evidence was not relevant and could prejudice the jury against her. But the appeal judges concluded that the photograph of Rafael proved there was an intimate relationship between the two of them, which provided a motive for the murder.

They both claimed that the murder was not premeditated, but this was also rejected by the judges. The fact that Jeffrey was tied up and clearly struggled demonstrated premeditation, and the fact that the couple had sex after the killing shows they were calm, and they also started a clean-up operation.

Martha's lawyers claimed that a recording of the 911 call from Raegene's house should have been submitted as evidence, on the grounds that she clearly accused Rafael of the murder in that call. But this was dismissed as a self-serving attempt to put all the blame on him, hours after the murder occurred. Similarly, Rafael's statement about finding Jeffrey's ring was not included in the trial and Martha's lawyers argued that this made the jury think she 'gave it to him as a trophy of some sort'. Again, the judges rejected this.

Six years later, in 2014, Martha tried another appeal, based on the fact that her lawyer advised her against accepting an offer from the prosecution to reach a plea deal. They offered her a twenty-year sentence and eligibility for parole after six years if she helped shore up the case against Rafael. Martha's lawyer recommended she turn it down because he was convinced the holes in the case were enough to save her from a guilty verdict. Again, her appeal was rejected, and it was no consolation to hear that her original lawyer regretted giving her advice to turn down the plea deal. She must regret it far more than he does.

Meanwhile, Martha has settled into the prison regime and advertises from jail for penpals, listing herself as a 'Sexy, Southern Voluptuous Lady'. She says she is seeking a gentleman for friendship, companionship and romance. She adds she watches the news to keep up with events, and late-night comedy shows and PBS documentaries.

I'm a full-figured attractive woman that enjoys meeting a variety of new people. I can strike up a conversation with anyone because of my flirty demeanour and quirky sense of humour.

My hobbies include acrylic landscape painting, Titans football, non-fiction books and a dazzling array of music. I want a man that is interested in getting to know me: my hopes, dreams and memories of an extraordinary life. Someone who is quick with a witty, sarcastic observation, but caring enough to sense my deep-down needs and desires. Because I don't have a family I am lonely. I want a compassionate, caring, kind, loyal guy who is also honest and trustworthy. Someone that I can open my heart to and share life's ups and downs.

She lists her earliest release date as 2029, and says her maximum release date is unknown.

5

All for a Life in the Sun

Tina Strauss had moved from the sun-baked enclave of her luxury home in Jamaica to the chilly north of England for love. But her passion for Tim Franklin, the man who had wooed her away from her wealthy husband, was no longer enough to keep her warm. She hated the cold, the winds, the endless months of the year when she had to have central heating blazing away. She could count on her fingers the number of days she could lie out in the sunshine, and even when she did it was a thin, watery sun that did not soak into her pale limbs.

She longed to be back in a hot climate, to feel real heat beating down on her, bronzing her arms and legs, and bleaching her hair even blonder. She yearned for the Caribbean, and she had made up her mind that seven years in North Yorkshire was enough. She was leaving, going to live somewhere warm because she could not face another dismal winter of ice and snow, huddling in scarves and thick coats. She did not have to consult Tim because she was a wealthy woman. It was her money that had set the lovers up in the luxury home where they lived, it was her money that would take her back to the sunshine, and she had told Tim. He didn't want to move, but that was fine with Tina: the love affair had run its course, and she and her fifteen-year-old daughter, Claire Louise, would be better off without him.

Tina, forty-two, had not started life in the sun-drenched Caribbean. She grew up in Droitwich, Cheshire, and her real first names were Elizabeth Louise, but she was known as Betty to her family. On moving to London as a young woman she had changed her name to Tina, and that was what everyone except her mother called her (her father was dead). In London she worked as the secretary to a Labour MP, a prestigious job that brought her into contact with plenty of influential people. Her northern vowels had been ironed out, and she was well integrated into the social scene.

She met and married Richard Strauss, a wealthy Austrian twenty years older than her, who had been running a wine business in London before investing in banana plantations in the West Indies. He later described himself as 'not quite a millionaire', at a time when a million pounds was the equivalent of more than twenty million today. Richard was not a dilettante investor: he was acclaimed as an expert in soil erosion, a serious problem for plantation owners. His unmarried sister owned a portfolio of valuable London properties.

Tina, as the wife of a wealthy white man in Jamaica, enjoyed a life of lavish luxury, with servants on hand for any menial tasks. Her daily routine of sunbathing, swimming, beauty treatments and tennis was punctuated by hosting grand dinner parties for twenty or thirty people. She was a very good hostess, and her charm and wit made her a popular member of the ex-pat community. She gave birth to her daughter in 1956.

It was a claustrophobic community compared to life in a city like London. The same roster of guests attended every party and the social calendar never changed. Occasionally a newcomer would arrive in Kingston, and there would be a frisson of excitement until they, too, were absorbed into the milieu. So when Richard told Tina that a young man would be coming to stay while they completed some business dealings, Tina could not have been more delighted. Tim Franklin, just a year older than her, was good-looking, intelligent, single (after a divorce) and a consultant carrying out a study of the financial viability of the banana industry. Tina was pleased to have him as a trophy to introduce to everyone else in her social clique, an asset that gave her some cachet as the young women vied for his attention.

At first Tina was simply enjoying being the one to introduce someone new and attractive to the mix. But before long she found herself enjoying his company for its own sake. Richard was always very involved with his work, and had never enjoyed the social scene as much as she did. He was concerned about improving soil erosion in under-developed countries, and while Tina could see how worthy this was, it didn't make for great conversation. Tim, on the other hand, had a lighter touch, enjoyed making her laugh and was a companion when Richard was away. When he suggested he needed secretarial help, Tina volunteered. Richard approved: he hoped it would give his wife an interest outside the monotonous round of socializing with the same people.

For a couple of hours each day, Tim and Tina were closeted together in the office. Their feelings for each other deepened when Richard had to spend a few days in hospital, having dislocated his shoulder in a riding accident. It is probable that this is when they became lovers, and Richard later expressed suspicion about Tim's motive in pursuing his wife. 'While I was in hospital he went through my private files and obviously discovered there was money,' he said.

It was a passionate, clandestine romance, and within four months of Tim arriving in Jamaica Tina had filed for divorce. She went to great lengths to hide her relationship with Tim because she knew that if she was seen as the 'guilty party' in the break-up, her maintenance settlement would be adversely affected. She was successful: when the decree nisi came through, she and Claire Louise flew to England, leaving Richard still hosting Tim as a house guest for another ten days while he finished his project.

At first mother and daughter lived with Tina's mother in Cheshire, and when Tim arrived he found himself a job as sales director for a hydraulic lift company based in Stockton-on-Tees, County Durham. Tina and Claire Louise moved to be near him, into a substantial, detached house, The Garths, with a large garden in North Otterington, and workmen arrived as soon as Tina bought the house to build a self-contained annexe. As she was still at war with Richard about the amount of maintenance he should pay for her and Claire Louise, it was vital to keep Tim out of the picture. If Richard discovered she was living with another man he would apply to drop the £200 a month (about £3700 today) he was paying her. His lawyers had already appealed for an increased maintenance payment of £300 (£5500), and she was worried he would employ private detectives to spy on her, and her allowance would drop further.

So Tim lived in the annexe, and was always careful to enter the property through his own front door. Prying eyes might suspect, but Richard would not be able to prove cohabitation. Inside, though, there was a communicating door between the annexe and the main house, concealed on both sides by a full-length mirror.

It didn't fool local residents, who always accepted Tina and Tim as a couple. Tina was well liked, and did her best to fit in and build a new life for herself in the community. She signed up for painting classes in nearby Darlington, regularly drove her red Mini to Bedale for cookery lessons, was treasurer of the church and had shifts pushing a Red Cross tea trolley around the local hospital. Claire Louise went to a private school in Darlington, fees paid by Richard. Tim was less friendly – some saw him as standoffish – but he was good at his job and got on well with colleagues.

For Tina, though, the small community – it literally had three houses – was as claustrophobic and a lot less glamorous than life in Jamaica, and it was not long before she began to chafe, mainly missing the sunshine. For a birthday present Tim built a windbreak in the garden, which gave her space to stretch out on a sun lounger, but she would rarely get an hour of sunbathing before the sun vanished behind the clouds.

Her frustration with her new life made her bad tempered, and Tim suffered as a result. Her rages were volcanic, and he knew to retreat behind the mirror when she unleashed streams of vitriol at him. She didn't bother to put up a pretence: she once hurled a wine bottle at Tim when they were serving dinner to one of his colleagues, John Fothergill, and his wife Helga. It later emerged that the fights were not one-sided: Tim was a controlling man with a dangerous temper.

When Tina announced that she intended selling the house and was moving to warmer climes. Tim made it clear that he did not want to go. On 23 January 1971, Tina took her daughter to the cinema, and that was the last time she was seen alive by anyone other than Tim and Claire Louise. She simply disappeared and failed to turn up at any of her regular commitments, even failing to hand over the church key, which she was always careful to do when she went away.

Tim announced to his friends the Fothergills that she had left him, and while they were not surprised that the relationship had broken down, they were baffled that she left her daughter with him, but took it as a sign that she did not mean to be away for long and had stormed out to punish Tim in some way. They invited Tim and

Claire Louise to stay with them for a few weeks, feeling very sorry for the pair. They did, though, notice swelling and bruising on Tim's hands, and a bump on his forehead. He said he had rowed with Tina before she stormed out, and that to get rid of his anger he had spent a couple of hours digging in the garden.

Meanwhile, Tim told a different story to neighbours in the village. He said Tina had gone to Cheshire to care for her ailing mother and for a while that seemed plausible, and even explained why, if she was worried about her, she hadn't handed over the church key. Tim and Claire Louise were now living alone together at The Garths and he was dropping her every morning at the bus stop for school, then driving on to his job. Work colleagues thought he was depressed, even on the edge of a breakdown, but excused it because he had, after all, lost the woman he loved.

Weeks went by, then months, and tongues were wagging. Tim and Claire Louise seemed to be very close, and in the seven months after Tina's disappearance they twice went on holiday together. Tina's mother was getting very worried. She had always felt a little overwhelmed by her daughter's lifestyle but Tina had been a dutiful daughter, and they'd always had regular contact. She had a couple of telegrams from Tina, one from Spain, but with no address. To her great surprise Tina did not send her a birthday card, something that had never happened before.

Local gossip escalated, and eventually reached the ears of Detective Chief Superintendent Arthur Harrison, head of the North Yorkshire Murder Squad. He wondered if the locals were exaggerating. Tina was a wealthy woman in her forties and she did not have to account for her movements to the gossipmongers; it was clear she had been in a relationship with a man who was not her husband, that it was a fraught relationship and she may simply have decided to leave him. It was the daughter, though, who puzzled him: there was no reason to believe Tina was not a good mother, and yet she had left her teenage daughter behind with her lover, not just for a few days but seven months.

So Chief Superintendent Harrison called at The Garths to make what he hoped were routine inquiries. Two hours later he walked back into the police station and said: 'We've got a murder on our hands.' He'd seen beads of sweat on Tim's forehead, he'd noticed him constantly wiping his palms, he watched as Tim's eyes darted about, never holding his gaze. It didn't take more than a few minutes in Tim's company for his gut instinct to kick in: this man had something to hide.

'I knew from the first moment … His eyes gave him away. They were shifty, nervous, strained. I didn't pay much attention to what he was saying at that first interview. I just kept looking at him. I knew he was lying, and as it went on he knew that I realized something was wrong,' he said later.

Tim gave Harrison the phone number and address for Tina's solicitor in London, but the solicitor said that they did not know where she was, they had no forwarding details and in seven months they had only heard from her once, a letter postmarked Malaga in Spain. The letter asked the solicitor to try again to increase her allowance from Richard. Tina's mother also expressed her worries about not hearing from her daughter: she too had had a telegram from Malaga, on the same date as the letter to the solicitor.

It didn't take long to check out Tim's passport, which showed he and Claire Louise had been in Malaga on the date the letter and the telegram were sent. It was enough evidence for the police to arrest Tim. His only question was whether Claire Louise would be looked after. For five hours under questioning at the police station he clung to the story of Tina walking out on him, even coming up with a story about meeting up with her in Malaga to explain the dates on the letter and telegram. Finally, he gave up. Sinking his head in his hands, he told the police that he had killed her and buried her close to the windbreak, the part of the garden she loved the most, and that he had done his best to give her 'a Christian burial'.

The following day her body was dug up, and it was clear she had been so badly beaten her skull, nose, cheekbone and jaw had been smashed. Round her neck was a piece of washing line, pulled so tight that it had forced her voicebox back against her spine. Also knotted around her neck was a man's tie, which he had used first but which was not strong enough. She was unrecognizable, and the police called on her local dentist for his records in order to conclusively identify her. Tim said that they had quarrelled violently while he was in the cellar trying to fix the boiler, and he threatened her that if she left him he would tell her husband that he had been living with her all the time. She attacked him, he said, throwing a box of screws at him and then picking up an iron bar. He wrestled the bar from her and retaliated. He smashed her head, but then put the washing line round her neck because, he said, he had a horror of anyone being buried alive and he needed to be sure she was dead.

After Claire Louise had gone to bed on that cold, wintry night, the weather that Tina so hated, he dug her grave and lowered her body, wrapped in a Spanish bedspread, a souvenir of happy times together on holiday. At his four-day trial at York Assizes his defence counsel argued, in an attempt to get a manslaughter verdict and a lighter sentence, that the attack on Tina was self-defence. He said: 'He placed her in the grave with tenderness and care … with heartbreak and an utter sense of tragedy.' Tim added, under questioning, that it was 'a comfort' to know that she was buried so close to the house.

But the prosecution argued he chose the spot behind the windbreak because nobody would see him digging the grave, and that it was a planned murder, not one carried out on the spur of the moment. Summing up, the prosecution barrister told the jury that the idea that he gave Tina a Christian burial was 'one of the worst pieces of hypocrisy you may ever hear.'

The jury agreed and it took them only ninety minutes to return a murder verdict. The motive may have been that he did not want Tina to move away without him, and he did not want to go with her. More sinisterly, it could be because he found Claire Louise increasingly attractive, and, after all, she was heir to a large fortune, making her far wealthier than Tina.

He was sentenced to life imprisonment, with a fifteen-year tariff. Claire Louise moved to live temporarily with her aunt in London, and then rejoined her father in Jamaica.

Ten years later Tim was released from prison on licence, when he was in his mid-fifties. He was accepted for a degree at Exeter University, where he was open about the long spell he had spent in prison. But he told a highly edited version of Tina's death, making it sound as if he was wrongly convicted for murder and that it was clearly a case of self-defence.

He was charismatic, intelligent and became almost a celebrity among the young undergraduates. One, twenty-year-old Kate Lock, was so taken with him that they became lovers and lived together for four years. However, she discovered he was controlling, had an explosive temper and, eventually and with great difficulty, left him. By this time, aged sixty, he was drinking heavily, and fifteen months after they split he committed suicide, leaving a note for Kate thanking her for the best years of his life.

It was some time later that Kate, now a journalist and writer, started to delve into his background. He had had a troubled childhood, with a father who was the illegitimate son of a Russian aristocrat with a very tough attitude to child rearing. She discovered that before he met her he had already been recalled to prison for starting a relationship with a young woman who was deemed too young and too vulnerable, and that it was his own sister who was so concerned she alerted his probation officer to the unsuitable relationship. Kate also knew that as she tried to leave him he was making overtures to another twenty-year-old.

As part of the detailed research she did on him for a book, she discovered that he had been violent towards his first wife, who left him because she believed he was too dangerous for their two daughters. Adding her own experiences to this, she knew the jury had been right with the murder verdict, and that other women who crossed Tim Franklin's path were lucky not to have suffered as acutely and as fatally as Tina Strauss.

6

The Royal Aide who Couldn't Take Rejection

JANE ANDREWS HAD HIGH ASPIRATIONS. WORKING AS A DRESSER and assistant to Sarah, Duchess of York, she mixed with royalty, the rich and the famous. For a working-class girl from Grimsby, it was an amazing and rapid rise, but one that Jane felt was nothing more than she deserved. She had no plans to ever go back to working behind the counter at Marks & Spencer. She saw herself fitting perfectly into the world of wealth and privilege, and quickly came to regard it as her right.

There was only one small problem. Unless she could net a high-rolling husband, she could not afford to keep up with the set she moved in. She needed someone to pick up the bills, and as an attractive, young woman with good connections she was able to land a couple of rich boyfriends. But, to her distress, they never seemed to want to marry her and make her a permanent part of their lives, probably put off by her obsessive jealousy and possessiveness.

For Jane, a girl who did not like rejection, it was hard to take, and her reactions were fiery and out of control. So out of control that she ended up in the dock at The Old Bailey, being sentenced to life in prison for murdering the latest boyfriend who wanted her out of his life, Tom Cressman.

Jane was born in 1967, the youngest of the family, with two brothers a few years older than her. Her father was a joiner, but work was
in short supply and her mother – a school assistant – was the one
with a regular wage. There wasn't much money to go round and they
lived, according to Jane, in a small house in Grimsby with no bathroom and an outside toilet. The lack of money meant the relations
between her mother and father were strained.

When her truancy from school was reported to her mother,
fifteen-year-old Jane took an overdose of pills she found in the
bathroom cabinet. She later claimed that although she was passing
in and out of consciousness, her parents did not call for help because
her mother would have seen it as shameful. She suffered from an
eating disorder and anxiety and, by her own admission, her sense of
worthlessness led her into unsuitable relationships with men, often
giving in to sexual demands for fear of rejection.

She left school with only three GCSEs, and signed up at a local
college to study fashion. At seventeen she had to have an abortion as
the result of another unsuitable and very temporary liaison. At twenty-
one she was working as a sales assistant in the Grimsby branch of
Marks & Spencer. Bored, she trawled through *Lady* magazine, where
top-drawer families advertise for staff, and answered an anonymous
ad for a personal dresser. She replied on a whim and forgot all about
it until, out of the blue, six months later she was asked to go for an
interview with the Duchess of York. Fergie, only eight years older
than Jane, was pregnant with her first daughter, Beatrice, and Jane
started working for her a month before the birth.

Jane later told a journalist: 'I was running away from my past. I
arrived at King's Cross with a suitcase and ten pounds in my pocket.
I got in a taxi and said: "Side door of Buckingham Palace." One of
the housemaids took me up to my room and there was a little posy

of flowers from Fergie and a card that said: "Welcome to the team, The Boss."

The two women got on well, and immediately the girl from Grimsby was immersed in a world of glamorous parties, travel and high profile charity work. It was a heady mix, way beyond anything she could afford on her £19,000 a year salary. She found herself chatting to Princess Diana and other members of the royal family, travelling first class and on private jets, eating the kind of meals you didn't get from the chippie in Grimsby.

But she was always aware that she was living this lifestyle off the back of The Boss. She craved the money to have the same lifestyle for herself, and less than a year after joining Fergie's staff she married a divorced IBM executive, twenty-one years older than her. It was a whirlwind romance, and it didn't last. After five years the couple split and Jane took the blame, admitting she'd had 'a few flings, I'm not proud of it'. One of her rumoured flings was with a royal bodyguard. 'She slept her way through the royal household,' recalled one former colleague. 'But she was very needy and she drove men away.'

Those around the York household were already remarking how Jane mirrored the duchess, dressing in a very similar style. They nicknamed her Lady Jane because by now she had ironed out all her Northern vowels, speaking with a cut-glass accent, and acting to the manor born.

After the birth of Eugenie, their second child, Fergie and Prince Andrew were increasingly living separate lives, the marriage breaking down at much the same time as Jane's. With her staff being reduced by the split, Fergie asked Jane to take on extra duties, which she willingly did, no longer just a dresser but an 'assistant'. And it was as an 'assistant' that Jane was fulsomely thanked by Fergie, in the introduction to one of her books, for her 'loyalty and kindness which knows no bounds'.

Jane was by Fergie's side as she endured years of press speculation about her private life, including the infamous toe-sucking incident with her financial advisor, John Bryan, and a rumoured fling with Texan multimillionaire, Steve Wyatt. She was with her as the duchess struggled to pay off the crippling debts she ran up, and travelled with her when she was an ambassador for Weight Watchers and other commercial ventures. The two women were close, swapping clothes and gossip. And then Fergie introduced Jane to Dimitri Horne, a Greek shipping magnate.

They started an affair and Jane moved in with him, but the honeymoon period did not last long because he made it clear that he did not want to marry her, and he soon wanted to end their affair. Jane went berserk, and Horne later told police she trashed his flat and stole a cheque from his brother's cheque book, which she tried to forge. To get her out of his life, Horne then put down a substantial deposit on a flat overlooking Battersea Park, in Jane's name. It was an asset that would stand her in great stead in years to come.

After just over nine years working for Fergie, Jane was made redundant. It came at a time of financial crisis for the Duchess of York, who had to cut her expenditure and staff. But there were rumours that Fergie's companion, Count Gaddo della Gherardesca, an Italian aristocrat, was showing too much interest in the flirtatious Jane. If she could dress like Fergie, and socialize with Fergie and her friends, why not make eyes at Fergie's boyfriend?

The redundancy shocked Jane. Her whole status was based on working for Sarah, Duchess of York. She became deeply depressed and particularly bitter that 'The Boss' had not told her in person that her services were no longer needed. It took her a few months to find another job and eventually, after a very brief spell in PR, she found herself, once again, working as a shopgirl, but at least in a very upmarket Knightsbridge jewellers.

Eight months after leaving her prestigious royal post, she was introduced to the man who would change her life – at the expense of his own. A mutual friend brought her together with Thomas Cressman, a former banker whose father was an American multimillionaire who had a huge chain of Ford dealerships across Europe, and had at one time been a director of Aston Villa football club. Tom was running a very successful business selling car accessories in partnership with the British racing driver, Stirling Moss, producing top quality car cleaning products for elite cars. He was the youngest of three children, and was educated as a boarder at Stowe School, followed by a business degree in Texas.

The relationship started well, and Jane quickly began to see it as a passport to the life she had grown to love and wanted to regain. Tom was sophisticated and well connected, with a collection of fast cars and a speedboat. What she needed, to cement her future, was a marriage proposal, and when she broke her wrist six months into the relationship (she later alleged that he broke it by being rough with her when they were dancing) it was an excuse to move in to Tom's house, in a fashionable area just off the Kings Road, Chelsea.

The couple were together for only two years, and there are two completely different versions of what their relationship was like. Jane said, in court and since, that it was a violent relationship in which Tom was sadistic, made sexual demands that she found un-pleasant and indulged in unusual sexual fantasies. His family and friends are furious that she tried to traduce his reputation. His mother, Barbara, knew him as 'a kind, affectionate and devoted son'. Her ex-husband, Tom's father, said: 'She tried hard to destroy his reputation but, thank the Lord, she didn't do it.'

Shortly before she murdered him, the couple took a trip to a water sport festival in Italy, where he piloted his classic Riva speed-boat across the lake with Jane by his side, and afterwards went to his mother's holiday home in France for a break. Friends of thirty-nine-year-old Tom believe it was while they were away that he broke the news to Jane that he had no intention of ever marrying her. According to a friend of the couple Jane asked Tom a blunt question, and he gave a blunt answer. She denies this, but she must have suspected he was not committed to her because six months earlier she found an email he sent to another woman: 'The girlfriend is getting a little bit like that pair of slippers I can't throw away! In some ways this is good, in some ways bad.'

The couple rowed a lot, and Tom complained to his mates about her possessiveness and mood swings. On the evening of Saturday, 17 September 2000, hours before Tom died, he phoned the police to say they were having a terrible row and said: 'I'm afraid we might hurt each other'.

Later that night she savagely beat Tom with a cricket bat while he was asleep and then stabbed him with a 7½ inch kitchen knife. She later admitted to a friend that she was covered in blood from the attack. She put a couple of pillows over his face to make sure he was dead. After, she showered and washed her hair, rigging the scene of the crime to look as if there had been an intruder and then drove off. Tom's body was found on Monday afternoon, more than thirty-six hours later, by one of his employees alarmed that he had not turned up at work or been in touch, and was not answering his phone.

Immediately a manhunt was launched for Jane, and over the next four days many of her friends and family, including the Duchess of York, received texts from her. 'Wot is going on. Just heard on news of this dreadful thing. All fine when I left Saturday evening.' She claimed she knew nothing about Tom's death, and made up a story about an anonymous blackmailer. Fergie texted back to her, urging her to come forward. She was found curled up under a blanket in the back of her VW Polo, in a layby in Cornwall, having taken an overdose of painkillers.

Charged with murder, Jane was given bail, with an 8 a.m. to 8 p.m. curfew, and went to live with her parents in Grimsby. But she needed a London base for legal meetings and appointments with a psychiatrist (she was later diagnosed as having a borderline personality disorder), and was allowed to stay with a friend, London socialite Basia Briggs, whom she met when she was involved with Dimitri Horne. What started as a one-day-a-week arrangement turned into Jane spending more time at the Sloane Square home of Basia and her husband than she did in Grimsby. Basia later told how she would sit up late pouring her heart out, wallowing in self-pity.

Jane was tried at the Old Bailey in May 2001, appearing every day dressed head-to-toe in black, as if in mourning. She claimed that she acted in self-defence because Tom was violent and abused her sexually, but there was no evidence for this except her word. Prosecutors pointed out that she had never complained of his violence, that none of her friends believed he had ever hurt her and that she lied to police during her interviews.

The jury of ten men and two women spent twelve hours finding her guilty of murdering the man she said she 'loved too much'. She was sentenced to life and ordered to serve a minimum of twelve years (later reduced to eleven), and taken to Holloway Prison. 'She murdered him in life and murdered him again in death by trying to ruin his reputation,' said Detective Chief Inspector Jim Dickie, one of the police officers involved in the case.

After the case Stirling Moss said: 'Tom was a bachelor who enjoyed his freedom. It would surprise me if he wanted to marry anybody.' Also, two of his previous girlfriends spoke publicly about how Jane's description of him as a savage rapist was not one they recognized, and police spoke to others who maintained he was never physically, sexually or psychologically violent towards them.

Tom's mother, Barbara, said:

> Jane was very jealous about Tom. On one occasion at a cocktail party an old friend who'd known him for twenty-five years came up and asked him if he was married. He said no, and she said: 'Oh good, I want to get married!' Jane rushed across the room and grabbed him by the arm and said: 'He's mine.'
>
> I think he had been trying to get her to leave of her own volition and she had threatened suicide on other occasions.

Harry, his father, and his second wife, Christa, who lived in Palm Beach, Florida, first met her in 1999 when Tom brought her to stay. Harry said:

> She had previously lived a high life for quite a number of years in the royal household. I think she looked upon Tom as someone who couldn't replace that, but would do his damnedest to bring her a little near to it again.
>
> I would have been happy for Tom to marry any girl he wanted to marry ... but I can honestly say she was not my cup of tea.

Harry added that she seemed very self-confident, and eager to drop into conversation her royal past.

She would pompously carry on about the things she had

done, the hotels she had stayed at, grand suites in New York or at The Cipriani in Venice. She was asked who paid her and she said: 'The Queen signed my cheque every month.'

Her friend Basia Briggs, who had realized during the three-week trial that Jane told conflicting stories, forced Jane to tell her the truth about the murder during one of their late-night talks. After Jane confessed, without contrition, about what she had done, Basia no longer wanted her in the house. Jane spent the rest of the trial living in a hotel.

She said Jane was not expecting a life sentence because, on the evening before the jury verdict, she turned up at Basia's home dressed in pink and blue, in contrast to the austere black she wore in court. 'She was expecting twenty months' probation and she got a life sentence. Nothing prepared her for that.'

Meanwhile, Jane Andrews' case was making headlines around the world because of her royal connection. And there would be more headlines in the years to come …

In 2003, she appealed to have her conviction for murder reduced to manslaughter, on the basis of new evidence about her disturbed state of mind at the time of the crime. She claimed that her brother, Mark, two years older than her, sexually abused her between the ages of eight and twelve, an allegation that her brother fiercely denied and which, according to his friends, brought him close to a nervous breakdown.

Was it just another callous lie by Jane to further her own ends? It was a devastating accusation to make, but the QC representing the Crown, opposing her right to appeal, argued that it was not a new accusation and that she had made it at the time of her trial. Rather than finding it difficult to talk about, as she claimed, he said she was:

'someone who wanted the world to know the details of her sexual relationships'. Her appeal was rejected.

At the time she was in Bullwood Hall Prison in Essex, and was later moved to another secure prison, Send, in Surrey. Other prisoners referred to her as 'Fergie's bird'. In the summer of 2009, eight years into her sentence, despite objections from Tom's family, the parole board approved her move to an open prison where she was prepared for release. She was transferred to Askham Grange open prison near York. Four months later she was moved to East Sutton Park Prison, in Kent, and on her first night there she made another suicide bid by overdosing on prescription tablets, and was held overnight in the prison hospital. Four days later she absconded, not returning to the prison for the 8 p.m. roll call. Police were alerted immediately and a search mounted. The description issued by the police was for a woman of slim build, fair complexion, with long, straight brown hair, wearing black jeans, a black bodywarmer and black trainers.

She was found in the early hours of the morning three days later, when she called a cab to take her and her parents, who had met up with her, to Grimsby. The cabbie, who described her as 'mud-caked', refused and called the *Sun* newspaper, and a journalist rang the police.

Her suicide attempt and her jailbreak were put down to her obsession with a man who had failed to visit her when he promised. The pair had made contact with each other when he, too, was serving a prison sentence, but when he was released he broke off contact because he was concerned that she was fixated on him. She wrote him love letters addressing him as 'husband' and bombarded him with phone calls, but when she went on the run he had panic alarms fitted because he was scared she would turn up at his home. She was not charged over the escape because prosecutors said 'it was not in the public interest'.

Jane was considered for early release several times, but each time she was not deemed to be sufficiently rehabilitated. It was fourteen years after her sentence (three years longer than the minimum term she could have served) that the parole board finally agreed that Jane was ready for release, in 2015. Tom Cressman's older brother, Rick, went to the hearing and read letters from other members of the family, opposing her release, but their objections were rejected.

Rick said, after hearing the decision: 'She is still devious, her personality hasn't changed. I don't know how they came to the conclusion that she is safe to release. I really hope they don't live to regret the decision and that nobody else suffers like Tommy did and like we continue to. I think she will remain a seriously dangerous individual. Any men out there in the wider world should give her a wide berth.'

It was her lack of remorse that made him fear that she had not changed. 'I have scant regard for her rehabilitation. As a family we have to live with what the parole board decided, but I really do hope it does not backfire on them.'

Her new freedom started well. When she left prison, Jane was able to move into a four-bedroom character cottage overlooking the sea, in the area of the country where she grew up. She had bought it before her release, funded by some canny property deals from behind bars. The flat in Battersea was initially rented out for £30,000 a year while she was in prison, and the money accumulated. She sold it in 2013 and used her £300,000 profit to buy a terraced house on the South Coast, which again she rented out until shortly before her release, when she sold it. Moving into her new home, which she shared with a budgie called Barney, she adopted the name Jane Lamb and started dealing in antiques – selling some of the royal memorabilia she had accumulated during her years working for

Fergie – at the stall she had in a Cleethorpes antiques centre.

One customer told a newspaper: 'She said she was selling the royal items because they had bad memories for her. She said they belonged to her and a wealthy ex-husband. She said she used to live in London but didn't visit anymore.'

But Rick's words turned out to be prophetic. She was back in prison two years after her release, accused of harassing an ex-lover, a married man, who later confided that she went to extraordinary lengths when he tried to finish their fling. She was sent to the secure New Hall women's prison near Wakefield, having told a colleague at the antique centre where she had been working that she was 'going away for a while looking after a poorly friend'.

'I get no pleasure in saying, "I told you so,"' Rick said. 'It was inevitable she would be recalled as she is clearly not ready to be let out. This is just a further unwelcome reminder of what Andrews did to Tom, and how she has left us all bereft and utterly devastated.'

Jane (now in her early fifties) was again released, in August 2019, moving from New Hall to a bail hostel. Again, Rick condemned the move with his sister, Cathy, joining him in appealing to the Parole Board to keep her in prison. 'It beggars belief. Any man who gets into a relationship with her will be at serious risk if he ends it, as she clearly cannot cope with rejection.'

This time the Parole Board has imposed conditions on her, recognizing that there are 'risk factors' when she gets involved in relationships. She has been ordered to declare any future romances.

7

Left in a Car Boot to Die

GOOD-LOOKING, CHARISMATIC, BOMBASTIC, SELF-OPINIONATED and, above all, manipulative – that's how those who knew Joe Korp described him. His wife, Maria, was quieter, a devoted mother, deeply religious and very hard working. They lived in a luxury, split-level, five-bedroom home with a theatre room and a circular drive to the front door, in five acres of land in a prosperous suburb of Melbourne, the second biggest city in Australia. Joe boasted proudly that it was the best house in the neighbourhood.

But Joe and Maria were not typical, wealthy, middle-class homeowners. Maria, fifty, was a machinist in a local factory; Joe, three years younger, had risen to be a manager with South Pacific Tyres, a subsidiary of Goodyear which manufactured tyres. Their home was the result of sheer hard work. Having bought a plot of land, the couple toiled to build the house themselves in their spare time, Maria later claiming to have carried every brick herself.

They worked on the redbrick building for seven years, gradually raising the (Australian) $500,000 that it cost. No money was spared, with high-end fixtures and fittings in the two bathrooms, including a spa bath. At the time of her death, in 2005, the house in Mickleham was valued at $1 million (over £400,000). There was a large plot of land outside, enough for Maria to cultivate a vegetable garden and, for a short time, she even kept a few sheep to remind her of her family home in Portugal.

The couple lived there with their son, Damien, eleven at the time, and Maria's daughter from her first marriage, Laura, who was twenty-six. Joe's children from his first marriage, Mia and Stephen, were occasional visitors.

Maria was Portuguese by birth, and emigrated to Australia in 1976 with her first husband, Manuel. They enjoyed their new country, especially after Laura was born, and they were both studying hard to learn English, settling in and getting on with their neighbours in Greenvale, a working-class area of Melbourne. Tragedy struck when Laura was only nine, when her father suffered a fatal heart attack, leaving Maria a widow at just thirty-three. She was forced to go to work to support herself and Laura, and took a job at South Pacific Tyres as a factory hand in the factory where Joe Korp was a manager.

Joe was then married to Leonie, whom he had known since they were both teenagers, when he courted her with hugely romantic gestures, throwing flowers into her parents' garden, riding his bike round and round her home. He was even dismissed from the army for repeatedly going absent without leave to visit Leonie. She said later: 'He was determined to catch me, and in the end he did.' They married in 1987 and had two children, Mia and Stephen, within three years. Leonie knew how controlling Joe could be within a relationship, forbidding her to wear makeup, ringing her several times a day to check up on her.

The exciting pursuit of a new love was a pattern that would repeat itself in his life: he loved the thrill of the chase, but found it much harder to settle down to the routines of a steady, married life. So when a young, petite widow with an alluring accent appeared on the factory floor, Joe made a beeline for her. Maria resisted his wooing, not wanting to get involved with a married man, but he spun her a yarn about how unhappy his marriage was making him. Eventually, he told Leonie he was leaving her for Maria, citing the news of two recent deaths in the family to justify his decision: life is too short not to follow your heart.

Despite her initial misgivings about breaking up a marriage, Maria was very much in love with Joe and the pair married as soon as his divorce came through in 1991; three years later she gave birth to their son, Damien. The couple worked hard, side by side, in any spare time they had to build their dream home, using money from Maria's home and from a payout she received for sexual discrimination from South Pacific Tyres.

The building work kept them both very busy, and it was not until it was completed that Joe began to feel the familiar restlessness within the relationship. He was a man who lived for himself, and he felt he was not fulfilled, sexually or emotionally, with Maria. Both Joe and Maria had their own studies in their palatial home, although instead of a computer in hers, Maria had a small religious shrine, with candles and incense, and she filled the space with pictures of her family. Joe, in his study, lined his shelves with memorabilia from his favourite Aussie Rules football club, Collingwood Magpies, and in pride of place was a shirt in the club's strip. He spent a lot of time on his computer, and discovered the world of online dating, soon making himself available for hook-ups with different women he met on sites where he called himself JoeK_40 and advertised himself as a 'Latino Lover', a single man, owner of a construction company.

There were plenty of takers because his photographs showed a good-looking man with thick, dark hair and a muscular physique, which he happily paraded. He also posted pictures of the palatial house that he and Maria built. He quickly discovered there were lots of women out there who wanted nothing more than a sexual encounter with someone new, and he was never short of offers. But Joe, despite his need for more raunchy sex than he was finding in his marriage, also liked the romance of a new relationship, so when he met Tania Herman, a single mother, online, it soon became more than a casual hook-up.

Joe would visit Tania at least once a week at her home in the town of Echuca, a two-hour drive away. Because of her young daughter they sometimes booked hotel rooms, but they also enjoyed sex in suitably remote spots in the great outdoors. He spun her the line that his marriage was deeply unhappy and he would leave his wife soon to be with her.

Tania, thirty-six at the time of Maria's death, had a troubled life. Sexually abused as a child, she had found it hard to settle down in relationships. Her first marriage ended in divorce after only five months. Another relationship produced a daughter, but after two years together Tania split from her partner. She married again, had another daughter, Taylor, but the pattern repeated itself and the marriage was soon in trouble and they split. She went through treatment for cervical cancer, including chemotherapy and radiotherapy, and was feeling low when she was introduced by a friend to the world of online dating and she met Joe Korp, who called himself Joe Bonte. They started the relationship that would end in two deaths and a lengthy prison sentence for her.

Tania gave Joe what he needed in terms of exciting sex. She was the opposite of Maria being tall, blonde and athletic, having been an amateur triathlete, a junior swimming champion and, on one occasion, had run a marathon. She was willing to join Joe in kinky meetings with other couples for group sex, shared his enthusiasm for outdoor sex and was always happy to experiment with new positions. But she also longed for a long-term commitment from him; she wanted a new life partner.

Joe, with his instinct for romantic gestures and the ability to speak fluently of love, showering her and Taylor with gifts, pledged himself to her and even arranged for her to move to a new address much nearer to him, in Greenvale. The rented house was signed for by both Joe and her, and her signature read Tania Herman Korp.

Maria was no fool and she soon sussed that her husband's trips to Sydney 'for business meetings' were a cover for a new affair. About eight months before she disappeared, Maria told her daughter, Laura, that she knew Joe was seeing someone else. She had found receipts for hotels, hire cars, meals; money had been withdrawn from their bank account; and she had found a picture of a tall, leggy, athletic blonde wearing Joe's football shirt and nothing else.

She even discovered Tania's name, and when Tania moved to Greenvale and enrolled her daughter, Taylor, at the same school as Damien, Maria saw her rival from a distance when she was doing the school run every afternoon to collect Damien. 'I saw the bitch,' she wrote in her diary.

Joe was torn between the two women, and on one occasion tried to finish with Tania, but typically did it in melodramatic fashion. He told her he was going to Barcelona to see his mother who had suffered a heart attack, and then one of his brothers phoned Tania and said Joe had been killed in a traffic accident in Spain. Tania went into meltdown, and had to be taken to hospital where she lay curled in a foetal position for three days. She even wrote words to be read at his funeral: 'You came to me on the wings of an angel. My world was complete. I love you with all my heart and soul ... Your sun shone on me. We were true soulmates.'

But the whole story was a pack of lies: he had not been to

Barcelona, he had not been involved in a car crash and he certainly wasn't dead. A couple of weeks later when he rang Tania, saying that he only had minor injuries from the crash, she was too elated to challenge the credibility of the story, although her family, who had deep reservations about Joe, were horrified that she took him back. Maybe he was trying to make a clean break from Tania, maybe he was testing the strength of her devotion, maybe he simply missed the thrill of their exciting love life.

Maria was understandably depressed and increasingly desperate about her failing marriage. She partly blamed herself, saying it was a punishment from God for taking Joe away from his first wife. She lost weight, and her co-workers at the hosiery factory where she now worked had to console her on more than one occasion when she burst into tears. They felt sorry for her but also wondered if she was perhaps a bit of a drama queen. A diary she kept at the time, written in Portuguese, was full of Joe's broken promises.

She immersed herself in her religion, and on nights when she could not sleep she wandered about the house reciting prayers. In the dust on Joe's car she traced hundreds of small crosses, as if to ward off the evil that was invading her home. She consulted clairvoyants and psychics as well as priests, and Joe would later rail against the cost of these charlatans, ignoring how much his double life was contributing to the family debt. At the time of Maria's death they were reportedly $500,000 in debt, which the life insurance on Maria, $300,000, would have substantially repaid.

Maria went to great lengths to keep Joe, growing her hair and dyeing it blonde to match her rival, and even became willing to participate in some of his unusual sexual demands. Did she agree to go on a swingers' website with Joe, as 'a happily married couple looking to have fun with another lady or couples'? The listing, with hers and Joe's pictures, appeared ten days before her disappearance, and could have been part of her desperate bid to keep her husband. Perhaps, more likely, it was a cover planted by him for what was shortly to happen. Certainly, her friends and family are convinced Maria would never have agreed to it. Laura, who worked as a hair stylist at a local salon and always had a bumpy relationship with her stepfather, worried about the damage his bullying and his selfish behaviour was doing to her mother.

Things at home were so miserable, and Joe was so overbearing and had even threatened violence, that Maria decided to change the locks and leave all his clothes outside in bags. When he returned he tried to pick the locks, and the police were called. On their advice Maria went to court to get a restraining order banning him from coming within 200 yds of the family home and from assaulting or harassing her. But a few weeks later she was at the courthouse again, Joe by her side, asking for the order to be lifted.

She said that after he had stayed away from the house for a few days they were now reconciled, and she wanted him back. The registrar was concerned that she looked nervous, as if she was in thrall to Joe, and suspected he was pressuring her to get the order overturned. The registrar agreed to lift everything except the condition about harassing and assaulting Maria. And he was right: Maria was definitely in thrall to Joe, who had wheedled his way back into the family home with promises that he would give up his affair and be a changed man, none of which he intended. He was covering his tracks for what would happen next.

To Tania he was saying the opposite. Maria, he made her believe, was the only thing that stood between the two of them being together, happy ever after. He demonized Maria, painting her as a demanding, difficult wife who was not interested in him and gave none of the emotional support he wanted from a lover. Tania, he was sure, would supply all of this.

Did he mean it? He was certainly convincing enough for Tania to believe every word, and she fell in with his plot for what he thought would be the perfect murder, getting Maria out of their lives forever without suspicion falling on either of them. Well, certainly not on him.

For months before they put the plan into operation Joe was grooming Tania, and he was so convincing that she later said: 'I never for one moment thought we would be caught.'

On the evening before Maria's murder, the same day that the restraining order had been lifted, Joe and Tania sat in Tania's car at a service station opposite Joe's workplace and he psyched her up for the plan. When Tania said she could not go through with it, he asked: 'How much do you love me? You have to get rid of her for me.'

So, in the early morning of 9 February Joe crept out of the family house and drove to Tania's home, arriving at 5.20 a.m. She joined him in the car with the equipment they had previously assembled: a swimming cap to make sure she did not shed any hairs at the scene, a balaclava, a pair of Joe's trainers which she put on (so that any footprints found at the scene of the attack could be explained as his), gloves and a long strap (the kind used to wrap around luggage). Tania wore dark leggings and a hoodie.

Joe drove into the three-car garage at the house at 5.50 a.m. with Tania crouching next to him. He left her hidden in the shadows at the corner of the garage, and inside the house he began his normal preparations for a day at work, having told Maria that he had to leave early for a meeting. Maria, who always started work early in order to finish her shift in time to pick up Damien after school, busied herself preparing lunch for Damien and a salad sandwich for herself. Joe left first and in the garage hastily embraced Tania, whispering: 'I love you. I don't want her to come out of this garage alive.'

Shortly afterwards Laura, asleep in one of the bedrooms at the back of the house, awoke to the sound of screams. She thought they came from the front of the house, from Joe and Maria's room. She went to Damien's bedroom and asked if he had heard anything. Damien said no and went back to sleep. When she went to her mother's room there was nobody there. So Laura went back to bed and fell asleep.

What Laura did not know until later was that the scream came from the garage, which was below her parents' room. As Maria went to get into her Mazda, Tania leapt out from the shadows, wrapped the strap round her neck and tightened it. Maria, although taken completely by surprise, managed to raise one hand inside the ligature, which gave her time to scream out for help, the screams that Laura heard. The two women grappled, and Maria managed to squirm around and see Tania's face, the only time that Tania and Maria ever looked into each other's eyes. They tussled and fell, Maria hitting the concrete floor, blood spurting from her face. Tania, bigger and stronger, eventually managed to tighten the strap around Maria's neck until she stopped gurgling.

Certain that she was dead, Tania loaded Maria's body into the boot of her own car and drove away with it. But while she and Joe had planned the murder carefully, they had not discussed what to do with the body, except that Tania should dump the car a long way from the house. Tania, both terrified and horrified by what she had done, and wanting to obey Joe's orders and also to save herself from a murder charge, drove through the busy, early morning traffic. She later heard slight movement and sound from the boot, which terrified her, but she drove on for over an hour, tears streaming down her face.

Eventually, she stopped the car on Dallas Brooks Drive near the Shrine of Remembrance in the Royal Botanical Gardens, with 89 acres of trees, gardens and lakes in the South Yarra district. She listened, but there were no more sounds from the boot. Making sure she still had the incriminating evidence of the strap, balaclava and gloves, she then emptied Maria's handbag and took out her phone and wallet. Did she also take Maria's wedding ring and the crucifix? They were never found.

Now Tania, a good athlete, ran as fast as she could away from the scene. Desperate to get home in time to take her daughter to school, she went to the motorcycle workshop where she knew her brother, Steve Deegan, would be at work. She turned up sweating and breathless, telling him that she had been for a job interview and had decided to run back. Steve, who knew his sister was a long-distance runner, was not surprised about the distance she claimed to have run, but something about her story did not add up. Steve distrusted and disliked Joe, and was disappointed that Tania had once again attached herself to a man he described as 'a scumbag'. The fact that Joe was a married man worried all Tania's family, but Tania assured Steve that Maria was a bitch; he'd leave her and marry Tania.

Despite his misgivings about her story, Steve gave her a lift home but by the time she had showered and changed, she was late getting Taylor to school and had to go to the school's admin office to sign her in, explaining that nightmares had kept Taylor awake. Taylor was not happy all day, crying on a couple of occasions and needing to hold the class 'comfort toy' to calm her down.

Although, according to their agreement, Tania was not supposed to make contact with Joe that day, she could not stand carrying the burden of what she had done alone, and Joe agreed to meet her briefly at the tyre factory. Under the pretext of taking him a ham sandwich, she turned up to tell him what had happened. She was deeply distressed by the fact that she had heard movement from the boot, but that was not what concerned Joe. It was the blood spilt on the garage floor that bothered him, and he was angry. He told Tania, who was upset and crying: 'Just pull through. You've got to be strong.' He told her to burn the evidence, including the strap, and she did at the place where she and Joe used to go for outdoor sex. But what about Damien?

Much later, when school ended at 3.30 p.m., Maria was not there to collect her son. This was normal because her factory shift only ended at 3.30 p.m., and it usually took her fifteen minutes to get to the school gate, so Damien played with his mates in the yard. Gradually the other pupils disappeared as their lifts arrived to take them home, and when Maria was still not there, Damien was taken to join the after-school club for children whose parents could not get to the school until later. It was unusual for the staff to see him there though: while Maria arrived a little late, she was never that late and totally reliable. The school started ringing her mobile, but getting no reply after several attempts, at 4.20 p.m. they rang Joe, who was at work.

Joe sounded perplexed. He was a good actor, and over the next hours, days and weeks he put on an Oscar-winning performance as the husband whose wife has mysteriously disappeared. He collected Damien and they went back to Mickleham. By 5.30 p.m., when there was no sign of his wife, Joe drove the route between her workplace and the school, ostensibly to check if she had been involved in a road accident. When Laura arrived home, Damien explained that Maria was missing, but Laura thought she may have simply gone shopping.

It was 7.30 p.m. when Joe went to the local Craigieburn police station and reported her missing. He told the police he had last seen her making lunch in the kitchen. The next, and important, check was with the company where she worked, and the police discovered she had not turned up for her shift that day, completely out of character.

Joe told the police he had been at work all day from 7 a.m., attending meetings at 8.30 a.m., 11 a.m., 3.30 p.m. and 4 p.m., all of which was true. He had been seen by many people, and had not left work all day, not even for a lunch break. He told the police that he and Maria had been having marital problems and that she was depressed, but he said he did not believe she would have committed suicide as she was religious and loved her kids. The thinking among the police officers was that she was so fed up with her unhappy marriage that she had simply run away, perhaps to punish him, intending to turn up again after a while.

Her mobile phone was off and untraceable. The police, not unduly alarmed at this stage, sent out a message to all patrol cars to look out for her Mazda. They checked with towing companies that it had not been towed away, and they sent a patrol to look around the car parks at local shopping centres. Calls to her friends and relatives drew a blank, and a check on her bank account showed she had not withdrawn money for two days.

When word got out that Maria was missing, Joe's brother, Gust, rang the police to say that he suspected his own brother may have had a hand in her disappearance. He mentioned that Laura had told him she was woken by the sound of screams at 6.30 a.m., and he told them that Joe had recently forced Maria to change her will. While helping Joe with a computer glitch, Gust had seen emails between Joe and Tania, not just loving ones, but one which said: 'I have to do it alone, I can't have you involved.'

Later that evening the police went to the house in Mickleham and carried out a thorough search, with Joe being exceptionally co-operative. In the master bedroom, with a large framed picture of Maria and Joe's wedding day looking down on them from above the bed, they discovered that none of Maria's clothes, toiletries or luggage was missing, which made it less likely that she had simply run away, and increasingly likely that foul play was involved.

The police could not make sense of Joe. He should have been the prime suspect but he had a rock-solid alibi, and he seemed genuinely very concerned for a wife he said he loved, despite the rough patch in their marriage. He was asked, more or less routinely, if he knew of anyone who had a grudge against Maria, and without hesitation he named Tania Herman, describing her as a 'former' girlfriend.

The following day a more desperate police search began, with a helicopter covering more remote areas. Suicide was increasingly looking like the most obvious solution, especially after a friend of Maria's turned up at the police station with a plastic bag that Maria had given her about a month earlier, with the instruction to take it to the police if anything happened to her. It was a bizarre and motley collection of bits and pieces, including the picture of Tania, Maria's diary and a letter that seemed to reinforce the suicide option. Addressed to Joe, Maria wrote: 'I love you very much. I cannot keep going. I have taken things into my own hands. I love you.'

At some point that day Joe and Tania met because he gave her the scrubbing brush he had used to bleach the garage floor, the blood-stained trainers and Maria's ear-rings, which must have been torn off in the fight. Tania took them and buried them near Greenvale Reservoir.

That afternoon Joe was asked to go to the police station for formal questioning. He was as helpful and amenable as ever, and still seemed to be genuinely very upset and puzzled by his wife's disappearance. Questioned about Tania, he described her as someone with whom he had had a casual on/off relationship, and that he had split with her but she refused to accept that their fling was over. He said she was 'a thorn in his side'. And he denied being involved with with Maria's disappearance.

As he drove away he was shadowed by an undercover police car, and the detectives saw him pull over and dump a plastic bag into a wheelie bin near the side of the road before driving on home. The retrieved bag contained a spare set of car keys, some documents and receipts, a balaclava, a walkie talkie set and, puzzlingly, some photographs of computers.

The police raided his house again, and, as before, Joe was co-operative and friendly, and still seemed disturbed by Maria's disappearance. One of the cops found him rummaging in the pocket of a pair of shorts in his bedroom, but the pocket contained only a security pass to his place of work.

At the same time that Joe's home was being searched, Tania had her first visit from the police. They questioned her about Joe and discovered that, as far as she was concerned, it was not a relationship that was over but was very much ongoing. She said she was his princess, he'd offered to take her on holiday round the world, and they were planning marriage and children. She had the love letters, texts and emails to prove it, including very recent ones. She also told them how, according to Joe, Maria was ruining his life with her crackpot religious charlatans and psychics, and how she had threatened to kill him and then herself. It was clear to the detectives that Joe had demonized Maria, and Tania really hated her. Then, in a waste paper bin, under some sweet wrappers, they found a list which included 'balaclava, knife, backpack, gloves, socks, shampoo, conditioner'.

When the police told Tania that Joe was professing undying love for his missing wife she was clearly shaken, but nonetheless said she could feel his love, and when asked if she thought Joe could have had anything to do with Maria's disappearance she said: 'Joe could never hurt another human being. It's not him.'

Early on Sunday morning, four days after Maria had been reported missing and the story had been splashed across the local media, a gardener at the Royal Botanic Gardens spotted a single car on Dallas Brooks Drive. It was the car in the news, the burgundy Mazda. When he approached it, there was a smell from the boot. He banged on it, but there was no response.

It only took minutes for the police to pick the lock. There was a strong odour of decomposing flesh from the bruised and battered body of Maria Korp. She had a large, open wound on her head, the skin was pale and there was blood around her cracked lips. But to the astonishment of policewoman Norelle Frazer there was a shallow movement of her breast. Maria was alive. Somehow. 'I just wanted to wrap my arms around her and tell her she was safe now,' Norelle said.

An ambulance rushed Maria to the Alfred Hospital where she was put into an induced coma. She was suffering from severe dehydration and her blood pressure was very low. There were ligature marks around her neck. She was immediately given a police guard.

Joe, the consummate actor, seemed to be thrilled his wife was still alive and begged to see her. But the police, now suspicious of his devoted husband act, re-imposed the restraining order that forbade him going near her. And it was Laura, at her mother's bedside, who noticed that her wedding ring, a simple gold band, and the crucifix she always wore, as well as her diamond earrings, were missing. They were not found in her car or at the Mickleham house.

Now it was time for another brother to go to the police, this time Tania's brother, Steve. He told the police how Tania had turned up at his workplace the morning Maria disappeared, and how she was completely under the spell of Joe, a man he and the rest of the family disliked intensely. He told how he had heard Joe and Tania casually discussing the murder of Maria, but he had not taken it seriously because they were so flippant about it.

Another call to the police came from the mother of one of Taylor's classmates, a little girl aged eight. She described how Taylor had told a group of girls that she knew who had strangled Maria, and it was her mum. But she swore them to secrecy because she did not want her mum to go to jail.

Tania was under siege, having been splashed across the media as Joe Korp's mistress, the other woman in a horrendous attempted murder. Reluctantly, and after a great deal of soul searching her brother, Steve, visited her with a concealed tape recorder under his clothes. He found her haggard from lack of sleep, desperately worried about the effect on her two daughters (the older one was living with her father) and her parents, and heart-broken because Joe was happy to stand in front of reporters and news cameras swearing his undying love for Maria. He was not taking her calls. She was distraught.

She did not make an explicit confession to Steve, but he encouraged her to talk to the police and told her she had to give Joe up. What Steve recorded was enough for the police to swoop and arrest Tania for attempted murder and in the police car, before she even got to the station, she made a full confession. Police found remains of the burned strap – all that was left were the metal bits – and they dug up the earrings, the scrubbing brush and the trainers. Forensic scientists were able to find the blood stains on the concrete floor of the garage, despite Joe's cleaning efforts.

He was charged with conspiracy to attempted murder and theft. The police found computers at his house, the ones that were in the pictures he threw away, and they discovered that these had been stolen from his employers, South Pacific Tyres. The security pass that he had been trying to hide also related to these thefts: in all he had taken $10,000 of equipment.

While Tania was held in custody, Joe was released on $150,000 bail, with his parents' home as surety. He was banned from contacting Laura and Damien. Tania's family took care of Taylor.

Four months after her arrest Tania came up in court, pleading guilty. She said: 'I'm one hundred per cent certain he befriended me for the sole purpose of getting rid of his wife from his life.' Because of her guilty plea, because she was genuinely remorseful and because of the element of coercion, Tania was given a relatively light sentence: twelve years with the chance of parole after nine. The judge in summing up said: 'I assess the prospects of rehabilitation as excellent.' He said she was 'blinkered, if not blinded, by passion ... The split second it took her to click on Joe Bonte/Korp's profile was the split second that changed her life forever.'

Tania was the star witness when Joe came up for committal proceedings, a pre-trial hearing to determine whether he had charges to answer. Despite his defence lawyers trying to blame Tania for the whole plot, it was decided he should stand trial. His bail was renewed. Laura applied to have Maria's will, which left almost everything to Joe, to be declared invalid, and the court agreed he should no longer be a beneficiary.

Maria was still alive, but barely. She was no longer in a medically induced coma, but she was unresponsive, her body was deteriorating and she appeared to have little or no brain function. She was being kept alive by receiving nourishment through a feeding tube.

As she had no legal guardian (a role that would normally fall to a spouse) the Public Advocate was appointed to look into whether she should be allowed to die.

The case caused huge controversy across Australia and among her relatives in Portugal. The advocate, Julian Gardner, tackled his responsibility with great care, and after talking extensively to all concerned, from family and friends to Roman Catholic ethicists, he came to the conclusion she should be allowed to die, and food and water were withdrawn.

The advocate also had to decide whether Joe, who had opposed allowing her to die, should be given permission to see her one last time, and he agreed that Joe could spend half an hour with her, under supervision, on the day sustenance was withdrawn.

The advocate made a public statement:

It is important to try to understand what Maria would have wanted. There is evidence that she wanted to keep her marriage together. She was a strong Catholic, so forgiveness would be part of her character. Also, I have to consider the presumption of innocence, so really I could not exclude him. It was not technically a difficult decision, but as a human being it was very difficult.

Joe spent half an hour at her bedside, and that night Maria died peacefully in her sleep. Her death meant that Joe's charge could be upgraded from conspiracy to attempted murder to conspiracy to murder.

He did not attend her funeral the following week because he was banned from seeing Laura and Damien. Instead, he held his own 'memorial service' at the house, attended by friends, family, a reporter and photographer. As ever, Joe loved an audience. On the day of the funeral he watched on television while Damien read out a letter expressing how much he'd loved his mother's 'cuddles, cooking, the way she helped with his homework'. Most of all he said he loved the way she loved him. Laura thanked her mother for teaching her to stand on her own in the world. After the service, Maria's children each released two white doves.

Later that night, police were called to the house that Joe and Maria so lovingly built. In the workshop at the back they found Joe's body, hanging from a metal beam. His feet were only three inches from the ground. Before he died he had phoned his first wife, Leonie, the mother of his two older children, telling her what he would do. She had screamed down the phone, begging him not to. Around himself he had built a shrine, with pictures of Maria, his football memorabilia and a note which said: 'My lovely wife, I'll be with you soon.'

Was it suicide? Or a failed attempt by Joe to grab attention, to further his cause as a wronged man whose mistress murdered his beloved wife? Had he lost his footing on the top bar of the stepladder and accidentally killed himself? There will never be an answer.

Tania was released from prison in 2014 and has expressed deep regret for what she did. She was met as she came out of prison by a woman who served time alongside her, and who became her lesbian lover.

8

Not One Dead Wife, but Two

For one wife to die in a terrible accident is a tragedy. But when another wife mysteriously disappears, it's beginning to look suspicious.

Drew Peterson appeared to be an upstanding member of the community, even if he didn't seem to have a very settled private life – he had married four times. Wives numbers one and two are the lucky ones: they walked away with nothing more than some bad memories. Numbers three and four paid with their lives.

Drew was born in Oakpark, a prosperous area on the west side of Chicago, in a household that was run on military lines by his father, a member of the Marine Corps. It was a regimented life: Drew and his two siblings had to be up early, make their beds, do their homework on time, do chores. But it was not a totally miserable childhood and Drew had time to join the local martial arts club and, by the time he was seventeen, had qualified for a pilot's licence.

He met his first wife, Carol, when they were at school, and they married when he was twenty and she seventeen. He joined the army after leaving school and, following a spell in the military police, realized that law enforcement was his goal. He signed on with the Chicago Police Department, doing well and moving to a plum job with the narcotics squad by the time he was twenty-four. Five years later he was Officer of the Year. He was friendly, well liked by his colleagues, the life and soul of any social event.

He and Carol had two young sons, and, like his dad before him, he ran the house as a military operation. Outside the home, though, he abandoned his strict moral code. He was good-looking, liked to flirt and it wasn't long before he was using his charms on any young woman he met. Off duty with his buddies, they would help him with his pick-up routine. One of them would start to pester a pretty girl, allowing Drew to move in and rescue her, ready to make another conquest.

Carol was soon aware what was going on, and after only six years of marriage the couple divorced. She may have felt wretched at the time, but she had a lucky escape and her sons, too, had the chance to live in a more relaxed household. Another young woman who had a lucky escape was his next fiancée, Kyle Piri, whom he met when he was called to the petrol station where she worked as a cashier because a customer had left without paying. They got chatting, Drew used all his charm and they were quickly engaged. Just as quickly she discovered how controlling he was, constantly questioning her, tailing her in his police car, shoving her to the ground and climbing on top of her to hit her. She rang the police and reported him for domestic violence.

One of Drew's friends on the force turned up and persuaded her not to press charges. Then a campaign of harassment started, not just by Drew but by his mates. She was issued with lots of parking tickets that were not left on her car, so the first she knew about it was a warrant for her arrest. Drew was the officer who turned up at her place of work with the warrant

She escaped his obsessive clutches only because he found a new object for his affections, twenty-three-year-old Vicky Connolly. She was reluctant to date him as she was going through a tricky divorce, but Drew the Charmer stepped in, bombarding her with love messages, sending her flowers, until she caved in. He swept her off her feet and in October 1982, just after her divorce was finalized, Vicky became the second Mrs Peterson. Vicky had a daughter, who moved in with them until she was seventeen, and at first Drew seemed happy with this arrangement, although he later claimed bitterly that Vicky put her daughter before him. Later his stepdaughter said he was abusive, but he maintained it was only because he liked to run the household with strict discipline.

Together the pair of them opened and ran a bar, Drew working shifts when he was not on duty. He ran into trouble at work, and an inquiry found him guilty of disobedience and failing to report a bribe, amongst other things. He was sacked, but the following year he appealed and was accepted back as a patrol sergeant, a role which meant a drop in salary. The family had to move to a smaller apartment, and tensions between the couple were surfacing. On one occasion he pushed Vicky to the ground and held his police revolver to her head, telling her: 'I can kill you and make it look like an accident.' His mantra was: 'If you are not controlling your wife you are not controlling your life.'

The marriage limped on for ten years altogether, surviving mainly because running the bar meant they could avoid each other much of the time. But Drew wasn't going to go without female company, and he now met Kathy Savio, an accountant, on a blind date. He admitted he was married but claimed he was going through a divorce and that his wife, Vicky, was a heroin addict. He sweet-talked Kathy into letting him stay over, even though it was Vicky's birthday the following day. Vicky tracked him down and it was the final straw: she filed for divorce.

Now if there was one thing Drew resented, it was the idea that he would have to split his property and possessions with an ex-wife. Carol got off lightly because after such a short, early marriage there was not a huge amount of assets to split. But with Vicky it was different: they owned a business together, a profitable bar. And if she was going to divorce him, Drew knew he would have to give her half of everything. Unless, of course, he could get Vicky out of the way permanently.

One evening Drew showed up at the bar earlier than arranged, to take over from Vicky. He told her to go off early. When she was driving home she discovered her car had no brakes. She lost control, rolling it three times, smashing her face and ending up in a coma for a week. When she came round she realized Drew had tampered with the brakes and that she was lucky to be alive. She remembered what he had told her about being able to kill her and making it look like an accident.

Vicky wisely decided to cut her losses and get out. She was genuinely afraid for her own life and that of her daughter, so she signed everything over to Drew. All her hard work building up the bar, all their savings, all their possessions: anything to be rid of Drew. It certainly saved her life, although he could not quite give up the one possession she wasn't prepared to give him: herself. She realized he was tailing her randomly as she went about trying to build a new life, and he was an expert at breaking and entering because she would sometimes wake up to find, terrifyingly, that he was in her apartment, standing over the bed watching her sleep. It was his way of continuing to exert power over her. She later said: 'Drew Peterson is a legend in his own mind.'

Poor Kathy was oblivious to all this, swallowing his lies about Vicky being a heroin addict. Although he had already been married and divorced twice, she and her family thought he was a good catch, with a respectable well-paid job, and not long after his thirty-eighth birthday Drew tied the knot for the third time. Kathy gave birth to two sons, Thomas and Kristopher, in quick succession, only nineteen months between them, but she was not as tough as Vicky, submitting to his violence, which was escalating. He dragged her around the house by her hair, beat her up several times and locked her in the basement. One of his older sons from his first marriage later testified to his father's cruelty towards Kathy. Talking about the marriage later Drew said that after the babies were born, Kathy's hormones 'went haywire'.

He was soon philandering again, and ten years after he married Kathy he found himself an even more compliant victim, the seventeen-year-old Stacy Cales. Stacy's life had been very difficult. Her father had been violent towards her mother, and her mother had had a series of mental breakdowns that meant long stays in hospital. She spiralled out of control, using drugs and alcohol to prop up her unhappy life and clocking up convictions for stealing alcohol. When they divorced, it was Stacy's father who got custody of her and three siblings – one sister had already died in a house fire. Then one night Stacy's mother simply disappeared, and has never been heard of since.

It was against this chaotic family background that Drew walked into Stacy's life, while she was working night shifts in a hotel. He was thirty years older than her, and she was below the age of consent, which is eighteen in Illinois, so by seducing her he was guilty of statutory rape, although nobody alerted the authorities. After all, he was a well-respected police officer.

She was easy to seduce, and as ever at the beginning of a relationship Drew was romantic and generous. He didn't keep his new affair quiet, and like her two predecessors, when Kathy found out she finally filed for divorce. It took courage because she was frightened of him, and with reason. After he moved out she rang 911 eighteen times, claiming that Drew was beating her up, was holding her at knifepoint or had not returned their two sons.

She was so concerned that she wrote a letter to the State Attorney's office, listing all the incidents of his abusive behaviour, detailing the huge debts he had left when he walked out and putting on record that she thought he might well kill her. 'He knows how to manipulate the system, and his next step is to take my children away. Or kill me instead … I haven't received any help from the police and I am asking for your help now, before it is too late.'

She told her sisters that, even if her death looked like an accident, they should know that it would, in fact, be murder by her ex-husband. As usual, Drew flexed his authoritarian muscles and reported her to the police for abuse, but the charges were dropped.

The divorce came through in October 2003, and a week later Drew married the pregnant Stacy in a small, quiet ceremony. But he had unfinished business with Kathy because although they were divorced, there was another court hearing scheduled to decide the split of their assets, which would include his police pension, the home and their savings. Not something Drew wanted to do and, unlike Vicky, Kathy wasn't giving up her rights. She had no idea how high a price she was going to pay for that decision.

The hearing was due for April 2004 and, as the date got nearer, so Drew became more resentful. Then the 'tragic accident' happened. One evening when Drew returned his sons to Kathy after an access visit, she didn't answer the door. He tried ringing her phone but got no reply. He took the boys back home, and then the following morning, when she was still not answering her phone, he contacted a neighbour and asked them to check out the house. Inside, there was no evidence of a struggle but upstairs they found Kathy's body in the bath. There was no water in the bath, just a large gash on the back of her head, and she was slumped forward.

Drew was next on the scene and he checked her pulse and then waited for the police. Because he was personally connected to the case, and he was a member of Chicago Police Department, the Illinois State Police Department was called in, a routine procedure.

Kathy's sisters, who knew their sister's fears, tried to alert the investigating officers that this was a murder scene, not an accident, but the conclusion was that Kathy had slipped, gashed her head on the back of the bath, then slumped forward concussed and drowned in the bath water. The water had gradually seeped away because the plug was not a tight seal. The coroner's jury was influenced by one of their members, a police officer who had served with Drew and who had assured them he was a good man who would never hurt his wife.

Drew showed no sign of concern. He started clearing his belongings out of the house on the very day that Kathy's body was found. His two sons moved in with him, Stacy and her two toddlers, Anthony and Lacy. A $2 million life insurance policy on Kathy's life paid out, the money going to her sons.

Now that he had Stacy completely in thrall to him, and after the birth of their second child, Drew shelled out thousands on cosmetic surgery for her, giving her breast implants and liposuction to remove any flab left on her tummy after childbirth. He was creating his own version of a perfect woman, but unfortunately for him real women have personalities and don't like to be controlled. Stacy began to wake up to the fact that this was not a normal relationship. He gave her a debit card with just enough money on it to pay for the groceries or petrol, and she had to ask him for more.

When another of Stacy's sisters tragically died of cancer, she suffered depression. She told her remaining sister that she wanted to get a divorce and go back to school and college to get some qualifications. This was not the type of attitude that Drew appreciated: he believed a well-controlled wife should be happy to stay home looking after the children and keeping the house in perfect, military order. He also did not like the fact that Stacy was studying for, and had nearly completed, a nursing degree as he did not accept that wives should have careers.

The couple reached their fourth wedding anniversary, but by this time Stacy had had enough, and she confided in a neighbour that they were splitting up and that Drew was leaving the marital home. The neighbour noticed a load of boxes in the garage and assumed these were for Drew's possessions.

But it wasn't Drew who left home, it was Stacy. Drew's version of events is that Stacy woke early on that Sunday morning, and told him she was going to her brother's house to help him with some decorating. He claimed he went back to sleep, then later woke up and made breakfast for the children. He said he heard from her again at 9 p.m., when she rang to tell him she had left him and was going away with another man. All she had with her was a bikini, and $2000 taken from the family safe (according to Drew). Her car was later found at the local airport.

Her sister, Cassandra, was trying to get in touch with her that day, and when she heard Stacy had gone to their brother, she rang him. The news that he had not seen or heard from Stacy rang very loud alarm bells, and Cassandra reported her sister missing that day, before the mysterious 9 p.m. phone call, which was the last time her mobile was ever used.

Again, the case was handed to the State Police. When he was

interviewed, Drew said that Stacy was like her mother, that she had left home before and always come back, and that he was not worried. But the police were hearing a different story from Cassandra and other members of Stacy's family, who knew that she would never walk out on the children. They got a search warrant, but in the initial search of Drew's house nothing suspicious was found.

As far as the local media was concerned, it was already a good story: a local cop's wife disappears. When they also uncovered the question marks over Kathy's death, interest in the case spread and soon there was a line of TV cameras and microphones outside the Peterson house. Initially annoyed, Drew came and went with a baseball cap pulled down over his head, and turned away from the cameras, refusing to speak.

Another search of the house and car using dogs trained to find bodies added fuel to the speculation, especially when it was reported that one of the dogs picked up a smell in the house. The dogs have a highly specialized sense of smell, and can detect traces of a dead body days and even weeks after it has been removed. Altogether, the house was searched four times.

Something else came to light that threw an even deeper cloud of suspicion over Drew. Two days after Stacy's disappearance his step-brother, Thomas Morphey, tried to kill himself, and when he was found he was admitted to a psychiatric unit for a few days. It was only when he was discharged that he went to the police to tell them that he had tried to commit suicide because he believed he may have helped Drew dispose of Stacy's body.

He said Drew had asked for his help moving a very large blue container from the bedroom at Drew and Stacy's home. He said there was a rancid smell. He helped Drew carry it out and load it into the boot of the car. He also told the police that on a previous occasion

Drew had asked Thomas if he loved him enough to carry out a killing for him, explaining that he wanted to kill Stacy because she was trying to divorce him. Thomas had a long history of drug and alcohol abuse, so Drew was easily able to discredit him. His evidence was partly corroborated though, by a friend of Drew's who told police they had bought three large blue containers from a cable company.

The search for Stacy, which had been carried out by police and volunteers, now switched to concentrate on a large, blue container. By the sixth day after her disappearance, local sewers were being searched, a lake near the airport was explored and the police were trying to find out where the last phone call on Stacy's mobile, which had been made at 9 p.m., had originated.

By this time, Drew had got used to the cameras outside the house and the most extraordinary series of events started with him giving Fox News a tour of the house. Then he launched a media blitz, giving interviews to numerous TV shows and newspaper reporters, all protesting his innocence, and gaining a reputation for his smart aleck answers. He appeared on *Larry King Live*, one of the biggest talk shows with over a million viewers, answering questions phoned in by the audience. His lawyer, Joel Brodsky, sat with him telling him which questions to answer. Drew clearly loved the limelight.

The issue of Kathy's death was now being addressed by the police, after some pushing from her sisters. Permission was given for the body to be exhumed. On the same day Drew tried to resign from the police, but the police chief at first refused to allow it, although later he was able to resign. To the annoyance of the department, they could do nothing to stop his $6000 a month pension because he was not, at this stage, a convicted criminal. His mother, who was publicly defending him, claimed the rest of the police department had turned their backs on him.

Two new postmortems on Kathy were carried out, one by a medical examiner paid for by Kathy's family and Fox News, who concluded that she died after a struggle and had been put in the bath after her death. The results of the second official postmortem have not been released.

Drew was still desperately trying to prove his case that Stacy had walked out and would return, yet in his many TV and radio interviews he never appealed for her to come forward and he refused to join the searches, despite reiterating he did not believe she was dead. He did try to throw suspicion on an old friend of hers though, Scott Rosell, whose twin brother she had dated when she was at school. But when police checked out the guy, he had a completely watertight alibi.

He was friendly with Stacy, and he told the police she had confided in him that she had lied to them about the evening of Kathy's death. She said Drew went out that night dressed entirely in black and when he arrived home late he told her that if anyone asked, he had been home with her all night. Scott was not the only one to tell the police her account of what happened; so did her sister Cassandra.

So now Drew was being investigated over Kathy's death *and* Stacy's disappearance. For anyone else it would be a deeply worrying time, especially if he was genuinely innocent. And especially if he was worried about his children: Kathy's two sons had lost their mother and now their stepmother, and Stacy's two children had also lost their mother. But Drew was loving his fifteen minutes of fame, revelling in the media attention, milking the publicity for all it was worth.

Three months after Stacy went missing he and his lawyer embroiled themselves in one of the tackiest stunts ever pulled. He phoned in live to a Chicago radio DJ, and after discussing the case the lawyer made an astonishing suggestion: why didn't the radio station make Drew the feature of their regular dating slot. In other words, he wanted them to offer a man suspected of killing two wives as a date for their female listeners. The DJ sounded interested but the next day the station pulled the plug on it, having finally twigged that it was a terrible idea.

Drew was having a high old time, travelling around the country, all expenses paid, to appear on TV shows. The frustration felt by the police must have been enormous. He was enjoying himself so much that he possibly even staged another stunt when, fourteen months after Stacy disappeared, he announced his engagement to twenty-three-year-old Christina Raines. If he really believed Stacy was alive and well somewhere then he simply wasn't free to get engaged, let alone married. Four months later the couple split, with Christina claiming the whole engagement was a sham to keep his name in the public eye. Apparently her father gave her an ultimatum that helped her 'come to her senses'.

In May 2009, Drew was finally arrested for the murder of his ex-wife, Kathy, just over five years after her death. Bail was set at $20 million, making sure he stayed behind lock and key. But being locked up did not initially stop the Drew Peterson media circus because he was giving radio interviews from jail, until a judge severely limited his access to the media.

It was another three years before he came to trial, mainly because of a legal wrangle that resulted in a change to the law in Illinois, with a new law, nicknamed Drew's Law, enacted just for this case. Drew was probably thrilled to have his name written up for posterity because by this stage he must have realized he was unlikely to ever see the outside of prison again.

The law means that hearsay evidence can, in some circumstances, be admitted in court. Normally hearsay evidence is not allowed – nobody can testify about what they heard someone else say about the accused because the accused must always have the right to cross examine anyone who says anything about them. But with Kathy dead and Stacy presumed dead, hearsay evidence was very important: Kathy's sisters needed to tell the court what she had said about Drew, and Stacy's sister and her friend Scott needed to repeat what she had told them about Kathy's death. The new law states that in certain circumstances hearsay evidence is allowed if the testimony is reliable and if 'the person cannot answer because they are the victim'.

The evidence was compelling. Kathy's sister told the court Kathy had asked her to take care of the children if she died, and that Kathy had been told by Drew that he could kill her and make it look like an accident. Another witness said Kathy told her how Drew grabbed her by the neck and said, 'Why don't you just die?' The jury heard how Kathy was seen with bruises and cuts on her arms, legs, stomach and thighs. The pathology evidence concluded Kathy was very unlikely to have drowned unless she was very intoxicated, and there was no evidence of alcohol or drugs in her system.

Stacy's voice was heard in court when her church pastor spoke about how she had told him about Drew forcing her to give him an alibi for the night of Kathy's death. It turned out she had told this to a lot of people, including her divorce lawyer, and her sister. If word was getting back to Drew that she was talking about his phoney alibi, it is no wonder he was keen for her to disappear completely.

When the trial ended, Drew was found guilty of the premeditated murder of Kathy. Before he was sentenced to thirty-eight years, he rocked the courtroom by screaming out 'I did not kill Kathleen,' the only time his calm demeanour cracked. Susan, Kathy's sister, shot back with: 'Yes, you did! Liar!' Then, savouring one of his last moments in the public spotlight, Drew made a long speech. Addressing the state prosecutor who brought him to justice, Jim Glasgow, he dramatically said: 'All aspects of my life have been destroyed. Never forget my face. Never forget what you have done here.'

After the case Jim said: 'We all got an opportunity to see a psychopath. When he got up on the stand and that shrill, kind of feminine screech that he didn't kill Kathy, that's the guy that killed Kathy. You got a glimpse into his soul.'

Kathy's family all paid tribute to her, and her brother Henry said: 'While he is in jail I hope Kitty is what he sees every night before he sleeps and I hope that she is haunting him in his dreams. He took Kathleen's future and now she has taken his.'

It seems that Drew did not forget what he believed Jim Glasgow had done to him because in 2013, not long after his sentence began, he was caught trying to arrange with another prisoner the execution of Mr Glasgow by a hitman on the outside. Unbeknown to him, the prisoner he was soliciting to find the hitman was wearing a wire, having alerted the prison authorities. Arrested and charged again, Peterson was given another forty years in jail, to start after his first sentence. This means he will be one hundred and twenty-seven when he is first eligible for parole.

Once again he grandstanded, giving a twenty-five-minute speech in which he claimed he only did the deal to help the other prisoner get a shorter sentence. By 2017, after several attempts at appeals, he was forced to accept he was not going to get out.

He continues to attract attention though. In 2017 he was attacked by another prisoner, and was moved to a high security prison at Terre Haute, in Indiana. True to form, he gave an interview to a journalist about how happy he was with the change, describing the new prison as 'living the dream'. He claimed it was cleaner and more comfortable than his previous abode, and was 'comparatively like a day care centre'. He said he spends his days watching sitcoms and movies, and earns pocket money working in the laundry. The only problem with his new life, he told the journalist, is that he misses women. 'I love women. I just don't have access to them here. If I get out there I am going to be dating again, but with the sentences I got, I doubt I'm going to see daylight for a while anyway.'

And, of course, he still insisted he had nothing to do with the death of Kathy or the disappearance of Stacy.

Meanwhile, Stephen, one of his sons from his first marriage to Carol, has taken on the job of bringing up both Kathy's and Stacy's children, and they still live as a family in the large, detached house that Drew owned, and where friends and relatives regularly put fresh flowers on a memorial to Stacy.

In a 2017 interview Stephen conceded that his father probably killed his third and fourth wives. 'Over time I finally came to the realization that maybe he did have something to do with it,' he said. 'Stacy has not come back. He never said he did it … but I'd probably say so.'

9

If I Can't Have You

IT WAS A BRIGHT MORNING IN SEPTEMBER 1935, AND SUSAN HAINES Johnson left the hotel where she was staying on holiday with her family and strolled to a pretty stone bridge over a stream in the picturesque Gardenholme Linn valley, about 2 miles from the Scottish town of Moffat. Stopping to lean on the wall and admire the view of the River Linn, she noticed a bundle wrapped in fabric on the boulders beneath the bridge. She screamed when she saw that the bundle had burst open, with what looked like a human arm sticking out.

She ran back to the hotel and returned with her brother. He clambered down, confirmed it was an arm, then they both dashed to the police station. Several more parcels were found by the police, all containing human tissue and body parts. They had apparently been tossed into the stream, which until a few days earlier had been swollen with rain water, but when the level dropped in dry weather, the grisly bundles were stranded on the banks of the stream.

The body parts were taken to the mortuary at Moffat, where two forensic doctors began the grisly task of piecing them together. By this stage the flesh was very smelly, and the maggots living in it would soon have a pioneering role to play in the development of a new science: forensic entomology.

The doctors soon realized that they actually had two mutilated corpses on their hands, and they also quickly understood that they were dealing with a clever murderer. Fingerprints had been removed from two hands so that identification would be impossible, teeth had been pulled out so that dental records could not be used, vaccination and operation scars had been removed, hair had also been removed (almost entirely) and one of the disembodied heads had had its eyes gouged out. Lips, ears and other soft tissue were missing, making it impossible to draw composite pictures of the victims. The way the bodies had been dismembered, with a knife not a saw, suggested that the murderer – perhaps a butcher but more likely a doctor – knew exactly where to slice through a joint.

At first the police thought that they were dealing with the bodies of a small, elderly man and a woman in her thirties, with the well-manicured hands and feet suggesting she was a woman who did not do manual work, and had the money to take care of herself. However, within a week the massive police search had turned up even more parcels, thirty in total, and it became obvious – there were three female breasts – the victims were both women. Most of these parcels were found on the banks of the River Annan, and it was later decided that this was where the parcels had been thrown, so that the water would propel them down to the sea at the Solway Firth. Some had already washed up in the tributary River Linn because of the high rainwater.

There were more clues from the parcels. A yellow blouse, which had been patched under one arm, was wrapped around one bundle. A child's romper suit was wrapped around another. Most importantly the *Sunday Graphic* newspaper was wrapped around another, and contained a special supplement of pictures of the Morecambe Bay carnival, an edition of the paper that was only sold in the Morecambe area of Lancashire; only 3700 copies were printed, and the date was two weeks before the body parts were found. Other newspapers used to pack the grisly parcels were older.

This was where the maggots came in. They were sent to an entomologist at Edinburgh University, and he identified that they were only twelve to fourteen days old, tying in with the date on the supplement. The maggots are now preserved in the insect archives of the Natural History Museum because this was the first time that insects had been used in forensic investigation.

The police now had an approximate date for the murders, and they turned their attention to Lancashire, and that's where they picked up the trail from the local police. Five days before the body parts were found, a local doctor in Lancaster had gone into the police station and claimed that his wife had 'once again' deserted him. Earlier the same day he had visited the parents of the family maid and claimed that their daughter was having an affair with a local youth and was pregnant, and his wife had taken her away for a discreet abortion. As abortions were illegal, he urged them not to go to the police.

The doctor was Buck Ruxton, a popular figure in Lancaster where there was no prejudice against his Indian origins. Patients nicknamed him The Rajah and poorer members of the community flocked to him because, in those days before the National Health Service (NHS), he never asked how they were going to pay, and never pursued debts against those he felt couldn't afford it.

He was an unusual character. He was born in Bombay, the son of a wealthy Indian doctor and a French mother. His real name was Bukhtyar Rustomji Ratanji Hakim. He studied medicine at London University, struggling because his English was poor. Unlike most middle-class Indians, he had not grown up speaking English but was fluent in French. He returned to India to complete his studies at medical school in Bombay, then joined the Indian Army Medical

Service with the rank of captain. He married an older Indian woman, probably an arranged marriage by his devout Parsee father, but his family were not pleased when he left his wife behind in 1926 to return to Britain.

He was always short of money, and chronically bad at managing his finances, and splitting from his wife probably cut him off from family funding. He went to Edinburgh to take his surgeon's exams, settling there under the name of Captain Hakim, giving himself the first name Gabriel. In Edinburgh he met Isabelle, known as Belle, who became his common-law wife. She was the manageress of a tearoom, where he spent hours lingering over the teacups to stare at her. She was a sexy-looking, haughty young woman, still married to a Dutchman from whom she had split. She and Gabriel were soon having an affair, and he spent a great deal of money helping her get a divorce. He was entranced, but an inferiority complex about the colour of his skin made him excessively jealous if she looked at white males.

He twice failed his surgeon's exams, and moved back to London, sponging off wealthy Indian families. Belle joined him, and the first of their three children, Elizabeth, was born. At this point he decided to buy a general practice, and when one came available in Lancaster he purchased it with money probably supplied by his parents. Before moving from London he changed his name by deedpoll to Buck Ruxton.

His relationship with Belle was always stormy, and he moved to Lancaster without her while she was back in Edinburgh with the baby, working as the manageress of a Woolworth's, but now that he had a house she rejoined him, and they resumed their tumultuous sexual relationship. Later, in court, Ruxton would say they 'could not live with each other but could not live without each other'. Their fighting had a strong sexual element, with wild lovemaking following vicious rows, with Belle going out of her way to provoke her husband, perhaps because they shared a sado-masochistic pleasure in physical violence followed by abandoned sex.

The doctor built up a practice that, in spite of his philanthropy, was prosperous, earning him more than £180,000 a year in today's money. But despite this, he lived beyond his means, feeding his lavish and bizarre tastes. The house was decorated with huge zodiac signs on the walls, and was painted bright green and yellow on the outside – very unusual in sombre, grey-walled Lancaster – and red and white inside. He even drove a white car with bright blue wheels at a time when almost all cars were black. He hated the dark, and from dusk every day the lights in the house were switched on, and stayed on all night. He had a bath every day, which may not raise eyebrows today but was considered extravagant at the time. Also, his clothes were changed every day and sent to a laundry. As his debts mounted, he turned to moneylenders.

He and Belle had two more children, Diana Rose and William Gladstone, known to the family as Billie Boy. The couple carried on fighting, and Belle twice complained to the police that 'Bommie', the name she used for Buck, was beating her. Buck was summoned to the police station and was very distressed, wildly accusing his wife of being unfaithful and screaming that he was going to kill her. The police sergeant on duty apparently told him to give the other man, the one he believed Belle was having an affair with, a good hiding, definitely not the sort of advice given today.

Buck calmed down abruptly, and told the policeman he would give his wife the money to go to her sister in Edinburgh. Before she could leave they had another passionate reconciliation, and she stayed. But only a month later police were called to the house where Buck was raging wildly because he said his wife was 'going out to meet a man'. He accused the family's maid, Mary Rogerson, of scheming with his wife to deceive him. He told the police: 'I feel like murdering two people in this house.' On another occasion, when he met Mary's stepmother, Jessie, he alleged that: 'Mary has been working in conjunction with my wife, deceiving me, and sometimes I feel I could choke them both … I would gas myself but for the poor children.'

He kept a diary of his relationship with 'my beloved Belle'. He claimed she tried to chloroform herself, precipitating a miscarriage, and that she twice left gas taps on in the children's bedroom and tried to poison his coffee. There is no way of knowing how true these allegations were, and on other occasions he wrote lovingly about Belle, including poems he had written to her. One entry said 'Belle is kissing my feet' but, two days later, he recorded that 'she has thrown a flowerpot at me, a knife and a chair'. On another occasion he recorded that Belle said: 'I would rather sleep in the gutter than sleep with you.'

They were not married, and he lived in fear that she would find out about his Indian wife. He said she accused him of having an affair with a nurse, and he was convinced she was having an affair with a twenty-five-year-old solicitor, Bobbie Edmondson, who worked at the town hall, immediately opposite the Ruxton home. A week before her death Belle went to Edinburgh with Bobbie and his parents and sister, and Buck convinced himself that she and Bobbie shared a hotel room. Hotel records later showed they actually had separate rooms.

The murder of Belle and their maid, Mary, took place on 14 September 1935, following a blazing row about Belle returning home late from a trip to Blackpool. She had been to visit two of her sisters and see the illuminations. She left Blackpool at 11.30 p.m., getting home in the early hours of the morning. Overwhelmed by his paranoid jealousy, he probably strangled Belle, then beat and stabbed her. Mary probably witnessed the attack. He bludgeoned and strangled her, also stabbing her before or after death.

The three children were in bed, and apparently slept through the carnage, which probably took place in the main bedroom. Immediately afterwards Buck made some attempts at cleaning up. At 6.30 a.m. the next day, a Sunday, he called on his cleaning lady, telling her that she was not needed that day as his wife had gone to Edinburgh. When the children woke he drove them to the home of a dentist and his wife, who lived in Morecambe and were friends of the Ruxtons. Then he went home, moved the bodies to the bathroom and began the long job of dismembering and parcelling up the body parts.

At about 4.30 p.m. he called on a patient, Mrs Hampshire, and asked if she and her husband would help him prepare the house for the decorators, due the next morning. The couple found the house in disarray, and at his trial Mrs Hampshire described seeing straw all over the floor, even protruding from under a locked bedroom door, and several rolled-up sections of stair carpet. In the garden there were more pieces of carpet and some half-burnt towels. Before they went home, the Hampshires were given some stained carpet and a bloodstained suit, on condition they had them cleaned. A decorator turned up the next day to paint the hall and stairway, although he had been booked to paint a different room. It's not surprising that gossip was going around Lancaster about the missing Mrs Ruxton and the maid.

When the body parts were initially found, Buck was relieved that they were being identified in the press as a man and a woman. He was still covering his tracks, telling the police his wife had deserted him and visited Mary's family. But her father and stepmother were not happy with his explanation. If it was normal for Belle to storm off in fury, it was completely out of character for twenty-year-old Mary to go missing, and 'she was not that sort of girl' to get pregnant. To have left without saying goodbye was unthinkable.

Mary's parents went to the Ruxton's home to try to make more sense of the situation, and this time he told them that his wife and Mary had broken into his safe and taken £30 (now worth about £180), and said they would return when the money was spent. They now had two different stories from him, so the next day they went to the police and recorded Mary as missing.

The police in Scotland and in Lancaster were talking to each other, and some of the clothes found wrapped around the body parts were taken to the Rogerson's home, where Mary's stepmother identified the yellow blouse, which she had bought for Mary at a jumble sale and patched herself. They also told the police that Mary had a squint in one eye, which offered an explanation as to why one of the disembodied heads had the eyes removed. Although they could not identify the rompersuit, Mary's parents suggested the police visit a friend of Mary's, where Belle and the children had lodged when they went on a brief holiday to Morecambe. The friend had bought the rompersuit as a present for young Billie Boy.

The same day as the clothes were identified, Buck was back at the police station complaining that malicious rumours were flying around about him, damaging his practice and his health. He demanded that the police search his house to quash the rumours, and even asked them to put out a statement that the grisly packages found near Moffat were not his wife and the maid. But the police had other ideas.

Buck was finally arrested a month after the murders, on 12 October.

Shortly before the police came for him he was with a newspaper reporter who described the encounter:

> He paced rapidly up and down the library floor ... ran trembling fingers through tousled hair, and occasionally thumped his forehead with the palm of his hand. Now and again he stopped, swung around, and almost screamed 'I did not kill my Belle. I tell you she has gone away, she will come back. Tell everybody I am not guilty. Tell them I loved my Belle too much to harm her.'

It was almost six months later that he came up for trial at Manchester Assizes. There was a massive amount of evidence against him: the charladies gave evidence about the state of the house: the strange yellow discolouration of the bath; and the sanitary towels in Mary's bedroom that discounted the theory that she was pregnant.

The trial lasted eleven days, and Buck was restless and unhappy in the dock. When a witness fainted, he gave the police instructions how to treat her. His defence was based on challenging the proposition that the two bodies found in Scotland were his wife and maid, and that the bloodstains found in his home were the product of years of medical practice. He was the only defence witness, and alternated between hysterical sobbing and loudly claiming that he had last seen his wife when she and Mary left for Edinburgh. When challenged about the physical abuse his wife had suffered he said: 'Who loves most, chastises most.'

It took the jury only an hour to find Buck Ruxton guilty, and the judge pronounced the death sentence. Buck saluted the judge, said 'I am very sorry' and then thanked him for 'the patience and fairness of my trial'.

In the condemned cell his behaviour veered between a haughty insistence that prison officers call him by his name not his prison number, and courteous co-operation with the staff. He wrote to a friend: 'Please do speak me fair in death. Try to be good to my children. They are my one flesh and blood. Do something for them.' After his signature he wrote one word: 'Crushed'.

He also wrote to the reporter who was with him shortly before his arrest, reminding him of their interview in the library. 'Pity! The library is no more. Only the bare walls of that spacious room bear mute testimony of my choice of treasures.' He talked of how he wanted his daughters to be medical graduates and his son either a solicitor or a doctor. 'My solicitor has Isabella's oil painting in life size. It is the talk of the art world. Could you help to get it sold for a fair price to raise an education fund for my children?' he wrote.

Unfortunately the painting proved to be worthless, and Buck's insurance policies were invalid because he was hanged, and he was declared bankrupt while in prison. The children went to a local orphanage.

Buck had launched an appeal, which was quickly rejected, and despite a petition from Lancaster residents asking for him to be treated with clemency, Dr Ruxton was hanged at Strangeways Prison in Manchester on 12 May 1936.

His story was not quite over. Among the huge crowd that gathered outside the prison to wait for the black flag to be hoisted, a signal that the prisoner was dead, was the chief crime reporter of the *News of the World*. A man sidled up to him and handed him an envelope, then disappeared into the crowd. The envelope was addressed to the newspaper's editor.

When it was opened, the journalists in the room expected another protestation of innocence. But the letter read: 'I killed Mrs

Ruxton in a fit of temper because I thought she had been with a man. I was mad at the time. Mary Rogerson was present at the time. I had to kill her.' The letter had been written the day after his arrest and entrusted to a friend with the instruction: 'In the impossible event of a verdict of guilty and if – God forbid – I am to die, I want you to hand the envelope unopened to the editor of the *News of the World*. But remember: it has not to be opened until I am dead.'

Why did he confess after maintaining his innocence for so long? He was a Parsee, and as part of his religious beliefs he did not want to die with a lie on his lips. By confessing at the very end he freed his soul for the four-day funeral rites that his widowed mother was holding in Bombay.

10

Did She or Didn't She?

DID SHE OR DIDN'T SHE? IS CAROLYN WARMUS A JEALOUS AND obsessed lover who brutally killed her rival? Or a woman who spent twenty-seven years in prison for something she didn't do?

She was released from prison in June 2019, aged fifty-five, needing acute medical attention for a brain tumour, having spent most of her adult life in a maximum-security jail. In her words: 'I was imprisoned … because I dated a married man.' But there are others who say – and the court agreed – that she killed her married lover's wife in a cold-blooded murder, for which he was originally the prime suspect, and that she had a history of obsessive jealousy. Campaigners are still fighting on her behalf, but it is unlikely that the truth will ever be known. It has been a long, drawn-out, controversial case. If Carolyn was innocent, then the real killer or killers got away with murder. If she was guilty, she has been an incredible actress over more than a quarter of a century.

Carolyn had a privileged early life in an affluent suburb of Detroit. Her father was a self-made multi-millionaire, his wealth coming from an insurance company he set up. He was estimated to have $150 million at the time his daughter went to prison (it would be almost double that amount today) and he owned eight jets, two yachts, fifteen cars, and estates in Michigan, Florida, Arizona and New York.

Carolyn and her two younger siblings, Tracey and Tommy, grew up with their mother, Elizabeth, after her parents divorced with great acrimony when Carolyn was eight years old. Her father left her mother for his secretary, who wore low-cut, sequinned dresses and wasn't a warm, welcoming stepmother to Carolyn. Over the years there was a succession of disputes, sometimes ending up in court, between the warring parents. When Carolyn was fourteen her mother also remarried, and Carolyn and her siblings moved back to their father's home.

Carolyn was bright, graduating from a prestigious state school with good grades, although she was overshadowed by her prettier, cleverer, more popular younger sister, Tracey. She took a degree in psychology at the University of Michigan and embarked on a series of disastrous romances, but ex-boyfriends reported her behaviour as obsessive, with her hiring a private investigator on at least one occasion to track an ex's movements. One ex, Paul Laven, had to take out a restraining order against her after, he claimed, she tried to run down his new fiancée in her car, stalked them and sent him a note claiming she was pregnant. She wrote to his fiancée: 'I guess as long as you keep letting him live in your apartment he'll just continue to pretend he cares about you.' The couple were frightened Carolyn would crash their wedding and reception, and she was restrained by a judge from ever having contact with them. One of her girl friends at university, Shari Odenheimer, said: 'She was attracted to guys who were attached.'

With family money behind her she was always very expensively dressed, and unlike most students she could afford to eat in the best restaurants. She was attractive, with fluffy, blonde hair and large, oval eyes and long legs, and could have made a good match. But, as her friend said, she seemed to prefer unsuitable and unavailable men, having an affair with a married bartender and, again, hiring a private investigator to tail him after he broke up with her, hoping to get pictures of him with another woman that she could send to his wife. She hoped that if his marriage broke up he would turn to her.

The private investigator she found in *Yellow Pages* was Vincent Parco, whose company claimed to take on 'unusual and difficult cases', and who taught a college class to aspiring private detectives called 'How to Get Anything on Anybody'. And his company did manage to give Carolyn a series of risqué photographs, as part of her scheme to rupture his marriage, but in the end they were never sent.

Carolyn certainly had a loose relationship with the truth, forging a document to get herself out of paying for the damages to another woman's car after an accident, and she was even suspected of credit card fraud while working in a casual job at a nightclub, although, with her family money it's unlikely she needed to steal money, and she was never charged.

Carolyn met Paul Solomons when, aged twenty-three, she went to teach at Greenville School, in one of the richest school districts in the country, where he was already established as a fifth grade teacher. Because it was her first full-time teaching job, covering for another teacher who was on maternity leave, Paul was appointed her mentor. Her classroom where she taught computer studies was opposite his. Before long Paul, who was thirty-eight when they met and had the swarthy good looks of his Lebanese ancestors, was having an affair with Carolyn, but she has always insisted that she believed he was divorced, and that she knew he had previously dated other young female teachers. He didn't wear a wedding ring, and he later admitted to having had two brief flings before he met Carolyn.

When she discovered later that he was still married and living with his wife and teenage daughter, Kristan, she says he told her it was an open marriage and that his wife, Betty Jeanne, an account executive at a credit company, dated other men, and that they took separate holidays; it was a marriage in name only. He told her, she said, that he would leave Betty Jeanne for her as soon as Kristan finished high school. Carolyn claims she naively believed him, but she still dated other men during their affair. She actually met Betty Jeanne at school events and tried to befriend her, showering her with gifts, but, according to Kristan, her 'distant and cold' mother did not like Carolyn.

Carolyn first met Kristan at after-school basketball practice, where she joined in, having been a talented player as a student. When Carolyn went for a meal with the whole Solomon family, she offered to take Kristan on a skiing holiday, and eventually her mother agreed. Kristan later said in court that when they were away skiing Carolyn asked her several times whether her parents rowed about her, and whether Betty Jeanne disliked her. On Kristan's fifteenth birthday Carolyn turned up with two expensive outfits for her and a bracelet, and the teenager admitted she was worried her mother would not like her receiving them.

Three months after the affair started, Paul sent Carolyn a card saying he was 'falling deeply in love' with her. But within weeks, by the end of 1987, he was trying to end the affair. Predictably, with her past record, Carolyn was not prepared to let go. When the summer break was approaching he told her: 'Carolyn, you know we're not going to be able to see each other over the summer.' According to Paul she was upset and crying, and said: 'Life's not worth living without you.' Her affair with Paul was back on again after the summer of 1988, and she told an old friend that 'she would take it upon herself to make sure she ended up with him. She would then end up with the family she wanted and live happily ever after.'

It was clear by now that Paul was not fully committed to the relationship, and again he struggled, in the face of Carolyn's perseverance, to break it off.

Early in the evening of 15 January 1989 a New York telephone operator handling the 911 line received a panicky call from a woman who screamed: 'He is trying to kill me!' She later admitted she could not remember whether the caller said 'He' or 'She'. The call was abruptly disconnected, so the operator automatically contacted the police. They tried to trace the call but the telephone directory gave them a wrong address. Several hours later, at 11.42 p.m., Paul phoned the police after coming home and finding his wife dead.

The television was blaring loudly but there were no lights on. Betty Jeanne had been shot nine times in her back and legs, but she had also been bludgeoned around the head with the pistol butt. There was no sign of forced entry, neighbours had not heard any gunshots and there was no evidence of a struggle, apart from the disconnected phone. Next to the body was a woman's black cashmere glove, which apparently was tested and found not to have any blood on it.

Detectives immediately suspected Betty Jeanne's husband. Paul told them he had spent the day with his wife of nineteen years, making love to her in the morning, enjoying the privacy of having the house because Kristan was away skiing with a school friend. Carolyn, he said, rang him and persuaded him to meet her that evening for a belated celebration of her birthday. He told Betty Jeanne he was going to a bowling alley, and he did go, and met a few friends. But he only stayed briefly and went on to meet Carolyn at a restaurant, the Tree Top Lounge, part of the Holiday Inn in Yonkers, fifteen minutes from his home. They had met there before, enjoying the dimly lit privacy. She arrived twenty minutes after Paul. He drank vodka, she drank champagne and they ate oysters.

According to Paul they talked about the future, and because he was trying to get out of his entanglement with her, he told Carolyn: 'I'd be happy to dance at your wedding and see you happy.' She replied: 'What about your happiness, Paul? Don't you deserve to be happy?' He said he told her that if anything happened to Betty Jeanne he would never get married again. After they left the restaurant the lovers went to her car where they had sex.

After Paul arrived home and discovered the murder, he called the emergency services. When police arrived he told them:

> I got home and the first thing I heard was the TV on very loud. I walked into the living room. The lights were out. I noticed that Betty Jeanne was on the floor. I assumed she was asleep. I touched her and she was cold. I went and turned the lights on. I turned her over and there was blood. I thought she had fallen and hit her head.

He was allowed to wipe and wash his hands, which were covered in blood, and this was later admitted in court to be a breach of investigative protocols as it would have helped remove any gunshot residue. At first he lied about his whereabouts, saying that he had been at the bowling alley all evening, but later changed this to admit he had been with Carolyn. It was argued at the trial that he was simply unwilling to own up to the affair, not trying to protect himself from suspicion. When his hands were later tested for gunshot residue the test proved 'inconclusive'.

Carolyn voluntarily agreed to four lie detector tests, all of which came to the conclusion she was telling the truth, and at this stage Paul was still the prime suspect. Lie detector evidence is not admissible in court.

When the friends from the bowling alley and a waitress at the Tree Top lounge confirmed the timings that Paul gave the police, the investigating team began to shift their attention to Carolyn. Her behaviour was suspicious. Immediately after the murder she spent a lot of time at the Solomon home, cooking meals for Paul and Kristan, and gave Kristan diamond earrings from Tiffany for her sixteenth birthday. When Paul, overwhelmed by her excessive attention, finished his relationship with her, telling her to stop calling him, he received a stream of letters from her including one which said: 'I hope you are going to allow yourself some happiness and spend some time with me.'

Instead, Paul decided that he wanted to spend time with another young teacher, Barbara Ballor, twenty-eight years old. With his wife dead, Paul was able to be open about his new affair, and Carolyn began her old trick of stalking the couple. On one occasion, having found out that Barbara was out of town, she turned up uninvited at Paul's home and they had drinks. He later claimed in court that he asked her straight if she had anything to do with the death of his wife. She said: 'Paul, I'm so glad you feel comfortable enough to ask me that. No, I would never do anything to hurt you or Kristan.'

A few weeks later, when Paul and Barbara flew to Puerto Rico for a holiday, Carolyn turned up at the same hotel. Spooked, Paul and Barbara fled, and Paul reported Carolyn to the police. Barbara took out a restraining order against her, and a couple of months later Carolyn had a breakdown and spent a week in a psychiatric hospital.

She later claimed Paul had rung her and told her to meet him in Puerto Rico as part, she said, of an intricate plot to frame her for the murder, and to make her look like an unhinged ex. If she knew she was being watched by the police as a possible murder suspect, tailing her ex on holiday was not exactly sensible behaviour.

Meanwhile, evidence against her was accumulating. Vincent Parco, the private investigator who had previously worked for her tailing her ex-lover, claimed she first asked him about getting a gun for her six months before the murder. 'She said there was a series of burglaries in her neighbourhood and she needed protection,' he added. But she also gave him other reasons for wanting a gun, telling him someone was out to harm her family. She cited the crash of one of her father's jets (true), but added that a mysterious woman was seen hanging around the airfield. Then she claimed her sister had been struck by a hit-and-run driver in Washington DC, and described the driver as an attractive, dark-haired woman, possibly living in Westchester, who was called Jean or Betty Jean. She told Vincent this woman was her father's former mistress.

When he was first questioned by police, Vincent denied all knowledge of a gun, but when forensic experts were able to match the shell casings to the machinist who made the silencer, Vincent saw the benefit of helping the police and prosecution lawyers in return for immunity from prosecution. Vincent, who was later a star prosecution witness, said that even when her illicit affair with Paul resumed, he was also in a relationship with her that he described as 'social, bordering on dating'.

It was in early January 1989 that Vincent had sold her a .25 calibre Beretta pistol with a silencer for $2500. A check on calls made from her phone found one to a sports shop that sold ammunition. Checking with the shop, the only person to have bought .25 calibre ammunition on the day the call was made was a woman named Liisa Kattai, but when police traced her she had an alibi. She told them her driver's licence had been lost or stolen a few months earlier, at a time when she was working with Carolyn. So was Carolyn using her identity? Shopworkers could not confirm her as the woman they served, but she could easily have been wearing a disguise.

Carolyn was arrested for the murder of Betty Jeanne in February 1990, and her wealthy father paid the $250,000 bail. The trial started at Westchester County Courthouse in January 1991, almost two years to the day after Betty Jeanne died. Carolyn made a major mistake if she wanted to convince the jury she was innocent. She arrived wearing an expensive pink suit and matching hat, and as she got out of the car her skirt rode up showing her legs up to the top of her thighs. Black stiletto heels and large sunglasses completed the look of a woman who was revelling in her role as a femme fatale.

It played into the hands of the media, who had already dubbed the case The Fatal Attraction killing, after the hot 1987 film that featured Glenn Close as an unhinged, obsessive lover, and was mainly filmed in Westchester, where Betty Jeanne was murdered. From her prison cell Carolyn later claimed she was tried in the media and there was 'huge prejudice' against her because of her looks and her love life, but her outfits and slightly melodramatic behaviour during the trial fed the impression that she was in some way enjoying the limelight.

The prosecution case was that, after pumping the bullets into Betty Jeanne, Carolyn calmly escaped the scene without any witnesses seeing her, and travelled to her assignation with Paul. They made a lot of the fact that, after the murder, she was capable of having passionate sex in her car with her lover. Prosecutor James McCarty said she had 'a consuming desire to have Paul Solomon for herself, and Betty Jeanne Solomon stood squarely in her way.'

With the best lawyers that money could buy, Carolyn's defence was formidable. Both Paul and Vincent were ripped apart. Surprisingly to many observers, both men had been given immunity from prosecution for appearing as witnesses. David Lewis, the defence lawyer, tried to portray Paul as a weirdo who had not moved out of the apartment where his wife was murdered, as a creep who had sold the movie rights to his story for $175,000 and as a liar who had repeatedly cheated on his wife. Paul admitted all of this, and the accusation of cheating on his wife was countered when it was revealed that Betty Jeanne herself had had a nine-year affair with her married, former boss.

Eventually, after the relentless cross-examination, Paul erupted in fury at the defence lawyer: 'You twist and turn words, manipulate facts of half-truths and incomplete reports to make them what they aren't. I'll accept my guilt for the affair but I only hope that when I'm punished and judged, that you are punished and judged for what you've done here.' Lewis replied calmly: 'As you know, sir, there is no court of law that will punish or judge you, because you made an agreement that you are immune.'

Vincent was also easy to discredit. His job, he admitted, involved lying, and it was his testimony alone that connected Carolyn to the murder weapon, which has never been found. Late in the trial a school nurse came forward to say Carolyn had told her she bought a gun from a private detective because she was 'terrified to live alone', but added that she had no ammunition. The nurse had not told the police because she thought it was 'common knowledge' that Carolyn had a gun. Vincent claimed Carolyn had told him she had thrown the gun off a parkway.

After ten days of cross-examination, Carolyn's team were beginning to feel confident. They were pushing the theory that the murder was carried out by Vincent, on behalf of Paul. They even had testimony from a man who claimed he heard Vincent and Paul in the public lavatory of a bowling alley discussing throwing a gun into the river, and Paul handing Vincent $20,000, and another man who claimed he had been approached by Vincent six months before the murder and asked if he would carry out a contract killing.

But the prosecution then produced Liisa Kattai, who had been working with Carolyn when her driver's licence was stolen, and this was the document used to buy the ammunition. The defence believed that they had the clinching piece of evidence, producing Carolyn's telephone bill on which there was no record of a call to the sports shop where the ammunition was bought, and a long call to her mother, which would not have allowed her time to travel to the Solomon's home to kill Betty Jeanne. It seemed like a clincher, until the phone company executives said it did not look genuine because it did not have their slogan 'Communications for the Next 100 Years' at the top. Only one of the two phone records for that day could be genuine.

When the case finished after eleven weeks it was all circumstantial evidence. There were no fingerprints, no murder weapon, no hairs found at the scene, no blood linking Carolyn to the crime, and many seasoned crime reporters were finding it a difficult case to call. The jury of eight men and four women was out for twelve days, wrestling with a verdict. They all agreed that the telephone bill submitted by the defence was fake, and that the evidence of the two men who alleged there had been a contract between Paul and Vincent to carry out the murder was not reliable, but it was hard to get beyond the lack of hard evidence against Carolyn. In the end, deadlocked at eight to four in favour of conviction, the judge was forced to declare a mistrial, and for the time being at least Carolyn was free.

'My family and I are devastated by the knowledge that this nightmare must go on,' Paul said. And he was facing more problems, with his school board under public pressure to remove a teacher who had admitted having affairs. By agreement, he was taken off teaching duties but remained employed within the school.

A second trial began in January 1992, in the same tenth-floor courtroom. (This time Carolyn brought a pillow into court every day so that she could rest her head.) A crucial piece of new evidence turned up on the eve of the trial – a bloodstained glove, apparently the one photographed next to Betty Jeanne's body, and which matched a pair of gloves Carolyn owned. The glove had apparently been found by Paul in a box in a wardrobe between the first and second trials – astonishingly, the glove photographed next to the body at the crime scene had been handed to him by the police and he had claimed, at the time of the first trial, that he had searched high and low and could not find it. One reporter who covered the case described the police handling of the crime scene as 'like the Keystone Cops'.

Tested again, the glove had small bloodstains on the fingertips. The defence furiously opposed its last-minute inclusion as evidence, arguing that there wasn't sufficient proof the glove was the same one photographed at the crime scene, and no evidence that it belonged to Carolyn. At the very least, the crime scene officers were guilty of shoddy work: it should have been bagged, listed and presented at the first trial, not found months later in a cupboard. No DNA testing was done on the glove. And the judge refused to allow DNA testing now, on the grounds that many people had handled the glove, and it would be impossible to get a pure sample. Had it been carefully bagged and stored by the police on the day of the murder, sampling would have been possible.

The judge allowed it to be admitted though, after evidence that Carolyn had bought an identical pair of gloves from a department store, and that fibres found on Carolyn's hands at the time of the first investigation matched the fibres from the gloves. The defence argued that the gloves were very common, a one-size-fits-all, and

ABOVE: Dena Thompson leaving Lewes Crown Court in August 2000, where she was standing trial for allegedly attempting to murder her husband.
Chris Ison / PA

ABOVE: Martha Freeman, who kept her lover in the wardrobe while her husband slept.

Mark Humphrey / Shutterstock

ABOVE: Drew Peterson, the US cop who murdered his third wife, and whose fourth wife mysteriously disappeared.

MCT / SIPA USA / PA

RIGHT: Dr Buck Ruxton, who said he could not live with his wife or without her. He murdered her and their maid – and paid for his crimes at the gallows.

Universal History Archive / Getty

LEFT: Jane Andrews, assistant to the Duchess of York, and the lover, Tom Cresswell, whom she violently killed because he would not marry her.

Shutterstock

ABOVE: Glamorous Carolyn Warmus, dressed for the first day of her murder trial as if she was going to a glittering social event.

USA TODAY Network / SIPA USA / Getty

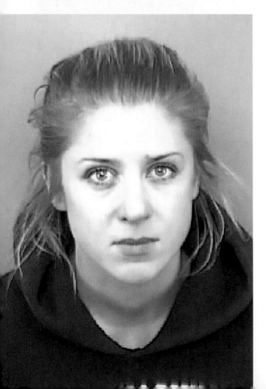

LEFT: Was she led astray by an older woman? Sarah Dutra, on trial for the murder of lawyer Larry McNabney, whose body was kept for weeks in a fridge.

San Joaquin Sheriff's Dept / Zuma Press / PA

ABOVE: Pharmacist Mitesh Patel who killed his wife Jessica with a 'bag for life', planning to spend the rest of his life with his gay lover.

© *KTD Media*

LEFT: Arminda Perry and her husband John. After he meticulously butchered her, he fed her flesh to their pet cat.

Shutterstock

ABOVE: Els 'Babs' Clottemans, the schoolteacher who killed her love rival by sabotaging her parachute.

©Yorick Jansens / EPA / Shutterstock

RIGHT: Emile Cilliers, the army sergeant who tried to kill his wife in a parachute 'accident' – amazingly, she survived, but with terrible injuries.

Jonathan Brady / PA

LEFT: They both made their livings providing kinky sex sessions for men, but in their private lives Margi Dunbar (left) and Christie Offord were lovers. After they fell out, Christie met a horrible death.

BELOW: John Tanner and his girlfriend, Oxford University student Rachel McLean. After killing her, he hid her body under the floorboards of the house she shared with friends.

just because Carolyn had a similar pair it did not prove that the one at the crime scene was hers. Nine thousand identical pairs of gloves had been sold, according to the supplier.

After the testimony of fifty-five witnesses and a trial that lasted four months, this time the jury was out for six days and came back with a verdict of guilty to second-degree murder, all jurors agreeing that it was the evidence of the black glove that most influenced them.

For the first time, the courtroom heard Carolyn Warmus speak, struggling through her sobs to say: 'I can only ask for leniency because I am innocent. If I'm guilty of anything at all it was simply being foolish enough to believe the lies and promises that Paul Solomon made to me.' But the judge was not lenient. He described the crime as 'a hideous act, a most extreme, illegal and wanton murder.' To the surprise and consternation of her supporters, instead of giving her the minimum sentence of fifteen years, he gave her twenty-five years to life.

Paul Solomon said: 'I beg of you all to allow Kristan and me and our families to go forward. I will not make another statement.'

Carolyn was moved to the Bedford Hills Correctional Facility for Women in Westchester County, the only maximum-security prison for women in New York State, and the place that would be her home for the next twenty-seven years. She swapped expensive restaurants and designer shoes for drab meals in dining areas shared with cockroaches, state-issued boots, showers that frequently didn't work, a regime where toilet paper was a prized commodity and where she was allowed just four hours of visits every month.

A year after her conviction, the case was before the court again when her lawyers asked the judge to declare a mistrial on the grounds that the prosecution withheld evidence and that Paul had committed perjury. Another private investigator, Anthony Souza, testified that he had been hired by Barbara Ballor, Paul's new girlfriend, three months before the killing, to keep Betty Jeanne under surveillance because Paul suspected she had a lover. Yet Paul had maintained at the previous trials that he had not started dating Barbara until several months after his wife's murder. Anthony said that his files had been confiscated when his home was searched in an unrelated case. He had followed Betty Jeanne for three days and found nothing more exciting than a trip to a Japanese restaurant, but the significance was who had hired him. Asked why he had not come forward before, he claimed he did not realize it was the same woman because at the original trials the headlines had been about Carolyn, not the victim.

Carolyn's lawyer also argued that the prosecution had not revealed that a second glove had been found outside the apartment building where the murder took place. The judge did not agree that this was enough to order a retrial.

It took nine years before a full appeal was heard in 1992, but the appeal court did not accept Carolyn's claim that there was not sufficient evidence to convict her, and the court also upheld the length of her sentence.

In 2004 she filed a lawsuit against the New York State Department of Correctional Services, claiming to have been sexually abused by prison guards. She alleged she had been raped and forced to trade sexual services in return for basic privileges. One prison officer was charged with sexual abuse, and Carolyn backed her claim with a sample of his semen that she had stored in plastic. She refused to testify in a court case against him, probably unwilling to have the media spotlight back on her. Four years after filing the lawsuit, after an investigation by the authorities, she was awarded $10,000 in compensation and her legal fees of $70,000 were paid. It's also worth mentioning that she had previously been accused of having a romantic relationship with a guard, who resigned. She denied the accusation and declared it was 'harassment'.

By now Carolyn no longer had the protection of her daddy's millions. In 1993 his companies collapsed and he was declared bankrupt. There followed a long series of legal wrangles over whether he had taken millions out of the companies for his personal use, hiding it in trust funds or in his wife's name, his mother-in-law's name or names of associates. The cars and the yacht and the planes were all cited. Eventually, in 2002, he was sentenced to ninety-seven months in prison for defrauding creditors, and after a series of appeals he finally started his jail sentence in 2007, so for eight years father and daughter were both behind bars.

Life went well for Paul Solomon. He continued to work at Greenville School until taking early retirement in 2011, when he was praised at a standing-room-only gathering organized by the school council, and presented with a coveted Silver Bowl Award for services to the school community. He taught at the school for thirty-five years. He was even honoured with a 'Paul Solomon Day', on 27 April 2011. He has now remarried.

Carolyn first appealed for parole in 2017, after serving twenty-five years, and it was then revealed that she had had eleven 'misconducts' recorded against her. This is not unusual for such a long stay, especially as some of the infringements are classified as minor. However, she was still protesting her innocence, and her lawyer argued that the killing had required a level of sophistication with a gun and brute force for the pistol whipping, which Carolyn did not have. They also, again, asked for DNA testing of the glove. Mainly because she would not apologize for her crime, her parole bid was turned down.

However, her second parole bid, in 2019, was successful, even though she continued to declare her innocence and delivered an attack on Paul, when asked by one of the parole board who she thought could have committed the murder. She said:

Well, the husband really benefited from her death. I found out – I didn't know at the time – that, you know, he had military training [he had been in the air force before teaching], that he had guns in his apartment. I did not know any of this. I didn't realize he was having other affairs. I found out at trial that he had already had large life insurance policies in place and benefited financially from her death through that, and through the media.

She was also asked what she would say to Paul Solomon now, after twenty-seven years in prison.

My heart just goes out to the family and I know at trial the husband – her husband and daughter testified and they did not express any love or concern towards the victim and the fact that she is dead … I mean, I lost my parents and I lost loved ones and it's heart-wrenching, and I honestly can't imagine what the victim's parents and siblings are going through. Nobody should have to go through something this tragic.

She ended by saying she regretted the affair with Paul. 'I'm just so ashamed and I just wish I could never have been involved with him whatsoever and, if I could change that, you know, I certainly would.' Coincidentally, in the week that she was finally granted parole,

Vincent Parco, whose evidence against her had been so crucial, was convicted of criminal charges accusing him of hiring prostitutes to blackmail a witness in a child sex abuse case. He was sentenced to between one and three years in prison.

Carolyn Warmus finally left prison on 17 June 2019. The campaign to clear her name goes on, but it is unlikely to ever change anything.

11

A Fit of Conscience

THEY COMMITTED THE PERFECT MURDER. THEY GOT AWAY WITH IT. And they could have taken the secret to the grave with them ... But then Colin Howell confessed, and now he and his partner-in-crime, Hazel Stewart, are serving long prison sentences.

Twenty years after they killed two people and managed to convince the world it was a joint suicide, they finally faced justice. Yet why did Colin confess? Did his deeply Christian beliefs finally get to him? Or was it because he was mired in debt, his second marriage was collapsing, he had a serious pornography habit and, as a much-respected dentist, he had been assaulting female patients while they were under anaesthetic?

His life was clearly out of control, and the memory of the crime was haunting him. When he talked to the police, he not only took himself down but he did nothing to protect the woman who was his accomplice and, at the time, his lover.

The story of Colin and Hazel is one of rank hypocrisy and selfishness. Both were upstanding pillars of their church, both professed a devout commitment to their Baptist faith and both had marriage partners who did nothing to provoke the cold, clever, calculated murders. Nothing, except being in the way of their passion.

Colin was born in 1959 and grew up in Belfast, the fourth of five children in a fairly prosperous family, his father working as manager at a government training centre. It was a religious household, and as a boy he went to church three times every Sunday. His ambition was to be a missionary. Having failed the entrance examination for grammar school, he went to an all-boys secondary school, where he worked hard and passed enough GCEs to take his A-levels. By this time the family had left Belfast and were living in Armagh. Again, he was a good, hard-working pupil and although his A-level grades were not good enough to get him a place at medical school, he decided instead to become a dentist, studying at Queen's University, Belfast, and graduating six years later.

His strict religious beliefs meant that he did not have sex until he met Lesley, who became his first wife. As a substitute he had developed a passion for pornography, buying top shelf magazines in those pre-internet days – a habit he would keep for the rest of his life.

Lesley was a student nurse at the Royal Victoria Hospital in Belfast, moving to Northern Ireland from Dublin, where she spent most of her formative years. She was attractive and popular, had led a less cloistered life than Colin, having travelled around with her student friends, and had more experience of relationships than him, having dated a few men (he had only had one short-lived relationship). But Colin's possessive and controlling attitude to women was already developing, and he ended up physically attacking a junior doctor who also took an interest in Lesley.

Colin probably made the running in the early days, but the relationship soon took off and became sexual. Perhaps because of religion, or simply because Colin did not like contraception, before they were married Lesley had three abortions, then illegal in Northern Ireland.

After they married they moved to Coleraine, where Colin had his first job in a dental practice. Lesley carried on nursing until their first child, Matthew, was born in 1984, followed two years later by Lauren. Colin's career was flourishing, and their social life centred around the Coleraine Baptist Church. Lesley did not enjoy staying at home, she missed her job and was lonely because in his free time Colin was doing more and more work with the church, taking on an active role as a youth leader.

He then established his own dental practice, but sank too much money into it, leaving the young couple with debts. At the same time, Lesley was resentful that she did not have the same lifestyle as other dentists' wives, with smart cars and clothes. They moved to a bigger house before their third child, Daniel, was born, and the mortgage plus the debt on the dental practice meant they were permanently living on an overdraft; they had to move in when some of the building work was unfinished, the rooms having bare boards and no carpets.

There were constant tensions between the couple. Colin was not a good businessman and Lesley hated living on a very tight budget. She also caught Colin out in his first extramarital affair, with a woman he knew from university. She rang the woman who assured her it had only been a fling and was over, but it still damaged Lesley's self-esteem. Meanwhile, the babies kept coming: another, Jonathan, followed quickly, and she found herself looking after four toddlers all under five years old.

Colin was always happy to do his share of childcare, but the dental practice meant he had to work long hours to cope with their ever-increasing overdraft. It was when he was taking his daughter, Lauren, to nursery that he first met Hazel Buchanan, an assistant there. He already had a nodding acquaintance with her, as she and her husband and children went to the same church, and Hazel often helped out looking after the younger children in the congregation, including the Howells' little ones.

Hazel was then shy and lacking confidence. She came from a large family, had grown up on a farm in the countryside and married Trevor Buchanan when she was eighteen and he was three years older. She was his first serious girlfriend, the love of his life. Trevor followed two of his brothers into the police force, where he got on well with his colleagues who nicknamed him Ted, and he was subsequently posted to Coleraine. Hazel, wrenched away from her large and supportive family, was lonely.

Colin began flirting with Hazel when their children went to the same swimming lessons. Parents were invited to join the children in the water, and Hazel was soon having swimming lessons from Colin, who was the only father to attend the classes. While the other mothers gossiped at the poolside over coffee, he was teaching her the front crawl, which involved him supporting her in the water. One day he ran his hand over her thighs and said: 'If I'm having wrong thoughts about you, you'll have to forgive me.' He wasn't expecting her reply: 'I'm not so innocent myself.'

The affair was on. Under the guise of teaching her how to play the guitar, when Colin turned up at her home he was greeted by Hazel wearing a denim mini skirt and a low-cut top. He later said: 'I knew I was not there for music lessons.'

Soon they were meeting whenever they could, which was made easier by her husband, Trevor, working shifts as a policeman. Colin would park away from her home and approach through woods at the back, climbing through a window that she left open for him, when her children Andrew and Lisa were asleep.

Hazel later told the police:

From this time on I began to feel there was more to life than merely being in the home. I found myself not depending on Trevor so much. Trevor saw a change in my attitude for which, for the most part, he was not in favour – he preferred me as I was before. This initially led to arguments between us and … a lack of communication set in. Colin was a different kind of person from Trevor in that he was friendly, more outgoing and easy to talk to, with plenty of chat.

The lovers communicated using a secret telephone code, and often spent hours late at night talking to each other when their partners were asleep, cleverly never speaking for more than ten minutes to avoid the call being registered on their automated statements, but ringing off and redialling after nine minutes. When Hazel became pregnant the couple were worried that the baby was Colin's, not Trevor's, and they managed to travel to London together for an abortion, taking care not to sit together on the flights there and back.

All the players in this drama were committed to their fundamentalist religion, and so when Lesley became convinced that Colin was having an affair with Hazel, she confided in their pastor, John Hansford. He spoke to Colin, who point blank denied that he was having an affair. When he later saw Hazel, she too initially denied the affair but later, tearfully, owned up to it, although she gave the impression it had only just started, and she insisted it had not been consummated. When Hansford again confronted Colin he backed this up, apologizing for denying the affair by saying it was not sexual. Nonetheless, he was forced to stand down from his many roles at the church. The pastor then told Trevor who reacted angrily.

Hansford said: 'It was obviously a desperately tense situation. Trevor was devastated and really, really angry. He managed to control his temper. Trevor and Lesley both felt a tremendous sense of embarrassment, shame and humiliation.'

Both families were allowed to continue attending church services, but there was a timetable to keep them apart, one family going to a morning service, the other in the evening. If they ever did overlap, they sat at opposite sides of the church, the Howells at the front and the Buchanans at the back. Both couples tried to reconcile, but Lesley started taking antidepressants, and she began to drink wine even when she was on her own.

Colin, who was already developing a taste for the dramatic confession, caused more emotional mayhem for her when he confessed to the pastor that the relationship with Hazel had been sexual. Dismayed, Lesley tried to kill herself by swallowing a handful of paracetamol. Hansford took her to hospital where she stayed for three days, and while there she told a friend who visited her that she could not go through with the suicide because 'I can't leave the kids.'

For four months Colin and Hazel kept to their promise of not seeing one another, but at the Howell household there was no reconciliation, with Lesley more and more obsessed about her husband's failings. She tailed him in the car when he went out running, she shredded his clothes and she ripped up family pictures. Trevor was coping in a much more restrained way, and it seems the Buchanan marriage was beginning to get back on track.

For Colin the separation from Hazel was close to unbearable. He later told the police: 'That four months period was a bit like I was choking … I didn't dare tell anyone, Lesley or John Hansford, what was really going on with me, the struggles I was having, and the emotions. I was making a deliberate effort out of duty and from my spiritual and Christian background, this was the right thing to do.'

When the pastor, who was counselling all four of them, told him the Buchanans were doing well and moving on with their lives, Colin became determined to win Hazel back. He decided to ring her, even though the pastor had told him she wanted nothing more to do with him. When he rang her 'it was like holding your breath, and when she said she was glad to hear from me it was like coming up for air'. They agreed that life in both of their homes was terrible, and that they desperately missed each other. Colin later claimed that Hazel said: 'I'll love you until I'm old and grey.'

It may have been at this moment that Colin decided he had to get rid of Lesley, once and for all, and Lesley clearly became worried that he was trying to kill her. She told a friend 'in case something happens to me' that when she was in the bath with a tape recorder, plugged into an extension cable, behind her, Colin came in and picked the tape recorder up and the lead came out and somehow fell into the bath, giving Lesley a shock. Luckily, it landed on her arm, which shot up because of the shock and the lead was tossed out of the bath.

Colin told Lesley not to tell anyone because he felt he had done something careless; Lesley, not sure whether she thought he was deliberately trying to murder her, told at least three friends. Years later Colin denied this was anything other than an accident. It happened only six weeks before the murders.

And then there was a death. Lesley's father, Harry, who had moved to live near his daughter after his wife died, and who loved spending time with the Howell children, was staying with Lesley and Colin when he had a sudden heart attack and died. Lesley was distraught. Years later many people, including Lesley's brother, Chris, were convinced that Colin had something to do with the death but it was impossible to prove. Certainly, Colin was up to no good: friends who loaned him their car found a passport in the side pocket of the driver's door. It had Harry's name and details, but the photograph had been crudely changed to Colin's. He later claimed to police that he used it to rent videos for his children, although it's more likely he was renting the pornographic films he was obsessed with.

After Harry's death, Lesley inherited the bulk of his money, totalling more than £240,000. She did not tell Colin how much she had, but he probably had a good idea, which helped provide a motive for killing her as he was, as usual, in debt. He also did not want the shame of a divorce and a custody battle, which he felt she would win. He later said he did not want his children being brought up by an alcoholic mother, but this was probably self-serving, as others who knew Lesley said that although she liked a drink, she was a long way from being an alcoholic. Colin later even told one of the psychiatrists who interviewed him after his arrest that he was sure Lesley wanted to die, and that he felt that by killing her he was helping her. He also claimed that she had said to him: 'I am going to Heaven soon. Maybe you and Hazel are meant to be together.'

It was a convenient conversation for him to remember, more than twenty years later, a conversation that he seemed to believe partially absolved him. Whether it happened or not, that night, as Lesley slept and her brother and his wife, over from England for the funeral, were in the spare room, Colin got in his car and drove off, probably to see Hazel. This was the beginning of the plot to wipe out the two people who stood in their way: Lesley and Trevor.

Although Hazel was at first disbelieving, Colin was charismatic and forceful, and before long she fell in with his plans to kill both their spouses and make it look like a double suicide. He said Hazel was mainly worried about the risk of being caught, threatening to slit her wrists if the police came to arrest her. Colin was able to assure her that the deaths would be painless, by carbon monoxide poisoning, and both the victims would be sedated so that they did not wake up. But he needed Hazel's co-operation and help. She was confused and worried, so he made sure that he never used the words 'murder' or 'killing' and later said: 'Our conversations were always sanitized to avoid the real horror of what we were doing.'

He gave Hazel six or eight sedatives, which he said belonged to his mother, and he asked her to move Trevor's gun because he was frightened if Trevor woke up while Colin was killing him, he might grab the weapon and shoot.

The night of the well-planned double murder was 18 May 1991. It was Daniel's second birthday the next day, and Colin had an excuse to spend time in the garage that afternoon, as he was meant to be assembling a slide for him. He took a baby's bottle with him, which he cut in half, squeezing the neck of it into a garden hose. Lesley was out for much of the day, going to the hairdresser and later having a sunbed session. She stopped to put petrol in the car, and the garage owner's wife noticed she was unsteady and seemed distracted. She was so concerned she rang Colin that evening to say she was worried about Lesley, not realizing she was playing into his hands by making her 'suicide' all the more plausible.

Colin made a point of keeping the children up late that evening, so that they were extra tired, and he checked they had all been to the toilet so that they were unlikely to need to get up. Then he blocked their door with a hockey stick. He was worried because Hazel was not responding when he tried to ring her, using their code. Eventually, much later, she rang him and he gave her the message: 'Tonight's on. We're going to do it.'

Later that night, after Lesley had fallen asleep in her nightdress on the sofa, Colin made the final preparations. He fed the hosepipe through the kitchen window, with the other end attached to the car exhaust with a tight seal made by the baby's bottle. He went back outside and started the car engine, then positioned the hose about six inches from her face, held in place by the quilt she had covered herself with on the sofa. He stood outside the room, away from the fumes. Concerned that she seemed to be stirring, he went back into the room and pulled the quilt over her more. She cried out 'Matthew' in a weak voice, the name of their oldest child, who was only six at the time. Colin later claimed to be haunted by this terrible, final appeal for help from a child. He held her tight and aimed the hosepipe at her mouth and nostrils until he was sure she had stopped breathing. Then he quickly left the room, took a few deep breaths because he could feel the fumes making him dizzy, went to the garage and disconnected the hose.

Back in the house he removed Lesley's nightdress and put a T-shirt and leggings on her body. He carried it to the boot of the car, put a blanket over her and loaded his bike on top. Then he took some family photographs and Lesley's Walkman, checked the children were still fast asleep and called Hazel. She was in bed with her husband, but she heard the click of their coded phone call and rang back to give him the all-clear to come round.

Colin freewheeled his car from the garage on to the road in order not to disturb neighbours, then drove to Hazel's home. She had moved the family car so he was able to reverse into the garage. Hazel let him in, and the whole murder procedure was repeated, this time in the bedroom where Trevor was fast asleep. Hazel had given him the sedatives, but Colin would later complain that she had not ground them down sufficiently, and when he glanced at a tuna roll in the kitchen he saw the suspicious-looking blue flecks. He was worried Trevor would wake up, as Lesley had almost done, and if he did he would be a more difficult proposition to hold down. And his fears were realized as Trevor did struggle against the hosepipe that

Colin pushed straight into his mouth, and the two men grappled together briefly before the fumes overcame Trevor.

According to his later account, Colin was nauseous from the fumes and ran into the back garden to vomit, but was relieved to be able to avoid being sick because he did not want to leave forensic evidence of his presence. Throughout both the murders he had carefully worn disposable rubber gloves. Back in the house, Hazel gave him some clothes to dress Trevor in, and then he was unceremoniously dumped next to Lesley in the boot and covered with the blanket and bike.

Colin told Hazel to light a fire in the grate, and she cut up and burned the hosepipe. She opened the bedroom window to disperse the fumes, and stripped the bed linen and put it in the washing machine.

So Colin drove off with two dead bodies in the boot of his car. A neighbour, who had been to the bathroom, heard a car drive away at about 3.40 a.m. and assumed it was Trevor starting an early shift. Colin took the bodies to the garage at the rear of Lesley's father's house. Harry's death twelve days earlier meant the house was empty – an important element, and one that convinces some of Lesley's friends and relatives that Colin was implicated in Harry's sudden death. He stopped on the way to hide his bike in a hedge.

Once inside the garage he manoeuvred both the bodies from the boot into the car, Trevor in the front seat and Lesley splayed in the back with her family pictures, her Walkman headphones on her ears and a tape of gospel music playing. He attached an old vacuum cleaner hose to the car exhaust and fed it in through the window. He switched the ignition on and beat a retreat, leaving what he hoped was the perfect scene of a double suicide, committed by two desperately unhappy people who were united in their misery at the betrayal of their partners. Then he made his escape.

A fit man who enjoyed jogging regularly, he ran hard and fast back to the place where he had concealed the bike, and then, as dawn was breaking, pedalled home. He did not encounter anyone, and was able to stow the bike and ring Hazel before any of the children woke up. He briefed her about what she must say to the police. Then he burned his clothes.

Before he alerted anyone to the fact Lesley was missing, he took out a note she had written after her father died and which, he felt, would underline her suicidal intentions. It was not dated, and she had crumpled it up and never given it to him. When he found it, he knew it would come in handy.

> Dear Colin, I'm just trying to go to sleep now, how long I don't know. Thank you for your help over the past few days and for the good times in our marriage. I don't know what to say to you because I don't know how I feel, but I have seen that life goes on after a few weeks of pain, and let's face it, Colin, I am nothing in comparison to what you lost in the one you loved awhile back. If I wake up in the morning, just let this be our secret, Lesley.

The first person he rang was one of the elders at the church, and after telling him Lesley was missing asked him to check out her father's house, as, Colin suggested, she may have gone there. But a cursory check of the house did not find anything. Another friend, also a church stalwart, came round and Colin told him that Trevor had been there the night before, there had been an angry confrontation and that afterwards Lesley had left in a highly emotional state. While the usual checks were being made at ferry and airport terminals, a second check was made at Harry's house, but the garage was not opened. On a third visit by two friends of the Howells, the smell of gas was traced to the garage and the bodies were found. Lesley seemed to have a smile on her face, according to one of the men who found her.

The news reverberated round the close-knit religious community, and both Colin and Hazel were blamed and condemned for their actions that had led to the joint suicide. What nobody suspected was that the two bodies in the car had been murdered. The families were shattered, and the pastor who had been counselling both the Howells and the Buchanans was criticized for not spotting the deep level of distress of the innocent parties. Hazel and Colin kept away from each other, and despite a sustained campaign by Colin to absolve himself from blame for his wife's death, they were both shamed into leaving the church and had to attend services elsewhere.

They did not stay apart for long. Only six weeks after the 'suicides', Colin pedalled across town on his bike and climbed in through a rear window at Hazel's home, just as he did when Trevor was working nights, and the two made love in the bedroom where Colin killed Trevor.

It was almost a year after the deaths that the inquests into the deaths of Lesley and Trevor were held. Both Colin and Hazel gave evidence about the state of their marriages, and about the events on the final nights of their partners' lives. They both lied convincingly, and the verdict was that Lesley and Trevor had taken their own lives. Colin and Hazel had got away with it: they had committed the perfect crime.

Colin and Hazel both profited from insurance policies, and Colin also inherited all the money that Lesley's father had left her. But the grand passion that had impelled them to commit the murders was spent, and although the relationship spluttered on for four years the sex was petering out. By chance they then discovered that the gas and air Colin used on his dental patients helped Hazel relax and climax during sex, and so he experimented with injecting her with powerful sedatives when they made love at her home.

Having sex with Hazel while she was effectively out of it, probably led to him sexually assaulting female patients while they were under sedation. When police eventually investigated, after his murder confession, they charged him with assaults on five women, but this is probably the tip of the iceberg. In 2011, after the murder case had been dealt with, he pleaded guilty to the assaults and the judge gave him a five-and-a-half-year sentence, to be served concurrently with his life sentence for the murders. He was also put on the sex offenders' register for life.

Pornography still had a powerful hold on him, and it became an obsession. He tried at various times to curtail it, but always came back to it and the birth of the internet opened up a massive new world to him. At the same time he was donating money to build orphanages in poor countries and doing free dental work among the destitute in India and Romania, he was a pillar of the church once again, and he played golf, squash and five-a-side soccer, as well as cycling and jogging. He seemed at first glance to be the self-made, successful man he portrayed himself as, even if some of his dental colleagues found his claims to be a great dentist to be self-aggrandizing.

In the aftermath of the deaths, Colin and Hazel reacted differently. Colin systematically wiped out any trace of Lesley in his children's lives. They were six, four, two and eight months old when she died, and the younger ones had no memories at all, and none of them were encouraged to talk about her. Hazel, on the other hand, kept photographs of Trevor and told her children stories of their father to keep his memory alive, taking them to his grave once a week.

Although Colin asked her to marry him, neither of them were enthusiastic about the prospect, and eventually it was Hazel who ended the relationship. She did not want to take on his four children, and she was worried about losing her police pension.

She started dating a new boyfriend and for a while the obsessive Colin stalked her, but after six years this relationship also petered out, partly, her ex claims, because he did not have enough money for the lifestyle she aspired to. She loved clothes, designer shoes and bags. After this affair she moved on to a better catch, retired police Chief Superintendent David Stewart, who became her second husband. She told him about the affair with Colin and the joint 'suicide' but did not admit to him, or anyone, that the deaths were murders.

Colin also married again, to a young American divorcee with two children. Within weeks of their marriage his new wife, Kyle, was pregnant. With six children already between them, Colin decided to build a lavish home for them all. His business was doing well, he worked hard and the family enjoyed lavish holidays. So Colin bought a plot of land in Florida, near Kyle's parents, to build a house. But to Kyle's astonishment, sixteen months after their marriage, he confessed to her about the murders, the first person he'd told; he begged her not to tell the police, and she didn't. He told her that he knew God had forgiven him, and she agreed to do the same – although it must have been very worrying to hear how her predecessor had met her end. She put her fears aside and went on to have another four children with him, bringing him a total of nine children and two stepchildren.

In 2007 a tragic accident killed Colin's oldest son, twenty-two-year-old Matthew, the boy whose name was the last word spoken by Lesley as she was dying. Matthew was in St Petersburg with university friends when he fell down a stairwell in the early hours of the morning.

Perhaps his death precipitated the chaos that followed in Colin's life, but the man who had never been very good at business began investing in an outlandish, get-rich-quick scheme based in the Philippines, and soon found himself mired in debt. He naively believed he was going to make millions, and instead he lost £353,000. His marriage to Kyle collapsed, and he was living in a caravan. A colleague, a fellow dentist, was so concerned about his mental health that he considered reporting him as unfit to practise. He owed £250,000 in tax and had taken £230,000 in advance payments from patients for cosmetic dentistry and implants that he would probably not be able to do.

With everything in his life spiralling out of control, he confessed to the murders, first turning to the church elders before contacting the police. It took him three days to tell the police everything, and he was held in custody for two years before he stood before the court in November 2010, almost twenty years after the murders, to plead guilty. It only took ten minutes for the court to accept his plea with his son, Dan, and daughter, Lauren, looking on, as well as Trevor Buchanan's two sisters and five brothers.

When he came up for sentencing the judge said that his confession was a mitigating factor, and instead of the maximum twenty-eight years he was sentenced to life imprisonment with a minimum term of twenty-one years.

Shortly after Colin's detailed confession, in which he in no way spared her, Hazel was arrested. When the police turned up at her home to question her, they had to wait an hour and a half because, ironically, she was at a dental appointment. When she walked in and saw them she put down her Louis Vuitton bag before getting into the police car. Unlike her ex-lover, she was allowed to live at home while on bail, and her husband and children stood squarely behind her as she protested her innocence. Over the next two years she was even able to carry on with her part-time job as a clerk in a pharmaceutical company, where she was popular with the other staff.

During this time her second husband brought his police-interrogating experience into play, and he asked her on many occasions about her involvement. He insists she was controlled and manipulated by Colin Howell 'like a frightened rabbit'.

She came up for trial after Colin had been sentenced, and he was the star witness against her. A packed courtroom heard him explain why he had finally confessed: 'I just knew that the time had come when the truth had to be told. I was overwhelmed by my conscience with hiding this crime for such a long time. I believed there were scars that needed to be put right, and I wanted to tell the truth. That was the only motive.'

Later, under cross-examination on his second day in the witness box, he said he was there 'under great personal shame. I have brought disgrace on myself and on many other people.' He spoke at length, going into long polemics about morality, control within relationships and about his perception of himself as a ladies' man. He contested statements he had made to a psychiatrist while on remand about Hazel being easy to control, and that 'she was very simplistic, not academic'. But he refuted the suggestion that he had seduced her, stating that it was the other way round. It was a long, verbose and self-serving performance in which he asserted time and again that Hazel had been a partner in the crime from its inception to the day of the killings.

He was in the witness box for four days, and he had given so much detail that, even if his motive had been vindictive, it was impossible to dismiss. Hazel's legal team had a difficult job on their hands. She did not give evidence, but her police interviews were played to the court.

I had to be strong for my children. My guilt was horrendous. My shame. I hated him. The relationship went on, but only because of him ... I was scared of him, not knowing what he would do ... But life has been horrible for me. I never got over it ... The thought of losing my children, losing David, is the hardest thing. I destroyed their lives, Lisa and Andrew. Colin's children didn't deserve this, or Lesley. Lesley was a lovely girl. Trevor was very good, too.

Summing up, the judge described Hazel as 'soft, weak and vulnerable', but he asked the jury to ultimately consider whether she had done everything she could to prevent the murders, or at least the murder of her husband. While the jury was out Hazel's daughter, Lisa, mouthed 'Mummy, I love you, Mummy, I love you' amid sobs. Her son, Andrew, held his head in his hands and her loyal husband, David, looked tired and drawn.

It took two-and-a-half hours for the jury to return their verdicts, and they found Hazel guilty of the murders of Trevor and Lesley. Her family, friends and even her work colleagues all submitted letters to the judge begging for her to be treated leniently, but two weeks later she was sentenced to serve life imprisonment with a minimum of eighteen years. She will be in her late sixties before she is released. Her family still believe she is innocent, and that she was wholly manipulated by Colin.

Only one of Colin's children, his daughter, Lauren, has stood by him. Kyle divorced him and went back to the States with the five younger children and her two from her first marriage, but not until she had been interviewed by police about why she did not report the murders when he confessed to her. Amazingly, Colin told the police that if she were charged he would be willing to testify against her.

Two years after being sentenced Hazel appealed, admitting her guilt to Trevor's murder because she had 'facilitated, assisted and encouraged it'. But she contested the guilty verdict for Lesley's murder. The three appeal judges dismissed the appeal after only a five-minute recess. In 2016 she tried again, asking the Criminal Cases Review Commission to refer her back for another appeal, but the commission did not take up her case.

The lovers will be behind bars for years to come.

12

Body in the Fridge

THE TV ADS SHOWED A HANDSOME MAN RIDING A HORSE, A WHITE cowboy hat on his head, ostrich skin boots on his feet. He looked wholesome, healthy and happy, a wide smile welcoming new clients to his business as a personal injury lawyer. 'Had a car accident? Injured yourself at work? Fallen over due to negligence by someone else? Ring Larry McNabney, he's the lawyer for you.'

The ads were still running on TV in Sacramento, California, in January 2002, and potential clients were still ringing Larry and *still* handing over hard-earned deposits for the services of this hotshot lawyer. Yet Larry had been dead for three months, murdered by his wife and her best friend in a bizarre pact that ended with one of them hanging herself in a prison cell and the other serving eight years in prison.

Larry was a larger-than-life personality, a brilliant lawyer who was acclaimed for his bravura court performances and his ability to assimilate information quickly and expertly. But he was a flawed character, with a drink problem that had seen him in rehab and a chaotic emotional life that had resulted in four marriages before he met his fifth wife, Elisa.

She was his undoing. From the moment she walked into his office to apply for a job, he was doomed. Even after she misappropriated funds from his clients, and he ended up being fined and in trouble with the legal authorities, he still adored her and went ahead with plans to marry her.

If Elisa had stopped at taking all his money that would have been bad enough. But she linked up with another woman in an unholy partnership that destroyed the genial Larry's business, his reputation and, ultimately, his life. Had the two women never met he may have survived, even if he was cleaned out financially. It was a rare conjunction of their distorted personalities that led to his destruction.

Elisa McNabney was, at first sight, the prime mover in the crime spree that ended with Larry's body being stuffed in a refrigerator and then buried in a shallow grave in a Californian vineyard. She certainly knew how to commit fraud, although her previous brushes with the law had all been for petty crimes. She was also an expert at conning men, with her good looks and her chameleon-like ability to fit in with their hopes and plans, only to move on when she'd fleeced them of their money. But murder? It took the catalyst of Sarah Dutra to bring about the horrific, painful and debilitating end with Larry being poisoned slowly over weeks with horse tranquillisers.

Elisa's real name was Laren Sims. She wasn't fussy about names: detectives who eventually, with great difficulty, uncovered her web of deceits, lies and cons, found as many as thirty-eight aliases that she had used over the nine years since she left home in Florida. She was born in 1966, in the small town of Brooksville, the middle of three children to respectable, middle-class parents. She had a lot going for her. She was good-looking and very clever, popular at school and a cheerleader. But she was also a teenage rebel, playing truant, hanging out at the bowling alley and drinking alcohol with other dropouts, and already discovering her gift for slickly talking her way out of trouble: more than one local cop tore up a speeding ticket when she charmed him.

She didn't finish high school, and she wasn't good at holding down a job, discovering early on that she could bounce cheques and her dad would bail her out. She tried marriage to one of the popular, local lads, but by the time she was twenty she was divorced with a daughter, Haylei, whom she adored. A couple of years later she had a son, Cole, born with cerebral palsy, and whose father was seventeen years older than her. The affair caused a scandal, which was topped a year later when she was arrested for burgling a house and stealing, amongst other things, Christmas presents. It was the idea of a boyfriend who told her that the property she stole was rightfully his. She was given probation but continued to bounce cheques, and eventually went to prison for nine months. Within weeks of her release she was in trouble again, for stealing credit cards.

At the age of twenty-seven and facing more time in jail for more petty offences, Laren decided to disappear. She cut off her ankle tag and took Haylei, who was seven, but left five-year-old Cole behind because he was in a special school, and going on the run with a disabled child would be difficult. Besides, he had a loving, caring father. She assumed the first of her many new identities, Elisa Barasch, the name of a woman she met while in prison, and whose social security number she knew. She left town, and her loving but despairing parents would not hear from her for ten years.

She moved to Las Vegas where she continued to live on her wits, using a host of different names to cash stolen cheques. She was not a typical, brassy Las Vegas girl, and always wore classy clothes and spoke politely, with a ready, winning smile. Men who hitched up with her often woke to find their wallets empty and their credit cards gone, and no doubt many of them just chalked it down to experience. And any who did lodge a complaint with the police … well, she was using a name that did not check out, and she was careful to leave no clues that would lead them back to the apartment she shared with Haylei.

Laren was always able to land a job, presenting herself well at any interview. She took a job as manager of a chiropractor's office, and used her charm on her colleagues and the patients, quickly becoming a popular member of staff. But the regular monthly pay wasn't enough for Laren, who somewhere along the line had developed a taste for the finer things in life. She was looking for a meal ticket, and one soon walked into her life.

Ken Redelsperger ran his own insurance agency, which was going well. He was earning good money, which he liked to spend on his outdoor hobbies: skiing, fishing, camping and water skiing. He was in his mid-thirties and had had several girlfriends, but never married. He said later that from the moment he saw Elisa he never stood a chance. He was instantly infatuated, and with her consummate acting skills she became everything he was looking for, adapting with ease to the outdoor life he loved, ingratiating herself with his mother, relatives and friends.

She told lies, as she always did, but even though he was puzzled by some of the things she said, he was happy to forgive her anything. He also really liked Haylei, and when the pair of them moved in with him he loved teaching Haylei how to ski, ride a motocross bike and fish. But soon after they moved in he realized Laren was running up huge bills on his credit cards and for a time they split up. But he took her back and, to the amazement of his friends, they married. She explained her lack of family by saying they were in Cuba – or was it Costa Rica? It was not easy, having to remember all those lies.

Ultimately, although Ken still loved her, he had to pull the plug on the relationship because she was bleeding him dry. After two years together – six months as man and wife – he realized he could not afford her. Even though his business was going well, he was not earning enough to support her extravagant spending. All in all, he reckoned, she took him for $30,000, and it couldn't go on. And he was constantly covering for her lies.

Laren, too, was getting itchy feet. She was tired of the chiropractor's office and quit the job. Looking for another one, now she no longer had Ken picking up the tab, she answered an ad to work as a secretary in the office of a local attorney, Larry McNabney, and she quickly had a new home for herself and Haylei. They moved in with Larry within weeks.

Larry was a hot shot, highly respected by other lawyers despite his drink problem. As his ex-business partner said: 'Larry was a better lawyer drunk than any other lawyer I ever saw sober.' When Elisa/Laren met him he was dry. After a short first marriage, he had had a reasonably long, successful second one, which gave him a son, Joe, a daughter, Cristin, and a stepdaughter, Tavia, whom he adopted. Eventually, the marriage foundered because of Larry's love for a good time, which involved large quantities of drink. In the following few years he had two very short marriages. But despite the chaos of his personal life, his business prospered and he had offices in Nevada – in Las Vegas and Elko – and in Sacramento, California.

By the time Elisa came into his life, he had been settled and living with a regular girlfriend, Cheryl Tangen, for seven years. Cheryl soon felt the full force of Elisa's arrival: 'He hired her in July and he left me in August,' she said. 'She made herself available to him twenty-four seven.'

Soon Elisa was promoted from secretary to office manager. She was adept at handling legal claims and was either aggressive or persuasive with big insurance companies, getting settlements for clients that exceeded everyone's expectations. She was a natural.

She was also a natural at moving clients' money around to her own advantage, and after more than $74,000 dollars went missing from client accounts, Larry was reprimanded by the bar, fined and had to pay the costs of the hearing, and he was ordered in future to be the only signatory on a client trust account. It was devastating for the reputation of a lawyer who prided himself on how well run his business was, but everyone involved in the case knew that the person to blame was not Larry, but Elisa.

She came up with a good cover story. Of course she did. She said she was using the money to pay operational costs for the offices, although the truth was that the money was funding her lavish lifestyle. Larry decided to move his main practice to the Sacramento office, and told friends he wanted to cut back on his workload. But instead of sacking Elisa for her behaviour, he married her, less than a year after her marriage to Ken. They rented a house in a posh, gated community.

They spent a lot of time together, and it's probably true she encouraged the wild side in him and he started to drink again. She later claimed he beat her, but other women who previously figured in his life all found that hard to believe. She also claimed he watched pornography, snorted line after line of coke, took heroin, used hookers and was drunk all the time. Furthermore, she cut him off from his friends and family, not allowing either of his daughters to stay close to him, and only tolerating his son, Joe, because she always felt she could get her own way with men, including a stepson.

Despite her picture of this debauched lifestyle, Larry was still meeting up with old friends to play golf, and was a regular and enthusiastic part of the quarter horse circuit. (American Quarter Horses are the most popular horse breed in the States, and get their name from being fast sprinters of distances less than a quarter of a mile. As well as racing they are shown and judged.) Larry owned and bred the horses, very successfully, and Elisa shared his hobby enthusiastically. If he was really living an out-of-control life, as Elisa later tried to portray, he was hiding it well from his associates and friends.

He loved the horse show circuit, and Elisa had grown up around horses and handled them easily. They had all the gear: expensive horseboxes, trailers, and among their horses was one that was doing very well, winning big prizes. It all cost a fortune, but Larry seemed to have it and everyone assumed the business was still prospering, even though he spent less and less time in the office. He seemed to have lost all his professional pride, once again letting the woman he knew had defrauded his clients handle the business side of the office.

Elisa, naturally, did not like the discipline of running the office. She wanted to be enjoying herself spending Larry's money, and that's why they took on another member of staff to help with the day-to-day work. Enter Sarah Dutra, the young woman whose malign influence on Elisa would culminate in Larry's murder.

On paper, Sarah sounded a much less likely killer than Elisa, who was steeped in deception and theft. Sarah was a university student, studying art at the University of California, and looking for work to help fund her. She was respectable through and through, bright, popular with other students and had never broken the law. Digging into her background, her father had been in trouble for embezzling the funds of a church where he was the pastor, but that scandal was long over and she didn't seem to be affected by it. Perhaps, though, it provided a clue to her amorality.

She was in her twenties, and in many ways looked like Elisa, both tall, striking and charming. They could have been rivals. Instead, they became the deadliest of allies, in thrall to each other, possibly even lovers. Their deep friendship started with a love for one thing: shopping. They loved clothes, beauty products, marijuana, drink and a good time. Elisa had access to the cash from Larry's office to fund this lifestyle for both of them, and not long after Sarah started work at the law office, other staff realized the two women were joined at the hip. They even boasted to the other staff that they had bought – and were wearing – matching underwear. They always bought two of everything, and splashed out a fortune on Gucci shoes at up to $500 a pair. Even when Sarah went to Italy on an exchange student posting, Elisa paid for her to fly back and forth so that they could still spend time together.

Larry didn't like Sarah, and the feeling was mutual. They were in a competition for Elisa, and there's no doubt Sarah was winning, as Larry (and even Haylei) were being sidelined more and more. Isolated from his daughters, seeing less and less of his son, Joe, and unable to keep up old friendships, Larry was now turning to the bottle. Larry's children, Haylei, the staff at the law office and anyone else who had dealings with them are in agreement: Sarah was the dominant, scarier one, the one who called the shots. Curiously, Joe insisted that there was real affection between Larry and Elisa right up to the last few weeks of his life, which makes it harder to believe what the two women did.

By the summer of 2001, Elisa and Sarah were smoking dope and taking handfuls of pills, mainly slimming pills. Both lost dramatic amounts of weight and were beginning to show physical signs of their debauched lifestyle. The office was in chaos and money was running dangerously low. The only way they could carry on funding their drugs and shopping habits was by keeping Larry working which, despite what Elisa later said about him, he was still capable of doing. And that makes their next act hard to understand.

They killed the goose that laid their golden eggs.

We will never know which of them first had the idea to poison Larry with horse tranquillisers. Perhaps it started simply as a means of subduing him. Certainly, Elisa had made jokes with friends about spiking his drinks so that she could get away from him. Some people felt the jokes were in bad taste, but nobody thought she would do it. Or, if she did, she would use sleeping tablets, nothing worse, to get away for a night's gambling. Then she began talking about divorce, and about getting a payoff from Larry.

Meanwhile, money was increasingly a problem, cheques for their rented home were bouncing and the two women were still racketing around together, going to parties, picking up men, Elisa passing herself off as single.

They may have been poisoning Larry slowly for up to a month before he finally died. By the time his body was discovered, it was impossible to tell how long the tranquillisers had been in his body, but the postmortem showed that there had been a long build-up. It was at about this time that Sarah later claimed Larry found the two of them in bed together, but whether or not they were in a sexual relationship has never been substantiated: it is only Sarah's word. It's certainly true that the two women were very close, even deceiving Haylei so that they could be alone together.

Things for Larry came to a head at a horse show at Industry City, a large suburb of Los Angeles. Two days before he had given Elisa an ultimatum: Sarah had to be sacked. This may have precipitated events. Larry was showing horses and Elisa was with him so he was happy, although some friends had already commented that he seemed tired and spaced out, and was drinking heavily. He wasn't his usual dapper self in the horse ring, looking dishevelled with his shirt buttoned in the wrong holes. Showing his horse he seemed confused by the routine, despite having done it hundreds of times.

That night he went to his room early, another odd event as Larry loved the camaraderie of his evenings with the horse crowd, and he usually had dinner with his trainer, the septuagenarian Greg Whalen. Later, Elisa came down to the hotel restaurant and ordered some soup for Larry, and white wine. Unbeknown to those who spoke to Elisa, Sarah was upstairs administering more poison to Larry. The women were putting horse tranquilliser into an eyedrop bottle and dripping it into Larry's mouth as he slept.

He was a strong man, and after a whole night trying to finish him off, he was still alive the next day. Leaving him in the room, the two women drove around trying to find a wheelchair. Failing to steal one from a supermarket, they eventually hired one and brazenly wheeled out the comatose Larry to the truck. It was 11 September – 9/11, the day the world saw two planes crash into the twin towers of the World Trade Center in New York – so two women with a 'drunken' husband in a wheelchair raised no eyebrows.

They drove to Yosemite National Park, planning to bury him. Elisa later said Sarah was willing to bury him alive, but that she could not do it. Sarah had a go at digging a grave, but the ground was too rocky so they drove on, back to the McNabney home. Both women, who gave different accounts of the last few days of Larry's life, agreed that he was still alive at this stage, albeit semi-comatose.

The next day Elisa went back to the horse show, where she sold Larry's truck and either gave away or sold his clothes, telling people he had left her. She had his Rolex watch on her wrist and a chain round her neck with Larry's diamond horseshoe ring dangling from it. Amazingly, because Larry had a history of going off on drinking benders, nobody questioned the story too deeply, even if they thought it odd. Perhaps the oddest thing though, and a subject of much speculation, was that Larry was on course to win a top place in the amateur quarter horse shows, and it was a strange time for such a keen horseman to bow out.

Back home in Sacramento, Larry was now hanging on, but overnight he finally died. Faced with a body, the two women decided to stash him in a large refrigerator in the garage. They emptied out the food, bent his body double and somehow stuffed him inside. Elisa later said: 'I wanted to kill him ... Sarah wanted to kill him ... He was jealous of Sarah. He was jealous of the horse trainer, who is seventy. He was jealous because he didn't like me to have anybody ...'

Two days later, both women were back in the office at Sacramento, and for the next four months they kept up a remarkable pretence that Larry was still alive. They took on new clients. They handled claims. They paid the staff. Larry was always 'away on a golfing holiday', or he'd joined a cult and found inner peace, or he was in rehab, or he was travelling around Europe, and so on. Ginger Miller, a new secretary who started work the week after the murder, was always told she'd missed him by five minutes or that he would be back next week. The two women even invited friends and family over for a Christmas meal, only to cancel at the last minute by saying Larry unexpectedly had to leave.

Telling lies came easily to Elisa, she'd been doing it all her life. But Sarah was no slouch and was soon up to speed, with those who knew them convinced that Sarah was the dominant, prime mover. They were both adept at forging Larry's signature. When the landlord at the office evicted them for not paying rent, they moved the business into the home where Larry was chilling in the fridge, and carried on milking the business for every penny, keeping up their wild spending habits. Things were so chaotic they were even being pursued by a Los

Angeles rental company for the return of the wheelchair.

By this time Ginger was having trouble getting paid, and had heard the two women telling so many conflicting lies to creditors and Larry's family that she was getting worried about what had happened to the boss she had never met. She had no idea, as she worked at the house, that he was only a few feet away in the garage. She rang the police to voice her suspicions and they began to investigate Larry's disappearance. But he was a man of unpredictable habits who had gone on benders before, so it was not red flagged as a major concern, even though he had not been seen or heard for three months.

Elisa and Sarah knew they couldn't keep him in the fridge indefinitely, and at one point they loaded the body into the boot of a car and drove to Las Vegas, partly to party and partly to find a place to bury Larry. Stoned out of their heads, they drove into the Nevada desert only to find once again that the sun-baked ground was too hard to dig a grave, so again Larry went back in the fridge. And as their debts grew, and they started selling off their possessions, so Elisa, Sarah and Haylei ended up sleeping in their only remaining bed together.

Finally, just before Christmas 2001, a couple of days before Larry's fifty-third birthday, Elisa decided to dispose of the body. On her own, she drove Larry to a vineyard 15 miles away. It was a rainy, muddy night, and at the far edge of a field she was able to dig a grave in the soft earth. Did she have help? Sarah wasn't with her, but detectives later believed she had someone, perhaps an undocumented illegal worker paid to keep schtum. She carefully removed all Larry's clothing, to eliminate any DNA evidence of her involvement, and drove around town dropping off items in different waste bins. Elisa later said she chose the vineyard because Larry's favourite wine was Chardonnay, and she wanted him to rest near the grapes he loved.

By this time, other people were talking to the police: clients who had been defrauded; Larry's son, Joe; and Ginger with her increasing worries. Elisa was fobbing Joe off with reports of Larry being in Costa Rica one day, the next day she said he was in Washington. The police contacted Elisa asking about Larry, and she could feel the net closing.

So she did what she had done before. She took off, changed her identity, disappeared. Just like last time, she took Haylei with her, driving off in her newly leased red Jaguar. When the business was eventually investigated, it turned out that she had defrauded it of half a million dollars, none of which she had left – in fact she had even borrowed $300 from the elderly horse trainer, who later found himself in trouble with the police because he had unwittingly helped her get rid of the fridge that had been Larry's last home.

She finally made the break with Sarah, telling the woman she had been so close to that she would leave a plane ticket for her at Sacramento airport, so that Sarah could fly to Scottsdale, Arizona, where Elisa was planning to attend a horse show. When Sarah got to the airport there was a ticket, but it was not paid for; Sarah had no money, and she soon discovered that Elisa's phone was disconnected.

No longer Elisa McNabney, Laren Sims – who was now calling herself Shane Ivaroni, among other aliases – was now heading to Kentucky, and then to her home state of Florida. As usual, she was quickly able to con her way into somewhere to live and work. She and Haylei moved into a beach house in Destin, Florida, a small resort in the Florida Panhandle, owned by a man she befriended in a casino. She walked into a job at an upmarket restaurant, claiming to be a wine connoisseur. She didn't stick the job for long, amazingly walking into another one as a legal assistant to an upcoming young attorney. Haylei, who kept her first name but used the same surname as her mother, also found a job.

It was at this time, after she had been on the run for two months, that a farm worker saw buzzards circling at the edge of the vineyard and discovered Larry's body. A missing person turned into a murder case, with the prime suspect the wife who had disappeared. Sarah was interviewed, and she gave a self-serving account that firmly put Laren/Elisa/Shane in the frame.

If she wanted to stay out of sight, Laren/Elisa/Shane couldn't resist getting up to her old tricks. The owner of the beach home where she was living discovered she had fleeced his credit card for $1000 and taken out a mobile phone contract in the name of his business. He promptly changed the locks and dumped her belongings, and she and Haylei moved into a motel and then sofa-surfed with friends they made.

Meanwhile, back in Sacramento, detectives made a breakthrough. They tracked down the address of Elizabeth (or Elisa) Barasch, the woman whose identity Laren stole when she first went on the run. The real Elisa took one look at the picture and told them she was Laren Sims. Tracking down her parents, the police discovered they had not seen her for nearly ten years. The net was tightening again.

The owner of the beach house, who had lost money to her, heard that she was now working for an attorney, and he dropped by the office to warn them about her. For the first time, they checked out her social security number and found out it belonged to a man. Then they got the registration number of the red Jaguar, and suddenly the police back in Sacramento had their biggest lead yet. They could not believe she was working in another law office.

Laren's sixth sense told her something was wrong the minute she arrived at work, and she wasn't hanging around to find out. She made an excuse about going to the doctor and rang Bob Sims, a man she had met a couple of nights earlier. They went to the movies together, and then she spent the night with him. Waking up the next day he discovered she had taken his pickup truck and $600 in cash, leaving him a note and the keys to the red Jaguar.

She picked up Haylei and headed north to Charleston. But Haylei was unhappy as she had made friends in Destin and now had a boyfriend. Laren had never been a perfect mother, but she loved Haylei so she turned the truck round and headed back, confessing all to Haylei on the way. She dropped Haylei at a friend's house, then set out again, alone. She was found sitting on the beach, gazing out to sea. When a policeman approached her she got up and walked towards him, later saying she didn't want to alarm children who were playing nearby. 'I'm the one you are looking for,' she said.

She said she didn't need a lawyer and spent three hours making a full confession to the police although, because she was always such an accomplished liar, parts of it are probably not true. She didn't spare Sarah, but she did show concern, asking how she was and making it clear Sarah was not there when the body was buried. When Bob Sims found out her true identity he was so relieved to have escaped lightly that he did not press charges for theft. That still left Laren with a 113-page criminal record.

Laren was vitriolic in her confession about Larry, claiming that he threatened to take Haylei away from her. She added that he knew the full story of her life (which is unlikely), and that he was already using horse tranquillisers as part of his increasing dependence on drugs, and all the two women did was up the dose to a lethal level.

Alone in her cell waiting for extradition back to California (the other states where she was wanted for petty crimes agreed to waive their claims), she wrote a long, loving letter to Haylei, urging her to live an honest life. She also apologized to her parents. 'Tell my mom and dad how sorry I am to have to put them through all of this. Please tell granddaddy I love him and please tell Cole I left him to protect him from me. I love you, my princess. You are the most deserved of all things good. Go to your new life with my blessing and my deepest hope for health and happiness. I will always be in your heart.'

Twelve days later, she hanged herself with carefully knotted sheets. She was cut down while still alive, but died seventeen hours later in hospital. She died under her right name: Laren Sims. She had survived for nearly ten years without that name, but it was hers in death.

Deborah Scheffel, one of the detectives on the case, paid tribute to her ability to live on her wits: 'She was very, very good. I've tracked a lot of criminals, but she was one of the best con artists I have ever come across. She was not a stupid woman.' Nor was Sarah, Detective Schieffel added: 'I met my match in Sarah. Conducting the interview was difficult. She wasn't your average homicide suspect … Who was Sarah Dutra? Take a look at Elisa McNabney, that's who Sarah Dutra was.' It is true Sarah had learnt from a master when it came to telling lies. But many of those who dealt with her before and during the trial believe it was Sarah who drove the cold-blooded, protracted killing of Larry.

At her trial, Laren's confession was ruled inadmissible, to the great disappointment of the prosecutor. Haylei was granted immunity from prosecution in order to testify: although she knew nothing of the murder, she knew about the financial frauds her mother was involved in. She was in the witness box on her eighteenth birthday.

Sarah showed no emotion, and never expressed remorse throughout the eleven-week trial, with her parents sitting in the front row clutching bibles. The basis of her case was that she was very much the subordinate in the relationship with Elisa, a dupe under the control of an older woman with a proven track record of lawbreaking, of whom she was afraid. Her lawyer described her as a 'babe' who fell under the spell of 'a black widow'. Despite testimony to the contrary, the jury, who were out for four days, seemed to accept this version because she was found guilty of the lesser charge of manslaughter, not murder. Jurors who heard the details of Elisa's confession afterwards, felt they had been misled. Sarah was sentenced to eleven years in prison, the maximum for manslaughter, and served eight, returning at the age of thirty-one to live close to her family.

Tavia Williams, Larry's adopted daughter who was very close to him until Laren put barriers between them, is clear that, although she had plenty of reasons to dislike Elisa, Sarah caused his death. 'If Elisa hadn't met Sarah, my dad would be alive today,' she said. And Sarah's family would probably add that if Sarah had never met Elisa, Sarah would never have become involved in a killing.

The truth is probably that the two women sparked something in each other, something that allowed them to act the way they did. Together.

13

Kinky Cottage

It was the 'Swinging Sixties' in London's trendy streets, but in the north east of Scotland the 'Permissive Society' was something only read about in the Sunday papers – until, that is, the goings-on at a small house nicknamed Kinky Cottage stirred the tut-tutting and vicarious curiosity of residents in Alford, a village 28 miles from Aberdeen.

The remote cottage was owned by Max Garvie, a good-looking, wealthy young farmer who lived 47 miles away in Auchenblae with his wife and young children. But Max was far from a traditional, kirk-loving, pillar of the community: he was obsessed with pornography, had sexual relationships with young men and women, and he dedicated the cottage to the pursuit of his pleasures, including orgies and swingers' parties. He even planted a screen of trees to hide the nudist area. He drank heavily and popped pills as if they were Smarties, always looking for the latest thrill.

Max met his wife Sheila when he was twenty-one and she was eighteen, in 1955. Sheila was the daughter of a stonemason who worked on the Queen's Balmoral estate, a puritanical, bad-tempered man. When she left school, she too worked at Balmoral, employed as an assistant housekeeper, before taking up a job as a secretary. It was at a Young Farmers' dance that she met Max, and there was an immediate, mutual attraction between the two good-looking youngsters. He was a great catch for a girl from a working-class background, owning his own 400-acre farm, and Sheila was the envy of the local girls.

For the first few years of their marriage all went well. Sheila gave birth to two daughters, Max worked hard on the farm and in his spare time piloted his own plane, which he kept at a disused wartime airfield north of the village where they lived, and which earned him the nickname The Flying Farmer. He started a flying club there, for other enthusiasts, and for a time performing stunts in the plane gave him all the thrills he needed. But then Max developed a passion for nudism, and he persuaded Sheila to accompany him on nudist holidays. The whole family went to a nudist camp in Corsica when Sheila was three months pregnant with their third child, a son. She later said she did not want to do it, but had to obey and please her husband. Their oldest child, Wendy, remembers being acutely embarrassed, being forced to walk around naked.

Max's obsession extended to founding his own nudist centre at the cottage in Alford, and he spent a fortune on mature trees to keep it private, with Sheila performing the opening ceremony. To the annoyance of Max, she refused to do it naked. Gradually, his new and debauched way of life took over. The plane, a Bolkow Junior, was used for jaunts to Holland and Germany where pornography was openly on sale (unlike in the British Isles at that time). He may well have traded in pornographic material: he certainly enjoyed it himself, filling the bookcase at the farmhouse with sex manuals while his regular farming magazines were tossed into the bin unopened. By this time he was a gentleman farmer, with staff taking care of the day-to-day running of his hugely profitable farm.

Max also took up photography, taking a total of fifty-seven nude photos of Sheila, and she discovered to her horror that he shared these with a friend who acted as navigator when he took the plane abroad. The friend let Sheila know by saying: 'I have seen more of you than you think.'

Although Sheila was reluctant to join in the excesses of Max's new, louche lifestyle, she enjoyed his money, and would travel down to London, coming back in the latest mini-skirts and skimpy tops that had yet to make it to the local shops, and with her neat figure and pretty face she attracted admiring glances from other men.

Max, a man of all-or-nothing passions, then developed an interest in politics and joined the Scottish National Party (SNP). Here he met Brian Tevendale, a good-looking twenty-two-year-old, the youngest child of an army major who had won the Distinguished Conduct Medal in the Second World War. The family lived at the Bush Hotel, in the village of St Cyrus, which his father owned. Brian had briefly been in the army, but was dismissed for going absent without leave.

Back in civvies, Brian was leading an unremarkable life as a barman until he met the Garvies. After an SNP meeting, Max invited the young man to go flying and very soon Brian was invited to spend the weekend at the farmhouse, where he met Sheila. At first Max probably wanted to seduce Brian, and he made a homosexual advance to him, which Brian repulsed. But then Max thought of another role Brian could play, by turning him into Sheila's lover.

Brian paints a lively picture of their time together. 'We used to go flying and drinking … He was a very charismatic guy. Then he started doing pills and he went all to hell. He had it all, and he was looking for more excitement.' He added Max would fly the plane while drunk, 'shooting up the traffic'. 'We went out on a Saturday night for a few drinks and when we went back to the farm I went to bed. A short time later Sheila was pushed through the door and the door was shut. She said she had been told to spend the night in there – or else.'

Max was titillated by the idea of his wife making love with another man, and the 'or else' was no empty threat: he was often violent towards Sheila. She was shivering, and they had to climb in bed together to keep warm. Brian admitted: 'She was a good-looking woman and I was probably quite chuffed about it all.'

Brian introduced his older sister, Trudi, a tall good-looking blonde, to the Garvies when he took them to her house one night. Brian was embracing Sheila when Trudi turned to Max and asked if he minded seeing his wife with another man. Max laughed and said that he liked seeing Sheila enjoying herself, and before long Max and Trudi were locked in an embrace, and Trudi became his regular mistress.

Trudi was married to a local policeman, Alfred Birse, and although Max at one time tried to line up another woman for Alfred, he was never a willing participant in Max's sex parties, only once taking part in a sixsome with the Garvies, Trudi and Brian. The *News of the World* later published 'The Secret Diary of Trudi Birse', and she wrote: 'I daydream back to those wonderful times when the foursome was new, when every experience with Max was new, when the foursome owned the world. I return to the memory of a weekend when we raced pell mell from Aberdeen to Edinburgh in Max's great bronze Jaguar, stopping at pubs and hotels along the way.'

They spent that night in two different hotels, Trudi and Max booked in as Mr and Mrs Garvie and Brian and Sheila as Mr and Mrs Tevendale. Trudi said that Max thought Brian would improve his wife's lovemaking – he described Sheila as frigid. He asked Trudi to question Brian about his sex life with Sheila and report back to him. Also, Max said he had had more pleasure from Trudi in two weeks than he had in his whole married life. Yet Trudi also claimed that after having intercourse with her in one bedroom, he would send her to a spare room so that he could have sex with Sheila.

Trudi confirmed the violence that Max was capable of, remembering one occasion when she had to wear a surgical collar because she had been beaten so badly, and also how he threatened to break Sheila's neck if she would not allow him to have anal sex.

At first Max was thrilled by the relationship between Brian and Sheila, but when they fell in love he became alarmed and tried to stop them seeing each other. Two meetings were held to discuss the future of the foursome. At the first, Max laid down the law: he and Trudi would not see each other, and Brian and Sheila would also break up. Sheila rebelled, telling the group that Max had used them all for his own selfish ends and he could not expect her to give up her lover. Max was furious and threatened to shoot her 'between the eyes'. When Sheila and Brian ran away to Bradford he pursued them and brought them back.

It was against this backdrop that the murder plot was hatched, but Brian and Sheila differ in their versions of its genesis. 'I can't remember how she worded it but she said it would be better with Max out of the way. I would have done anything she wanted,' said Brian.

In the early hours of 15 May 1968, Max was shot in the head as he slept in bed at the farmhouse. Brian recalled being terrified as he made his way to the farm that night with his friend Alan Peters, who was only twenty at the time, and who drove them there in his car. 'I don't think I realized what was going to happen. It was only later that reality hit.'

He claimed Sheila let them in through the kitchen door and took them both into the sitting room and gave them drinks. Then she took them to a room opposite the main bedroom and told them to wait there. She had given Brian her husband's loaded .22 rifle. On her signal, Brian went into the bedroom, possibly put a pillow over the end of the gun to make sure there was no sound, and shot Max. Downstairs, the three of them drank a bottle of whisky before wrapping up the body and stowing it in the car. Alan and Brian drove to an underground culvert that ran from Lauriston Quarry to the west side of Lauriston Castle, near the village of St Cyrus.

Brian said: 'I knew I would get caught, but Sheila and I continued our affair and she told people Max had gone flying and not come back. She acted like a weight had been lifted from her. I had to keep hoping we would end up together otherwise it would all have been for nothing.'

After three days Max's sister reported him missing. Although Sheila said he had gone flying, his plane was still at the airfield, with one of his cars. Neighbours reported seeing another plane take off from there, and for some time it was thought that Max had gone with a friend, perhaps on one of his runs to buy pornographic material.

A description of him appeared in the missing persons' section of the *Scottish Police Gazette*:

Spends freely, heavy spirits drinker, often consumes tranquillisers and Pro Plus tablets when drinking. Is fond of female company but has strong homosexual tendencies and is often in the company of young men. A man of considerable wealth and until four years ago completely rational. Of late has become very impulsive, probably brought about through addiction to drink. Has threatened suicide on at least one occasion. Deals in pornographic material and is an active member of nudist camps and an enthusiastic flyer. May have gone abroad.

The body was undiscovered for ninety-four days until Sheila's mother, Edith Watson, tipped off the police. Edith knew all about the state of her daughter's marriage to Max: Sheila had asked for help from her mother, from a solicitor, from a clergyman and from a friend, a hotelier, but they had all advised her to stick with the marriage for the sake of the children. Max had also confided in Edith his fears about Sheila and Brian being too close, and she had apparently promised him that if anything happened she would make sure Brian did not bring up his children. He threatened that he would have Sheila put away in a clinic in London.

When Max had been missing for three months, Sheila told her mother that she was sure Brian had something to do with his disappearance. Edith, who disapproved of Sheila's continuing relationship with Brian, went to the police – she almost certainly never imagined her daughter would be charged with murder, and she later testified in court that Sheila did not know where the body was hidden because she asked her mother about the time of the sea tides.

Brian immediately took the police to the place where he and Alan had stowed the body, and by torchlight a policeman shuffled along the culvert until he came to a pile of stones, with a toad sitting on top. In local folklore a toad hopping over a foot means a death, and when the stones were removed the remains of Max Garvie were found. He had a fractured skull and a gunshot wound to his neck. Brian claimed in his first statement that it was an accidental killing, with the gun going off as Sheila struggled with Max. He did not name Alan, but said that Sheila had called him to the house and told him Max had asked her to do something unnatural, and that they had struggled and the shotgun went off. He admitted disposing of the body.

Sheila was arrested within a few hours. Her daughter Wendy

remembers her saying to the children: 'I won't be long. I love you.' Wendy did not see her for more than ten years.

After their arrest, Brian said he and Sheila had a few moments alone at the police station, and she told him to keep quiet or to take the blame. She made it clear she wasn't going to implicate herself.

The ten-day trial at Aberdeen High Court was a local sensation, and big news nationally, too. The trial began on a chilly November day, but despite the weather police had to put up crush barriers to control the crowds that stretched in a queue round the elegant court building. It was what lawyers dub a 'cut-throat' trial because all three defendants were separately represented as they were blaming each other.

Alan Peters said in court that the murder was premeditated, and that both Brian and Sheila were involved, but although he was present he had no part in it yet he did admit to helping remove and hide the body. His story tallied largely with Brian's court version: Sheila either let them in or met them at the door (there was evidence that the door was not locked) and took them to the bedroom. He said Brian hit Max with the butt of the rifle before shooting him. He added that he was afraid of Brian who threatened 'if I did not assist in any way I would get the same.' He described himself as 'the fly drawn into the web'.

Sheila's version was different, claiming she was asleep in bed next to Max when she was woken by someone touching her arm. She thought at first it was one of the children but quickly realized it was Brian. She said he led her into the bathroom, and after hearing thumping noises he returned and said: 'He won't worry you any more.'

During the medical evidence, when Max's skull was held up in the court, one of the jurors fainted and the case proceeded with the remaining fourteen members (in Scottish law a jury consists of fifteen). The juror was not the only person to collapse: Sheila's mother, Edith, who had triggered the arrests, had to be taken home by ambulance when she collapsed before giving evidence on the first day of the trial. She returned the next day to tearfully tell her story.

Brian was the only one of the three who did not speak in court in his own defence. Sheila looked tired and pale as she was questioned, and there was some controversy afterwards as to whether she should have been allowed on the witness stand when heavily sedated with tranquillisers (Vallium and Librium were new drugs at the time).

Under Scottish law Sheila's solicitor had lodged a pre-trial notice of intent to attack the character of a dead man, and her barrister duly made it clear the kind of man Max Garvie was, the kind of lifestyle he led and how much pressure his wife was under to join in his debauched ways. But his attempt to portray the three months during which time the body was missing as 'a nightmare' for Sheila was undermined by a photograph of her at a picnic, with another man fooling around and lying on top of her.

Trudi, Max's mistress, told the court how she and her brother, Brian, and the Garvies went around as a foursome, staying in hotels and at the cottage. When she was not able to be there, she said Max and Brian would toss a coin to decide who slept with Sheila, but after Max lost twice he insisted they all slept together. Trudi's evidence was a great disappointment to Sheila's defence team because before the trial she had appeared to support Sheila's version of events, but in court she said Sheila had told her about taking Brian and Alan upstairs.

Sheila, as well as being on trial for murder, was also on trial in the court of public opinion: the prosecution did not mince their words about her, describing her as 'Lady Macbeth,' 'Lady Chatterley', 'the brain' behind the murder and 'as hard as nails'. Max Garvie, it was claimed, was 'destroyed by a Frankenstein of his own making'. The louche lifestyle was effectively used as evidence against her.

Hundreds of people queued outside the court on the day the verdicts came in, the queue forming from 2.45 a.m. onwards. Those lucky enough to get seats in the courtroom heard Brian and Sheila both found guilty of murder. Brian's verdict was unanimous, in Sheila's case two of the jurors disagreed and it was a majority verdict. Brian and Sheila both received life sentences, and kissed and embraced each other before being led separately from the dock. Alan Peters received a 'not proven' verdict, which in Scottish law meant he walked free.

During the trial the three innocent victims, the Garvie children, stayed with relatives in a hotel in Crieff, 100 miles away, and the staff shielded them by hiding away the newspapers. Many years later Wendy, who was twelve when her father was murdered, recalled the evening of his death in a way that seemed to confirm the version of events that Brian told in court. She remembered her mother had been drinking gin and orange that evening, and made the children go to bed early, telling them: 'No matter what, don't get up.' She said her mother seemed agitated.

Three months after they were sentenced, the passion that drove Sheila and Brian to murder was spent. In a letter from her cell at Gateside Prison, Greenock, Sheila told Brian, who was incarcerated 80 miles away in Perth Prison: 'I have decided to have nothing more to do with you ever again.' She asked him to get rid of her old letters. It was a blow to Brian, but after they were both released in 1978 (she in September; he in December), they never saw each other. He said he believed she broke off with him because, while they remained a couple, she was being denied access to her children.

Brian later said: 'Having Max out of the way meant we could get married and I assumed that was her motive. Looking back now, I'm not so sure. There was a lot of money to be gained from it, and I was under her spell. If I could go back now and undo it, I would. But when I did what I did I was stupid and naive and probably thought I was in love ... Nothing eases your conscience.' He had lost all affection for Sheila: 'I can't say I feel anything about her now. She has her life to get on with and I have mine.'

While she was in prison the three Garvie children, Wendy, Angela and Lloyd, were looked after by their grandmother, Edith, until she died a year later, and then afterwards they were raised by foster parents in Lanarkshire. They shared their father's million-pound estate.

When she came out of prison, Sheila lived in Aberdeen, running a guest house that belonged to her aunt. She married a Rhodesian-born welder, Donald McLellan, but the marriage only lasted two years, and shortly after their divorce she married drilling engineer Charles Mitchell. They were together until he died in 1992. Sheila then moved to Stonehaven, where her mother had lived, just 20 miles from the scene of the murder. She re-established contact with her children but her daughter, Wendy, had a troubled relationship with her siblings.

Wendy spoke of the shadow the murder had cast on her life. 'My dad is dead but I forgive my mother, and she knows that ... What happened that night has ruined lives, including mine ... The terrible legacy lives on and I don't think I will ever escape it.' She also said: 'My father was a difficult man, very domineering and difficult to live with.'

When her mother came out of prison Wendy was twenty-two

and they met in a pub. 'It was very difficult and she didn't seem to want to talk about what happened,' Wendy said. Sheila's last months were spent in a care home, because she was suffering from dementia. She died in 2014, weeks after her eightieth birthday.

Brian also married when he came out of prison, and he and his wife ran a pub. He said he was always honest with her about his past, and she had already heard lurid and exaggerated stories about him. The couple were planning to emigrate to Gambia when he died at Scone, Perthshire, of a suspected heart attack when he was fifty-eight.

The case seemed to bring misfortune to everyone involved. Alan and his wife had two children, but they were divorced five years after the court case. Trudi's marriage to Fred also ended in divorce and he got custody of their three children. He died of cancer in 1985, and Trudi, who was working as a housekeeper, also died of cancer three years later.

In 2015, the detached five-bedroom farmhouse, which had been expensively renovated and a large extension added, was put on the market for £749,000 by Lloyd Garvie, the son of Sheila and Max, who was only two when his father was murdered. It is protected by an electric gate and screened by trees, and much of the original farmland had already been sold off for housing development.

14

Killed by a 'Bag for Life'

IT STARTED WITH A DRAMATIC 999 CALL. 'HIYA, I THINK WE'VE BEEN burgled and my wife's been attacked ...'

The call came from Mitesh Patel, and it sounded very convincing. Interspersed with sobs he told the emergency operator that he had walked in to find his house ransacked and his thirty-four-year-old wife, Jessica, on the floor, her hands and feet bound in duct tape, and there were marks around her neck.

He sounded distraught as he pleaded with the operator to get someone to the scene, and to ring his dad. He said: 'I've just come home. I was just out, I went out to get something to eat and to see the lads at work and pick up my laptop and I just came home and the house is ransacked.' He cried as he added: 'She's got blood dripping out of her nose on to the floor. *Baby, wake up, please baby wake up.*' He told the operator that her hands were cold, and she was unconscious. The operator talked to him, trying to calm him, until the police arrived at the door of the semi-detached house in Linthorpe, an upmarket suburb of Middlesbrough.

What they found when they entered was the house in complete disarray, every drawer pulled open, clothes strewn across floors, furniture overturned and the body of Jessica on the floor of the living room, lying in the recovery position but without any hope of recovery. Mitesh had removed the tape, as instructed by the operator.

Jessica had been strangled, using a 'bag for life', which is made from strong plastic.

The scene of the burglary was convincingly arranged, and the 999 call was an Oscar-winning performance. Money had been taken from Jessica's purse, and £2000 and an iPad taken from the house. At first police had no reason not to accept Mitesh's story at face value and, worried that violent intruders were on the loose, an armed response team was sent to the road. Local residents who came out to see what was happening were told to get back indoors, and parishioners at a local church were ordered to stay there until given the all clear. The police also appealed to neighbours and local drivers to look for suspicious people in the road on their CCTV and on their car dash cams. But when one of the policemen at the scene noticed three scratches on Mitesh's neck, which he said came from an injury at the gym earlier in the day, they began to question his story.

Then the postmortem results came in, showing that Jessica had been injected with insulin and had also been suffocated with the same bag, which contained traces of her blood and saliva. The suffocation probably came when Mitesh heard her stirring after he believed he had strangled her. Under her fingernails the pathologist found traces of Mitesh's DNA, as Jessica struggled for her life.

The CCTV camera that the Patels had installed only a few months earlier on their Victorian redbrick home appeared not to be working, and police discovered that the hard drive was missing. They found it when they searched the house, hidden in a suitcase full of clothes under a bed, and watching it they were able to put together the true sequence of events. The footage showed no intruders had broken in between Mitesh leaving to establish his alibi (he even sent Jessica a text telling her which pizza he had ordered, although he had already killed her), and returning to make the 999 call. They also found syringes full of insulin in his laptop bag, and one empty one. Very quickly, the double life of Mitesh Patel was unravelling.

Searching the Roman Road Pharmacy that the couple, who were both pharmacists, owned and ran, they found a roll of duct tape that matched the tape used to bind Jessica. Staff at the pharmacy filled them in on the state of the marriage and, in particular, on Mitesh's secret gay life. Mitesh would leave his phone on the counter at times, and they were aware that he was using the gay dating app Grindr. One member of staff saw him on the shop's CCTV footage, embracing and kissing another man when the shop was closed.

It is ironic that the modern technology that Mitesh loved, telling neighbours they should follow his lead and have CCTV installed, eventually led to his downfall.

Weeks before Jessica died, he told a neighbour that his wife was very trusting 'and one day she will end up getting murdered'. He also told a call handler at a life insurance company that his wife 'lives in this bubble where she thinks nothing is ever going to happen. One day she will end up getting murdered.'

A seventeen-year-old who worked at the pharmacy told the police how Mitesh had asked him to demonstrate how to access the dark web, and wrote down instructions for accessing it. While they were scrolling through the dark web together, Mitesh looked up sites for drugs, guns and hitmen, and on a second occasion, when he asked the youth to show him again, he looked up 'insulin' and 'suicide'.

The police quickly discovered that Mitesh had been plotting to murder Jessica for five years, and she had only stayed with him because she longed for a child and really wanted to make a success of her marriage, even though she told a friend who worked at the pharmacy that 'Mits' wasn't very interested in sex. She had earlier told her uncle, while on a family holiday to Spain, that the couple had not had sex for ten months.

Mitesh, thirty-seven, also wanted a child and delayed the murder plot in the hope she would have a baby that he could take with him after her death, when he started his new life in Australia with his 'true love and soulmate', Dr Amit Patel (no relation; he came originally from West Yorkshire and had been working as a GP in a health centre before emigrating to Sydney in 2016, after divorcing his wife). When Mitesh realized this could take a long time, he decided instead to use the embryos the couple had frozen after four rounds of IVF, and which would be his after her death. This meant he brought forward his murder plans.

Mitesh and Jessica, who were both Hindu, met as children through the tight-knit Hindu community of West Yorkshire, Jessica coming originally from Leeds, with Mitesh's family living in Halifax. They both studied for pharmacy degrees at Manchester University. Mitesh later said he lost his virginity with Jessica in 2008 when they became engaged and added, questionably, that he did not have a homosexual relationship until 2012 when he met Amit.

Mitesh and Jessica had been running the successful Roman Road Pharmacy not far from their home since 2015, three years before her death, and they moved into their home at the same time. Although they kept up the front of being happily married, cracks were beginning to show from the time Mitesh fell in love with Amit. Not only did he maintain his double life, but he also began to treat Jessica with disdain and disrespect, calling her 'stupid' on more than one occasion in front of the staff.

One of her younger sisters, Minal, described him as 'increasingly controlling and cruel. He would put her down, say things in a jokey manner, but they were negative things ... about the way she dressed and looked. We could tell it was hitting her confidence because she became quite reserved and quiet.' He prevented her visiting her family as a means of proving his dominance, and told her father, Jayanital: 'I am the dominant one, I can do whatever I want … It is good that she never questions me.'

Her family were increasingly worried about her. It was not long after the start of Mitesh's relationship with Amit that one of her sisters saw some texts between the two men on his phone, with a reference to a 'love toy'. She took a screenshot, and later showed it to her sister. Recriminations and denials followed, with Mitesh promising to change his ways. But on the evening before Amit – who had also married but then divorced his wife – was flying out to a new life in Australia, he spent the night at their home, and Jessica later told her work friend that Mitesh went into the spare room with Amit 'and never came out until the morning'. Challenged, he said he had been helping his friend print out a boarding pass.

He told Amit that he had married Jessica because she was in love with him, and because marriage to her would provide cover for his true sexuality, which was difficult to reconcile with his strict Hindu upbringing. At the same time, he was reassuring Jessica that the homosexual relationship was over.

It was not until Amit left the country that Mitesh launched into a promiscuous gay lifestyle. Although he kept in touch with Amit – and Jessica complained that he spent all evening in his study talking to his lover – he signed up for Grindr and other gay dating websites, hooking up with men for casual sexual encounters. One other user of Grindr complained to the website about him because he was claiming to be single, and the man had seen a local newspaper story about him running a pharmacy with his wife.

When Mitesh went to a family funeral in India he paid 2000 rupees (about £21) to a male prostitute, and even when he and Jessica went on holiday to Fuerteventura, in the Canaries, only weeks before her death, he was in constant touch with Amit and also online looking for local men for sex. Jessica, in a desperate bid to make him give up his ways, told his brother Namesh about his gay relationships, but nothing changed.

Jessica, to her distress, was aware that he brought men home to their house for sex in the spare room, using a lubricant and condoms he kept in the marital bedroom. Despite all of this, they were both keen to start a family, in fact Mitesh was obsessed with the idea of having children. He was a fantasist, and told his personal trainer that he and his wife had eight-month-old twins, a boy called Aaron and a girl, Zara, saying he was making handprints of them every month, and that he was recording a song for their first birthday: 'You Are My Sunshine'.

Jessica was initially happy to go through IVF, but after three unsuccessful rounds she said she wanted to stop because of his gay relationships, but he told her that if she didn't go ahead with it: 'I'm telling you this, then we are parting ways.' She agreed to another cycle resulting in three embryos that were frozen at a clinic in Darlington, but she was reluctant to have them implanted and told him she did not want to bring up a child in a household in which gay pornography was stored on his phone and he was using gay apps. Mitesh texted her: 'I think you are mad, you can forgive me but I won't forgive you for this. I'm being honest with you. The only person I want and have wanted is you. I love you and I can assure you that if I didn't, we would have parted. If you want, I won't talk to anyone. Like always, I will sacrifice myself.'

The prosecution at his trial maintained that this was the moment that the murder plot came forward because, with access to the frozen embryos, Mitesh and his lover could start a family when Mitesh flew out to join him. He no longer needed Jessica. His other motivation was pure greed: Jessica's life insurance policies were due to pay out £2 million on her death.

As they searched his house, police discovered more clues: under a drawer liner, face down, was a picture of Mitesh with his lover, Amit, taken in 2012 when they were on holiday together. It was not a graphic picture, but it was puzzling because it had been concealed. They also found a list of 'Items needed for Australia'.

During the three days before his arrest, he kept up his performance as a tragic husband who lost a beloved wife. Her sister, Minal, recalled: 'He grabbed me, he buried his head in my shoulder, sobbing and sobbing. He said if he ever got his hands on the murderer he would kill him.'

Once arrested, he was questioned by the police for thirty-two hours before being charged. He did not deny his gay relationship with Amit, and admitted having sex with 'a handful' of other men. After his arrest, police used the iPhone Apple health app on his phone to track his movements, in what is thought to be a legal first in the UK. They downloaded critical information from the health app, which uses motion processors to monitor a user's steps, registering the difference when the user goes up stairs.

The evidence was used in court to show the killer's frantic movements as he ran around the house ransacking rooms to stage the robbery, after he had strangled his wife. It also showed that when he first returned after going out to visit the pharmacy and buy pizza, the trip he used as an alibi, he had gone upstairs to hide the house CCTV hard drive before phoning 999 to report the attack on Jessica.

A similar health app on Jessica's phone showed the handset moved fourteen steps at 7.44 p.m., the exact time that Mitesh left the house to create his alibi. He said she was alive when he left, but her phone did not move again until a police officer picked it up where Mitesh had left it outside by the front door, trying to make it look as if it had been dumped there by the intruder.

More evidence piled up. His online search records included one for 'I need to kill my wife', 'insulin overdose for a healthy non-diabetic woman', 'plot to kill my wife, do I need a co-conspirator', 'hiring hitman UK' and 'how much methadone will kill you?' His online history showed he had watched a video on how long it took to die from strangulation. He also researched 'funeral arrangements for a Hindu wife' and 'rebuilding your life after the death of a spouse'.

Prosecutors claimed that Dr Patel was kept informed of all the developments in the murder plot. In a message to Amit he described Jessica as 'a thorn in our side', also saying: 'if she can cause us upset, we can do the same to her.' Another message, sent when he was with Jessica on holiday in the Canary Isles, read: 'You know this plan, do you think we will succeed?' Dr Patel replied: 'Only you know the answer.' When Mitesh messaged, 'Do you think it is a bad plan?' he received no reply. He messaged again: 'I am telling you, her days are marked.'

The couple talked about the possibility of Jessica having a baby, with Amit saying, 'She might be around for eighteen years', to which Mitesh replied: 'No, because I will curse it if I lose you. What are your thoughts if she goes early? Will you love it like your own?' On 2 May, Mitesh messaged his lover: 'Hi baby, ten days.' In fact, it was twelve days before he murdered Jessica.

Immediately after the murder there was no contact between Mitesh and Amit, which the court heard was an arrangement made in advance so that police would be unaware of the relationship. But even on the day of the murder, Mitesh had been visiting several gay websites. After his arrest he spent six months in prison awaiting trial.

At the start of the twelve-day hearing at Teesside Crown Court, the judge Mr Justice James Goss QC told the jurors they would be excused from sitting on the jury if they used the Roman Road pharmacy, or if they had used the Grindr dating app in the past seven years.

Opening the case, prosecution counsel Nicholas Campbell QC pointed out the irony of the plastic bag that was used as the ligature to strangle Jessica being a 'bag for life'. And he told the court that when Mitesh had the embryos, he had no further use for Jessica.

Forensic scientist Nicola Taylor used a mannequin to demonstrate how Jessica could have been strangled with the plastic bag, either by her husband attacking her from behind or, if she was on the ground, with the bag being pulled tight around her neck. Blood and saliva, which came from Jessica, was found inside the bag, and the bag was damaged in parts, which may have been caused by Jessica fighting to yank it from over her head.

Speaking in his own defence about 'the prison of his marriage', Mitesh said, when asked how he felt about his brother hearing about his double life: 'I cannot explain how I felt. It was the fear of being exposed as a gay Asian man, that was one thing, and the other was that I was not going to let Jess down. I had married Jess and all her dreams were going to come crashing down … I should have been honest with myself and I should not have married Jess.' He said that he felt great shame about not being able to have a family, and culturally he would have been allowed to leave her, but he assured her he would not do that.

Questioned about why he had not tried to revive his wife with CPR when he found her, Mitesh replied that he 'lost his bearings' and panicked. Mr Campbell said: 'And you weren't going to waste your time trying to revive the dead, were you?' Mitesh later told the court: 'I am going to get into trouble for something I have not done. I have my parents and my wife's parents in the gallery.'

Summing up, Campbell said:

This murder was the culmination of five years of planning. He made some very real and obvious mistakes. The evidence reveals he set aside, in his planning, the means to kill by using insulin and had researched other means, not least strangulation.

Having attacked her and left her for dead, he then goes about making it look like a burglary. He takes money from her purse. Was it then he heard her stirring?

He also remarked that the marriage was 'far from *The Waltons*'. However, defence counsel Toby Hedworth QC argued that being a bad husband and a cheat and a liar did not make Mitesh a murderer.

It took the jury only two hours and fifty minutes to return a unanimous verdict, and when 'Guilty' was pronounced there were cries of 'Yes!' from the public gallery, which was packed with family and friends of Jessica, all wearing black sweatshirts with the message in white on the front: 'JUSTICE FOR JESS'. On the back were her dates, '16.09.83 to 14.05.18', followed by: 'MISS YOU'.

Before sentence was passed, three members of Jessica's family gave victim impact statements to the court, expressing their deep heartache. Her father, Jayantital, told of hearing someone in a movie say: 'There is nothing heavier than carrying your own child's coffin'. And, he added: 'It is very true. I have felt that weight.' He said that he felt he had let down Jessica's mother, who had died some years previously, by not protecting her.

Her grandmother, Jai Shri Krishna, made a statement that was read out by Jessica's stepmother, Roshni Patel: 'My heart cries. I can't forget, and pray to god that my dear sweet granddaughter finds peace. A completely innocent girl received such a big punishment.'

Jessica's younger sister, Divya Patel, made the longest statement, on behalf of herself and her sister and the three cousins who had grown up with them in the same home.

The words 'Jessica is no more' shattered our lives in an instant. The next day we visited Jessica in the morgue for the first time. Seeing her lying there motionless behind a glass window, the reality began to hit that she was truly gone.

For two days we believed it was a burglary that had gone wrong. Nothing could prepare us for what was to come. Not only had we lost Jessica but Mitesh, the man we watched marry our sister, was arrested for her murder. We had to wait an agonizing five weeks, which seemed like forever, before we finally had Jess back to perform her final rites.

The one thing we hoped and prayed for above all else was that in her final moments she did not suffer. The cruel reality is that she did in fact suffer, she knew exactly who her killer was and he mercilessly ignored her attempts to fight for her own life as he ended it. We can only imagine the fear and panic she must have felt. Thinking of that moment makes our hearts so heavy.

Only Mitesh can truly answer why he did this. Everything he has done has been for purely selfish reasons. He could have divorced her, taken everything he wanted, he did not need to take her life. He had no right to take this evil, cruel, malicious step.

Then turning to face her brother-in-law Divya added: 'We do not just pray, we know, she will be free of you forever as she will rest in heaven while you will rot in hell.'

Mitesh showed no emotion as the judge, Mr Justice James Goss, told him:

> You are a selfish man, business driven, wanting a very successful life and wanting to retire at forty. You were also wanting to commit to a life with another man on your own terms and you well knew that insurance policies would realise two million pounds on Jessica's death.
>
> You have no remorse for your actions. Any pity you have is for yourself ... Mrs Patel clearly loved you and was a dutiful wife. She wanted nothing more than to have children and live a normal life. The difficulty is that you had no sexual attraction to her; you were attracted to men.

He went on to say that Jessica was 'lonely, often upset and controlled by you.' He said Mitesh's messages to his lover revealed him to be 'needy and callous', and he used his wife 'whilst indulging your own desires and whims'.

The following day Mitesh was back in court for sentencing. The public gallery was so packed that the press covering the trial were moved into the jury benches (the jury had done their duty the day before, and were no longer in court). He was jailed for a minimum of thirty years, and walked from the dock silently, his hands clasped in front of him. The judge said that a thirty-year minimum sentence was reserved for cases where the seriousness of the offence is 'particularly severe', adding: 'This is such a case.'

After the case ended, the Senior Investigating Officer attacked

Mitesh for putting the family through the agony of a trial. 'Even when faced with overwhelming evidence, Mitesh chose to inflict further pain and suffering on Jessica's family by not admitting his guilt, exposing her family to his deceitful, dishonest and wicked ways throughout the trial.'

Questioned about the role of Dr Amit Patel in the murder, the police said they had spoken to him during the course of the investigation, as a witness.

'It would not be proper to go into any detail about Amit. It would unduly prejudice any further proceedings, should they ever be taken against him.'

The Roman Road pharmacy was 'closed indefinitely' after Mitesh's arrest. At first, while police carried out forensic tests there, the pharmacy remained open with a locum pharmacist dealing with prescriptions. A typed notice apologised to customers 'for any inconvenience' and thanked them for their custom over the last few years.

Mitesh was immediately suspended from the pharmacists' register when the trial ended, and six months later the General Pharmaceutical Council struck him off permanently. At the time he was in HMP Frankland, and did not use his twenty-eight day chance to appeal against the decision. He'd had a previous warning from the pharmaceutical council, in 2016, for storing a controlled drug, methadone, on a shelf and not in a locked drugs cabinet. It is a small infringement compared with murdering his wife, but set against his internet search 'How much methadone will kill you?' it is more than possible he had deliberately made the methadone available for a staged robbery, a murder plot he later abandoned.

15

The Go-Go Dancer and the Cat

JOHN PERRY WAS ONE OF THOUSANDS OF MEN WHO FLY OUT TO the Far East for holidays that involve more than sunshine. They go to enjoy the sexual favours of young, pretty women whose only desire is to please, both in bed and out, as long as the price is right.

John had just gone through a bruising divorce, so two weeks in Manila, the steamy capital of the Philippines, was the break he felt he needed. And the petite go-go dancer who was flashing her sultry eyes at him every time she gyrated past his table in the sleazy night-club was definitely the antidote to the bitter wrangling he had been going through with his ex-wife. When her dance was over she joined him at his table, and a financial deal was agreed.

John liked that. Always frugal with money, he enjoyed the fact that a price was fixed in advance, and he knew exactly what he was getting for his investment. Arminda Ventura, only 4 ft 10 in tall, looked very young, but she was twenty-one and already had a baby daughter. She was very experienced at this kind of work, and knew exactly how to please.

For two weeks she moved into John's hotel room, pandering to all his desires, even washing his clothes. She was the sort of woman he liked: one who obeyed his every whim. He had been married twice, both times to British women, but he had found them too in-dependent, with minds of their own. His frustration with them had always boiled over, and he had been physically violent. Arminda, in contrast, was all accommodating, and treated him with the respect and reverence he felt he deserved, as well as providing hot sex.

At the end of his blissful two weeks, John travelled back to Higher Kinnerton, North Wales, a small, pretty village close to the border with England. He found himself thinking about Arminda, and not just because he missed her sexually. What John wanted from a woman was the house kept clean, meals on the table and unquestioning obedience. He wanted to be lord of his own home, and he had been unable to find a woman who would treat him with the deference he felt he deserved. Arminda, he was sure, would never step out of line. And if he gave her and her child a home, in return she would be his servant, as well as sharing fun in bed – which he wouldn't have to pay for.

Bar girls in the Philippines, Thailand and other countries in the Far East all dream of the rich Western man who will sweep them out of poverty and into a life of, what to them, is luxury. Sharing cramped rooms in the back streets of Manila makes a two-bedroomed bungalow in Wales seem like a palace, a palace with constant electricity, a fridge, a car. Some girls find husbands through agencies, some, like Arminda, from holiday romances. Far more cling forlornly to promises made by Western lovers who have no intention of fulfilling them.

For the lucky ones who do land a husband, the reality is often not what they dreamed about. They leave the hot, gaudy, noisy streets of their homeland for the dreary grey skies of Britain, living isolated from anyone they know apart from their husband, unable to speak their own language to anyone, puzzled by the closed doors and drawn curtains of their new country.

Arminda had no idea of the downside of her new life when she excitedly boarded a plane for the UK less than a year after her first meeting with John, holding her two-year-old daughter. For her, a major part of the deal was that her little girl would go to school in her new, adopted country, and there would be money to shower the little one with toys and pretty clothes. It had taken a bit of negotiation to get permission for her to come, and her immigration papers were dependent on her marrying John. Within a month of him meeting her at the airport, she became the third Mrs Perry, even changing her first name to the more English-sounding Annabelle.

At first it seemed promising. Both John's previous wives found his fastidious standards impossible to meet. He would walk in after a day at work and run his finger over cupboards, checking for dust and twitch the curtains because they had not, he felt, been carefully aligned. He expected a hot, freshly cooked meal when he arrived home from his shift at an engineering works 5 miles away in the village of Llay. Both his first wife, Julia, and his second wife, Susan, later talked about constant beatings and hectoring lectures. Julia claimed he even shouted at her for over an hour for not cooking his peas properly. And Susan? 'He bashed me about so much I sometimes did not recognize myself,' she said. 'He tried to strangle me once and I thought he was going to kill me.'

At first, his choice of a third bride seemed to be working out well: both were getting what they wanted from the bargain. Arminda was more compliant that her emancipated predecessors, and happy to kowtow to his autocratic whims – for a while. But soon cracks in the marriage started to appear. He was moody and difficult to live with, as both his previous wives knew.

The pretty little Filipina missed the fun and variety of her previous life, and her instinct to please men went beyond servicing her husband's sexual needs. When the couple went to pubs and clubs she was quick to jump on to the dance floor, and to dance in the only way she knew, the sexually provocative routines she had learnt in the girlie bars of Manila. John later complained that at an Anglo-Philippine party in Birkenhead she snuggled up to other men she was dancing with, and he caught her kissing another man. 'She was very provocative, rubbing herself up and down him and swinging her breasts from side to side in front of him. She was kissing him all over his chest.'

He claimed he followed her outside when she left with this other man, but he was attacked when he tried to separate them. He said she would lead men on, whispering to them that she was not wearing knickers and in some cases slipping her hands down a man's trousers in public. The uninhibited sexuality that had attracted him when he was on holiday in the Philippines did not translate well into a faithful marriage back home. Did he beat her for her transgressions? He almost certainly did, because it was the way he tried to control the women in his life.

Undeterred, Arminda started a passionate affair with a neighbour, Barry Burns, who at thirty-two was fifteen years younger than John. He called round from his home in the next street to make love to her three times a week, while John was working the night shift.

By late 1990 it was clear to Arminda and John that the terms they had negotiated were not working out. Arminda tried to leave on several occasions, but she had no financial support, no close friends or family to take her and her daughter in, so she ended up returning to John. In the end, after someone explained to her that if she divorced John she could get financial support from him for herself and her daughter, she went to see a lawyer and filed for divorce. Furious, John rang the Home Office and tried to get the two of them deported as illegal immigrants, but officials saw through the pack of lies he concocted.

After long-drawn-out legal negotiations a divorce settlement was drawn up. John was forced to agree to give Arminda a settlement of £15,000 (£34,000 in today's money), plus a small sum of maintenance each week for her daughter. When he received a letter which gave the date of the divorce hearing, he seethed with anger and resentment that he would have to give any of his hard-earned cash to a bar girl he had rescued from a life of poverty and transient sexual encounters in Manila. He decided there was only one solution: murder Arminda.

If she disappeared, it would be easy to explain her absence as she had left home before, and those who had met her, and observed her behaviour around men, would accept his story that she had gone to London to work as a prostitute, or that she had flown back to the Philippines. He even drew up a list of the differing costs of divorce and murder, totalling them on a piece of paper. Death, predictably, was much cheaper than divorce.

He later claimed that he killed Arminda after a furious row when he found an explicit letter she had written to her lover Barry Burns, describing him as 'the best sex instructor'. He claimed that when they rowed she said she no longer wanted her daughter, and that she died in a struggle after she threatened to commit suicide by slashing her wrists with a carving knife. He described how he tried to resuscitate her by blowing into her mouth, but did not realize he should have blocked her nostrils and all that happened was that blood spurted out.

But that version is contradicted by the typically thorough preparations that John, a man who paid great attention to details, had made. He set about the task meticulously. Just as he liked his household to be well organized, his murder plan was equally rigorous. He asked a friend at work, who had previously trained as a butcher, how to dismember a body. Although John did not confide his plans, he gave enough away for his mate to know that he was talking about a human body, not an animal carcass. The friend told him to follow the joints, and threw in the gruesome information that human flesh is very like pork, and cooks and carves in a similar way. His mate thought it was just an interested, if macabre, enquiry, at best a murder fantasy. Not the real thing.

At about the same time John, who had always preferred night shifts, asked to be transferred to the day shift, which gave him access to huge vats of acid that were stored in a part of the building closed at night. He also bought *The Reader's Digest Family Medical Adviser*, which included a detailed diagram of a human skeleton.

The exact details of Arminda's death are unknown, but it was committed while her daughter, by now eight years old, was asleep in the house. Then John bundled up the tiny body of his wife and stowed it in the boot of his car, immediately afterwards cleaning up any obvious evidence of her death at the crime scene.

He came very close to organizing a perfect murder, and may have got away with it, but … The first neighbour to appear on his doorstep was Janet Wilson whose boyfriend, Barry, was having the affair with Arminda. Janet came round to have it out with Arminda, but John answered the door and told her that she had gone away. Janet noticed that the carpet was soaking wet, and saw splashes of blood on the doorframe and on a plastic bag. John hustled her away quickly, and did not seem to want to talk to her about the affair that affected both of them, which Janet found odd.

With Janet out of the way, he drove for forty minutes to a wood near Oswestry and dumped the body, hiding it quite carefully but leaving it accessible for him to recover. The following day he was not due in work, and he took Arminda's daughter to stay with friends. He then collected the body, brought it back to the bungalow and began the grisly task of dismembering it in the bath. Even though she was tiny, her body would have been stiffened with rigor mortis, and manhandling it would not have been easy.

He remembered from his schooldays the statistic that seven-tenths of the human body is water, and he believed that if he cooked the flesh the water would evaporate and he would be left with man-ageable amounts to dispose of. He had an impressive collection of tools for the job: a hacksaw, electric drill, hammer, chisels and a selection of knives. Pieces of flesh were hacked off and placed in a roasting dish and cooked in the oven. It was a long, difficult job, and he worked painstakingly and steadily.

He then collected Arminda's daughter and somehow concealed from her what he was doing whenever she was at school or in bed. The cooked meat was packed into plastic bags: a pathologist would later say it was 'meticulously and uniformly diced, like meat prepared for beef stew'. The intestines were put into a plastic container nor-mally used for home brewing, with more pieces of cubed meat and skin put into another one. These two containers were moved to the garage, and a large pan of human fat was put to one side to solidify.

He was particularly concerned about getting rid of his wife's head because of the risk of her being identified. His determination never wavered, and his stomach was strong enough to carry out his grue-some plans. He shaved her hair and baked the skull until the flesh fell off. The brain, which he later described to the police as 'grey slurry', was tipped into a bucket that was filled with strong liquid detergent, which dissolved it. He shattered Arminda's skull with the electric drill and the hammer, and the shards of bone were put into a supermarket carrier bag.

His plan was to get rid of the small parcels of human meat in tiny graves scattered around the countryside, confident it would be devoured by wild animals. He had already started dropping small cubes of meat in roadside gutters, and there was a green plastic bag full of more diced flesh in the boot of his car. He'd also found another way of getting rid of the remains: feeding them to Katie the cat.

Another twenty-four hours or so and John Perry may have got away with a perfect murder, leaving nothing of Arminda behind as evidence of his crime, so carefully had he planned it all. He told neighbours she had taken off again, probably heading for London, and as she had been known to walk out on him before, he was confident no questions would be asked.

But there was one neighbour who saw a great big flaw in his cover story. Yes, Arminda had disappeared before but she had never left her beloved daughter behind. Whenever she split from John, her daughter, whom she adored, went with her. Now the neighbour was aware that the child was still living in the bungalow with John, and she was also puzzled by the late-night banging and hammering, *and* the drain at the back was blocked with a lot of soap foam.

The neighbour rang the police and a constable visited the bungalow. John confirmed that Arminda had disappeared, but he said she had gone away before without saying where she was, and on one occasion she had been away for ten days. He said he would report her missing if she was not back by the following weekend.

The neighbour was not satisfied, and she rang the police again to say that the nocturnal drilling and hammering was continuing. It was shortly after midnight on 28 February 1991 that Sergeant Derek Frost and Inspector Ross Duffield parked outside the bungalow in Myrtle Avenue. They knew it was a strange time to make a routine inquiry, but there was something about the neighbour's persistence that made them curious. True to what she told them, the lights were on and there were noises coming from inside.

When John opened the door to them, the first thing that hit them was the smell of cooking. It smelt like a Sunday pork roast in the oven. But this was the middle of a Thursday night. Spread open on the floor was the *Reader's Digest* manual; John had a cut on his finger and a blood smear on his face. He was cool under questioning: the scratch on his face came from brambles when he was out walking, he told them, and he had cut his finger carving meat, and that was almost certainly the truth.

He explained that he and his wife were on the brink of divorce, and that it was typical of her to take off, always to return eventually. 'She's just gone off with some man or other,' he said, and he told the police that he had given up on women and was going to live alone with Katie the cat. But when they insisted on searching the house, for the first time his cool demeanour fractured. He'd been caught. He admitted strangling her, saying she put up no resistance. Then, chillingly, he added: 'I've done one good turn – I fed her to the animal.'

Within a short time a pathologist, Dr Donald Wayte, arrived to catalogue the grim discoveries. He described John's methods as 'almost obsessively tidy. Everything had been put in bags, everything was very tidily placed and very carefully done.' He estimated that it must have taken twelve hours of very hard work.

At the time the police turned up on his doorstep, John was at work drilling the skull into small pieces, but there was enough of it left intact for the pathologist to piece together the jaw, and to conclude that she had suffered a vicious blow to the back of her head. Arminda's denture was found in John's jacket pocket. Dr Wayte later said: 'I got everything from the house and put it in the boot of my car. I was able to rebuild her.' But he agreed that the missing flesh could well have been eaten by the cat.

John Perry came before Mold Crown Court in November 1991, charged with murder. He pleaded provocation, but the careful preparations he had made proved he had been hatching the plan to kill Arminda for some time. His work colleague, the trained butcher, described the conversations they had about dismembering a body, and the financial details of the divorce, which John believed were unfair, were produced. In his defence, Barry the neighbour from the next street, confirmed that he had been having an affair with Arminda and that she got hysterical and threatened to commit suicide when he tried to break it off.

John claimed in court that he was still in love with Arminda, and that her death happened because she provoked him. But despite telling the police on the night of his arrest that he intended to spend his life with only Katie the cat for company, they discovered he flew to Thailand two months before the murder and while there bought the company of another willing bar girl.

The jury voted ten to two in favour of a murder verdict, and John Perry was sentenced to life imprisonment. The judge described him as 'chillingly and ruthlessly efficient' in his systematic cover up of the murder. A police spokesman said he was 'one of the most gruesome and inhuman murderers in British criminal history'.

Watching him be sentenced for killing his third wife were his two previous wives. 'I'm not at all surprised that his violence led to him killing someone. He was like a wild animal when he lost his temper,' Julia said. Susan commented: 'He deserves to be locked up for a very long time because he is a danger to women.'

16

Desperate Measures

It was an unusual way for a woman to kill another woman: in a frenzy Mary Wheeler slashed the throat of her rival, and then murdered the eighteen-month-old daughter of her lover and his wife, a little girl she claimed to love. Mary was at the end of her tether: the man she adored had married his other lover, had a baby with her, while still continuing his illicit relationship with Mary.

Mary Wheeler was a young woman who was born and died during the reign of Queen Victoria. She started life in Ightham, a pretty village in Kent, but at an early age moved with her family to Stepney, London, growing up at various addresses in the tough, poor Mile End area. Her father was always in work, unlike many of his contemporaries, and although she was the oldest of five children they were never destitute until his death from an accident at work.

Mary's basic education taught her to read and write well, she developed a passion for books and her handwriting showed she had paid attention at school. She suffered from epilepsy from early childhood, though her fits were infrequent. Nonetheless, with no suitable medication, she endured headaches and those around her saw her whole personality change before a fit. She had a job as a nurse to a young child but lost it because her fits increased as she grew older, and the family she was working for felt she could not be left in charge of their baby son. Mary said to her mother: 'I can't tell what is the matter with my head.'

The worry about her illness and her father's death deranged Mary, and she tried to hang herself, being found just in time by a neighbour and her mother. It was a tough time for the family, and eventually her mother and the youngest child went into the workhouse, and Mary used the remains of her father's insurance money to keep the younger children together. But things got worse, and eventually the family were evicted, Mary going to live with a mother and her son who had been sharing their lodgings. She lost touch with her mother, but some time later reappeared, very smartly dressed, to say that she was going to work abroad. It was another five years before the family saw her again, when she was twenty-three, telling them that she had travelled all over Europe and announcing that she was now married to John Pearcey, a carpenter. In fact she had been back in England for at least three years, and her relationship with John was already over when she was reunited with her mother. She took the name Pearcey and used it for the rest of her life, although the couple were never actually married – possibly because Mary was not free to marry because she had married another man while she was abroad.

She was not the prettiest of girls, but she was described as having 'lovely russet hair and lovely blue eyes', with nicely shaped hands and pale skin. She was tall for the time at 5 ft 6 in, and strongly built. There was something that drew men to her.

Before she broke up with John she met Frank Hogg, who was at the time managing a grocery business belonging to his mother, just across the road from her home, and it was her friendship with him that was partly responsible for the break up. At first she carried on living in the rented rooms in Camden Town she had shared with John after he moved out, but then moved to rooms in Priory Street, Kentish Town, which were paid for by another of her lovers, Charles

Creighton. Charles lived in the suburbs with his wife and family, and only visited her once a week, which gave her plenty of free time for other entertainment.

Her neighbours believed Charles was her father and were very impressed by how regularly he called to see his daughter. Left alone for the rest of the week, she drank quite heavily, especially during one of her frequent bouts of depression. Frank Hogg, who by this time was working as a furniture remover, employed by his brother, helped her move house, but he claimed to have no idea about Charles because she told him she had a small private income to support herself. She also told him she had been married to John Pearcey and was entitled to be called Mrs Pearcey. What initially impressed Mary about Frank was that he had printed business cards, which she felt made him a cut above the usual local men in what, at the time, was a working-class area of the city.

Frank lived just under a mile away from her new home with his mother and his sister, Clara. He was a likeable man but weak, and could not face telling Mary that he was not going to marry her. She would leave a lighted lamp in her bedroom window as a signal to him that she was alone and able to receive him, and she clung to the hope that he would change his mind and make her his wife.

These hopes were finally dashed when Frank broke the news – he was going to get married, and that the woman who was to be his bride, Phoebe, was three months pregnant when the banns were read. Mary felt that Phoebe – a maid to a family in Rickmansworth, Hertfordshire, and who was seven years older than her and always in poor health – had deliberately tricked Frank into marriage by getting pregnant.

Mary was still genuinely in love with Frank, and desperate to keep the affair going. Her letters to him illustrate the depth of her passion.

Before he married Phoebe she wrote: 'Do not think of going away, because my heart will break if you do. Don't go, dear. I won't ask too much, only to see you for five minutes when you can get away, but if you go quite away, how do you think I can live? … NO, no you must not go away. My heart throbs with pain only thinking about it.'

Even after his marriage, she desperately clung to the love affair, writing to him:

> You ask me if I was cross with you for coming only such a little while. If you knew how lonely I am you would not ask. I would be more happy if I could see you for the same time each day, dear. You know I have a lot of time to spare and I cannot help thinking. I think and think until I get so dizzy I do not know what to do with myself. If it wasn't for our love, dear, I don't know what I should really do, and I am always afraid you will take that away, and then I should quite give up in despair, for that is the only thing I care for on earth. I cannot live without it now. I have no right to it, but you gave it to me, and I can't give it up.

She had met his mother and sister before he married, so when his wife, Phoebe, and within a few months a daughter, also called Phoebe (but known affectionately as Tiggy), moved into the same family home, Mary kept in touch with the whole family, visiting each other from time to time.

'I love you with all my heart and I will love her because she will belong to you,' she wrote to Frank, referring to his new wife.

The Christmas before her death, Phoebe and Frank spent Christmas Day with Mary, sleeping the night in her bed while she slept on a couch. When Phoebe was ill eight months before her death,

Mary volunteered to nurse her, and visited every day until Phoebe's family, concerned that she was not being properly looked after, took her back to her mother's home for ten days until she recovered. Frank later maintained that Phoebe, his mother and sister had no idea that his relationship with Mary was sexual.

On one occasion he managed to take Mary away with him for work, when he was delivering furniture to a village in Bedfordshire, and for two days they behaved as a happily married couple. But Mary was still plagued by her epilepsy, and just four days before the murders she visited her mother and said: 'It comes and goes again, but I'm never without it very long. In the dream I see a great arch-way and through it I go to darkness, dreadful darkness, that seems to hide something more terrible beyond.'

In those days before telephones became commonplace, it was quite normal for small boys to earn money by delivering notes for a penny a time. On 23 October 1890, Mary sent a note, entrusted to a young boy, to Frank's wife, Phoebe: 'Dearest, come round this afternoon and bring our little darling. Don't fail.'

Phoebe had not been well again for a few weeks, and did not feel like making the visit. She showed the pencilled note to her sister, who agreed with her that she should not go to Mary's home. How-ever affectionate Mary's note sounded, she was, as Phoebe probably suspected, her husband's ex-lover and she feared that the relation-ship was on again. Mary waited for her to come, with all the blinds in her house down, which was unusual but meant that the main room could not be seen from the street. She explained this by lying to her ex-husband, John Pearcey, when he passed by and saw her waiting outside for her guest to arrive, saying she was in mourning for her younger brother who had just died.

Finally accepting that Phoebe was not coming for tea, Mary

waited until the next morning and then sent another note. This time Phoebe felt it would be obviously rude to ignore a second invitation, and despite the seething jealousies between the two women who both loved the same man, she tried to keep up the pretence of a cordial friendship.

So that afternoon, pushing eighteen-month-old Phoebe in her pram, Frank's wife walked the short distance between their homes to visit her husband's mistress, pushing to one side any forebodings she had. It was at teatime, around 4 p.m., that neighbours heard noises from Mary's house. There were sounds of crockery breaking, and the baby could be heard giving a scream and then crying.

The neighbours believed that Phoebe and her baby were members of Mary's family, and assumed it was a family row, something that would blow over. Charlotte Priddington, who lived next door, had borrowed a wicker dress stand from Mary and returned it by putting it over the fence. She called 'Mrs Pearcey' five or six times to ask if everything was OK, but received no answer and heard no more noises, so put it out of her mind.

In fact the noises were the sounds of a vicious, frenzied attack on Phoebe by Mary, who hit her rival on the head and then slit her throat. The baby, Tiggy, had been given a toffee to suck, probably to stop her crying. She was lifted back into the pram, and when nobody was about Mary hauled the mutilated body of her mother and dumped it on top of her. Whether she planned it this way or not, the baby was suffocated by the weight of her mother's corpse on top of her.

Then Mary set out on a grisly evening walk pushing a pram containing two dead bodies. It was hard work: the combined weight of the two corpses was 9 st 10 lbs. She met a neighbour she knew, but did not stop or speak. 'When she saw me she dropped her head over the handles [of the pram] and she had difficulty pushing it up the hill,' the neighbour said.

At 7.10 p.m. a woman's body was discovered in a pile of rubbish at the side of Crossfield Road, Hampstead, a mile away from Mary's home, by a clerk who was returning home from work. 'It was very dark and I noticed something lying by the side of the road – a house was being built there. It was a woman lying with her face covered. I passed but walked back and found the body in the same position.'

He went to the police station and returned with a sergeant. The dead woman's head was wrapped in a cardigan, which the policeman pulled off to show Phoebe's bloodstained face with a huge gash in her neck. The clerk rushed to get a doctor who confirmed she was dead. The body was taken to Hampstead Police Station, and then to the mortuary. The doctor who examined her found she had a fractured skull and her throat had been slashed with such force it had nearly severed her head. Her head and arms were bruised, as if she had been trying to defend herself.

Later that evening, a police constable patrolling his regular beat found a heavily bloodstained pram in Hamilton Terrace, about a mile from where Phoebe's body was found. It was not until the following morning that eighteen-month-old Phoebe was also found, three miles away from Mary's home, in a field in nearby Finchley, her body not damaged. Medical examination showed she had been suffocated, probably under the weight of her mother's body.

Frank Hogg and his sister, Clara, were not immediately alarmed when the two Phoebes did not come home that evening. Phoebe's father, who lived in Chorleywood, Hertfordshire, was very ill, and Phoebe had warned Frank that if she had news his condition was worsening she would take the baby to visit him. Frank had been working all day with another man; his movements were accounted for. He then called round to Priory Street, Mary's home, at about 10.10 p.m. but the light signal was not showing so he left. The following morning, after talking to Clara and his mother, he caught a train to Chorleywood, but discovered his wife and daughter were not there.

In the meantime, at about 9 a.m., Clara went to see Mary to see if she knew where Phoebe and Tiggy were. She asked if the pair had visited Mary the day before but she said no, she had not seen anything of them. Pressed, she admitted that Phoebe and the baby had been round, and Phoebe had asked her to look after Tiggy for a while, and also to lend her some money. Mary said she could not do either: she was going out, and she only had a shilling in her purse. She said she did not tell Clara immediately because Phoebe had asked her to keep the request secret.

Clara then persuaded her to go to the local station to check whether there was any record of a woman with a pram, which had to be checked in when taking a train. Mary said she would, and then turned up at Frank and Clara's home half an hour later. Clara noticed scratches on Mary's hands, which she said was the result of killing mice, and there was blood from the mice smeared on her dresser.

At this point the landlady came in and showed Clara a newspaper report of an unidentified female body, and the pram was also mentioned. Clara, devastated, felt the description matched Phoebe, and asked Mary to go with her to the police station to find out more.

The two women were taken to the mortuary to see the body, and Clara said: 'I cannot recognize the face but I am sure it is her clothing.' Mary said, 'That's not her', and she tried to prevent Clara looking at her sister-in-law. After one of the policemen washed the blood from the face, Clara confirmed it was Phoebe.

Frank left Chorleywood as soon as he found his wife was not

there and went back home straight away, where his mother showed him the newspaper. He was about to go to the police station when three policemen arrived, and took him to the mortuary to identify Phoebe.

The following morning, a Sunday, a hawker called Oliver Smith was on building land at the side of Finchley Road when, inside the hedge and in a clump of nettles, he saw the body of a child lying face down. He immediately went to the police station, and the body of little Tiggy was taken to the mortuary to join her mother. Frank had the heartbreaking task of returning to the mortuary to identify his daughter.

He was the first to fall under suspicion, and he admitted to the police that he had been having an affair with Mary when they found a key to her house. Mary's jittery behaviour at the mortuary, and the fact that they now knew she was a love rival, sent the police round to Priory Street to interview Mary and search her home. They found bloodstains in the kitchen, a bloodstained carving knife, and there was matted hair and blood on a poker. There were signs of a struggle with two of the kitchen windows broken. A bloodstained rug smelt of paraffin, where attempts had been made to clean it.

Her behaviour was bizarre. She played the piano, sang and whistled loudly, and when asked about the bloodstains and the broken windows said: 'I was trying to catch some mice and I broke the windows.' She later explained the blood by claiming to have a nosebleed. She was arrested, and bloodstains were found on her clothes. She was wearing two wedding rings, and one of them was later identified as Phoebe's. 'Why,' she said, 'do you charge me with this crime? I would not hurt anyone', a stance she maintained until the end of her life.

Mary's trial was at the Old Bailey, starting on 1 December 1890, and the circumstantial evidence against her was overwhelming, but she maintained her innocence and remained calm throughout the trial. John Pearcey, her former lover, identified the cardigan found wrapped around Phoebe's head as the cardigan jacket he had left behind when he moved out.

The defence largely majored on whether Mary would have been strong enough to carry out the murder and dispose of the bodies. She did not speak in her own defence because the law then did not allow a defendant to speak in court.

The trial lasted three days and the jury took less than an hour to return a guilty verdict. She was asked if she had anything to say and replied, in a calm, quiet voice: 'I can only say that I am innocent of this charge.' Sentencing her the judge, Mr Justice Denman, put on the black cap worn when handing down a death sentence and proclaimed she should be 'hanged by the neck until dead'. Asked if she had anything to say she replied: 'Only that I am innocent of the crime.' She walked from the dock without help, her back upright, but apparently 'wept bitterly', according to the wardress who accompanied her, as she went to the cells.

Throughout the trial the courtroom was crowded: there were scuffles among spectators trying to get seats, and those who failed to get in congregated around the doorway. What surprised and offended many of the reporters was that the spectators were largely female, and the men who did attend court were usually accompanying their wives or sisters, who were enjoying the gruesome details.

The *Pall Mall Gazette* reported:

Hour after hour did these ghoulish women, armed with opera glasses, sherry flasks, and sandwich boxes, hang with eager curiosity upon every movement and look of their miserable sister, whose fate was so firmly fixed from the outset. To the end they stayed, for the solemn closing scene had special attractions for them. These women were not the wives and daughters of labourers and costermongers, but ladies of gentle birth and no inconsiderable position.

Waiting in Newgate Prison for the date of her execution, which came two days before Christmas 1890, Mary tried to get in touch with her lover, Frank. He was given permission to see her but refused to visit. When he did not turn up she wept inconsolably.

While in the condemned cell Mary was guarded constantly by three teams of wardresses, as prison officers were then called. She apparently slept well, and certainly did not lose her appetite: bacon and eggs for breakfast, chop or steak for dinner, tea and then supper and a bottle of ale before bedtime.

She was aware of the executioner peering through the peephole in her cell, sizing her up for the length of rope needed. 'Oh, was that the executioner?' she asked one of her guards. 'He's in good time, isn't he?'

Her case came at a time before appeals became part of British law, but her solicitor worked hard to get her a stay of execution on the grounds that she was insane, based on her epilepsy. But three doctors who interviewed her for over an hour concluded that there was no evidence of insanity and 'the law must take its course'.

The day before she went to the scaffold, she wrote to her solicitor that she still loved Frank, and added: 'He might have made death easier for me.' She seemed to have no concept of the agony he must have suffered, having his wife and daughter murdered by a woman whose affections he had encouraged. When the case was over, he moved away from the Camden area.

Mary left behind a mystery that has never been completely solved. During the last few days of her life she asked her solicitor to place a personal advert in a Madrid newspaper, although nobody knew of any connection with Spain. It read: 'M.E.C.P. Last wish of M.E.W. Have not betrayed. M.E.W.' She refused to explain it, but a possible explanation came after her execution, when *The Sunday Times* received a letter from Perpignan, a French town near the Spanish border, which read: 'We thank you for trying to save Mrs Pearcey – Mme Previst (Miss M. E. Wheeler).' The letter was signed with the symbol of a Maltese cross, and the only interpretation put forward is that Previst was the surname of someone Mary met and married on her travels in Europe.

Despite her imminent death, Mary refused to confess to her mother or her solicitor so that they could appeal for clemency and win a reprieve. On the night before her death, the wardresses reported that 'her fortitude was remarkable'. The next day she was asked by the Sheriff of London if she had any final statement and she said: 'My sentence is a just one, but much of the evidence against me was false.'

On her way to the scaffold, she was described as looking 'pale and wan' but was still composed. She told the three wardresses with her that she could walk without support, but when they said they would accompany her she replied: 'Oh well, if you don't mind going with me, I'm pleased.' She kissed each of them. The executioner, James Berry, a man of many years' experience, later described her as the calmest person present at the execution.

A crowd of about 300 waited outside the prison for the flag to be hoisted showing that she was dead, and as it went up they cheered. There was little sympathy for her, especially because she had murdered a small child. She was buried in an unmarked grave inside the prison precincts, and a short time later Frank sold the pram and some of his wife's and daughter's belongings to Madame Tussaud's, who made a model of Mary for the Chamber of Horrors. Bizarrely, the toffee that was lodged in little Phoebe's throat was included in the display. Thirty thousand people visited the exhibit within the first few days of it opening.

There were later theories that Mary was the real Jack the Ripper, based on the fact that she slashed her victim's throat. But that's where all similarities end. Another well publicized theory said she was the daughter of Thomas Wheeler, who was hanged in St Albans, Hertfordshire, after another sensational murder case.

During a robbery that went wrong, he blasted a farmer in the face with a shotgun and paid the ultimate price for his crime. It was a neat story: two murderers in one family, both hanged for their separate crimes, ten years apart. The fact that Thomas Wheeler's young daughter tried to hang herself after the shame of her father's death made the story even more sensational: she tried to die by the noose, and eventually was put to death by it, which was another parallel with Mary's attempt on her own life after the death of her father.

The story is, however, not true. Genealogical research has uncovered the more prosaic story of a girl who learned to survive in the tough streets of London's East End in Victorian times.

17

The Exotic Dancer with
Two Boyfriends

CATHERINE WOODS WAS AN AMBITIOUS AND SELF-ASSURED YOUNG woman. Dance classes from the age of three had given her poise and confidence, she had grown up to be very pretty with a dazzling smile, and she was sure she had what it takes to make a career for herself in dance and theatre. After all, at dance competitions judged by Broadway professionals, she was always singled out and told that if she worked at it she could go far.

Her hometown of Columbus, Ohio, didn't offer her the opportunities she needed and so, brimming with ambition at the age of seventeen, she left a happy family home to make the big move to New York in 2001. It was not just a big move in terms of distance: it was a massive move in terms of lifestyle, and especially in the cost of living in the huge, sprawling metropolis.

Her parents, Jon and Donna, were not happy with her leaving, but they accepted that Catherine was set on taking her talents to Broadway, and she argued that she had to go while she was still young enough to have her big break. 'If I don't go now, I never will,' she told them.

Dr Jon Woods was director of the 225-member marching band at Ohio State University, and a local celebrity because of the band's key role in supporting the college football team, the Buckeyes. Although he had hoped that Catherine, his oldest child and a talented trumpet player, would follow him into music, he had no doubt that dancing was her true love, and she was good at it.

Catherine graduated early from high school and then her parents loaded all her possessions, clothes, dance shoes, photographs, dancing awards and the stuffed rabbit she was given as a baby into a minivan and drove all day until they were dazzled by the skyscrapers of New York. It was a classic story of an ambitious, creative, hard-working young person, determined to make it to the top. As one of her dance classmates from Columbus said: 'To make it in New York you have to eat, sleep and breathe dancing. If your heart isn't into it that much, you might as well not do it. Catherine's was. She really wanted it.'

She found herself a tiny apartment, with a futon that doubled as a couch, a miniscule fridge and a bathroom so small that you could stand in the shower but not turn around. It was all she could afford, especially as she was spending up to $100 a week on dance classes at the famous Broadway Dance Center, where 40,000 students tap, pirouette and chassé their hearts out in the hope of landing a role on stage. She took voice and acting lessons and applied for audition after audition, at the same time earning her rent by teaching dance to children, and waitressing.

New York was lonelier than she imagined, as well as more expensive. She kept in close touch with home, ringing most days and visiting regularly. It was on one trip home that she met David Haughn, an aspiring rap artist two years older than her, who was selling his CDs in car parks. His early life was a great contrast to hers: his mother had addiction problems, he grew up in foster homes and was a high school dropout. Something sparked between them, and two months later he moved to New York and into the tiny apartment with Catherine.

It was an on/off relationship. On the one hand David idolized her, but on the other he seemed unable to find work and pay his share of the bills. Financially things were very tight, even though Catherine's parents sent her an allowance, and it was against the huge worry of how to find the rent money that, after nearly three years of struggle in the Big Apple, she became an exotic dancer, working in a topless bar.

Friends and other dancers, including those who have made it professionally, stressed that she was not a sex worker and that plenty of others have done this while waiting for the break that lands them a place in the chorus line of a big show, hoping that it would lead to even greater things. She obviously didn't tell her parents, and her calls home were still all about classes and auditions; she described the Privilege nightclub where she was dancing as 'an off-Broadway show'. However, she had money for the bills, with dancers earning between \$1000 and \$2000 a week, depending on how many shifts they took.

Catherine would, from time to time, order David out of her flat. He would disappear for a while, but she always relented and took him back in again, especially after she discovered he was living in his car. She could now afford to pay the rent on a bigger flat, and she slept in the bedroom while David was confined to the futon in the living room. By the middle of 2004 he was no longer her lover and simply her room-mate. He was working nights as a doorman at a neighbouring apartment block and earning extra cash walking dogs.

It was at this time that Catherine met Paul Cortez, five years older than her and a personal trainer and yoga teacher at a health centre where Catherine went to exercise when she couldn't get to her dance classes. He was very different from David. Although he, too, had a working-class background, having been brought up in the Bronx by his divorced mother, he excelled academically, winning scholarships to elite private schools, and graduating from Boston University's Theatre Arts Program with a degree in theatre. This gave him common ground with Catherine, and while she was waiting for her big break as a dancer, he was waiting for his as an actor, while writing songs for a rock band.

He and Catherine hit it off, and he introduced her to his mother, who went on an outing to the zoo with her son and his girlfriend. She was thrilled he had met a girl who had so much in common with him.

The two men in her life did not realize at first that they were rivals, but eventually they got to know about each other. Catherine assured Paul that David was her ex, but Paul was very unhappy about David sharing her flat, and the two had various uncomfortable meetings and phone calls, with David later claiming that Paul threatened him.

Like David, Paul fell deeply in love with Catherine, but unlike David he could not come to terms with her working as an exotic dancer and begged her to quit. Catherine refused, partly because she liked having her own money, and partly because she was an independent girl who was not going to be told what to do by any boyfriend. However, when she confessed that she may have been drugged and raped by a customer at the club, it was too much for Paul. He phoned her father and painted a very black picture of Catherine's New York life, claiming she was a sex worker and a drug addict.

It was enough to bring Dr Woods hotfoot to New York on the next available flight. To his great relief he found Catherine well, clearly not on drugs and not a sex worker. She told him to ignore Paul, describing him as 'overbearing and stressy'. And when her father rang the club, the staff did not know her because, like so many girls, she used an alias, calling herself Ava. Her father was reassured. But the next time he went to New York would be with Donna to face the terrible task of clearing out their daughter's possessions from the tiny flat after her death. She had come to New York with a dream; she would leave in a coffin.

Unsurprisingly, when her father told her about Paul's call, she was very annoyed and insisted she did not want to see him again. But the ban didn't last, and they were soon meeting up and in close contact through texts and phone calls right up to the afternoon of the day she was murdered, seven months after her father's visit.

Catherine was killed on 17 November 2005, and there are only two suspects: David Haughn and Paul Cortez. Which one of them did it? The investigation hinged on a critical half hour early in the evening. David and Catherine had been out together walking Catherine's dog, a Chihuahua called Josie, and a black Labrador that David was temporarily looking after. They returned to the apartment block at about 5 p.m., then David took the Labrador with him to buy some food and get the car to take Catherine to work for 7 p.m. After he left, Catherine phoned her friend Megan Wilkins, another exotic dancer, and the call ended at 6.10 p.m. Later, Megan said that Catherine was saving money in order to be able to give up dancing in clubs to concentrate on getting her career break.

At some time between 6 p.m. and 6.30 p.m. Catherine's neighbour found the black Labrador in the hallway, running loose, and it escaped through the main door when it was opened by a delivery man. The neighbour managed to catch it and brought it back but, getting no reply from Catherine's apartment, looked after it in his own flat.

Another neighbour, Aaron Gold, in the flat above Catherine's, was on the phone when he heard scuffling and a woman's scream, and a small dog yapping. He went outside his apartment, still on the phone, and looked up and down the hallway, but there was nothing to see and no further noise. Aaron reckoned that he heard the scream at about 6.28 p.m., and he stayed on the phone until 6.40 p.m.

At 6.49 p.m. David pulled up outside the block in his car to take Catherine to work. She did not come down, which was unusual, so he headed up to the flat, encountering the neighbour with the black Labrador who handed it back to him. Inside the apartment David found Catherine lying on the floor in a pool of blood, and he immediately rang 911. When the call was replayed later, the most noticeable thing was that he didn't sound upset or stressed, and when the operator asked him to describe the injuries he kept repeating that he did not want to look. He was probably in shock, and this can sometimes result in people sounding calm and detached.

When the emergency services arrived it was clear that Catherine had been stabbed many times, both her cheek and hand had been stabbed clean through, and her throat had been slashed at least twice from behind, the cuts so deep that her head was almost severed. There was a boot print on her back, suggesting she had been forced face down while her head was yanked up to slit her throat. Experts later said it would have taken five minutes for her to die, and they must have been a terrifying and agonizing five minutes.

In her hand were some blonde hairs, there was a bloody bootprint on the bedspread, and there was blood on the walls that later revealed, after the application of chemicals, a handprint invisible to the naked eye. The police were able to lift a fingerprint from this handprint.

At first David was a natural suspect. He was the last person to see her alive, he had access to the apartment and he had clothes on hand to change into, which the murderer would have needed because he would have been covered in blood, and no blood was found anywhere else in the flat except in the shower.

But CCTV from a neighbouring apartment block corroborated David's timeline, putting him in the car at the time he said he returned. He was also doing everything he could to help the police. When they asked him if there was anyone he thought had a motive to kill Catherine, he named Paul Vincent, the first and middle names of Paul Cortez. When detectives started digging into Paul's movements that afternoon, he became the prime suspect.

They knew from phone records that he tried to call Catherine several times before 6.30 p.m., but then the calls ended abruptly. When they asked him where he was when he made the calls, he said at home. But mobile phone data showed he actually made the calls in the vicinity of Catherine's flat: if he had been at home his calls would have gone through a different mobile phone mast. There was also CCTV footage of Paul standing outside Catherine's apartment block. Paul was lying, and as far as the police could tell David was not. Paul was now the frontrunner in the search for a murderer.

On 2 December, hundreds of people packed the Methodist Church near Catherine's home in Columbus for her funeral. The entire Ohio State University marching band arrived in six coaches, bringing the congregation to tears with 'Amazing Grace' and other gospel music. Two of her childhood friends performed a ballet in her honour. Afterwards, the teacher who had given her dance lessons from the age of three until she left for New York at seventeen, held a reception at the dance studio where Catherine had first worn her leotard and pointe shoes, the walls decorated with pictures of her starring in local productions.

The story of the murder of the pretty dancer was making headlines, and Paul's picture appeared in the media. Then the police had a breakthrough: a woman in New York came forwards and claimed she had been date-raped by Paul Cortez, and she was able to pick him out in a police identity parade. It was enough for the police to arrest and fingerprint him, and charge him with sodomy. The fingerprint matched the print they had obtained from the bloodstained wall at the murder scene.

This was all the police needed: Paul was charged with second-degree murder on 23 December 2005. (Three months later the rape victim decided she did not want to pursue the case because it was too painful to relive the memories. As Paul was facing an even more serious charge, she probably decided to hitch her justice to Catherine's.)

Once he was under arrest the police searched Paul's home and struck lucky when they found his handwritten diary. Since he cannot have failed to know he was a suspect, why on earth did he keep the diary? Its contents were incendiary:

- 'She thought I betrayed her when I told her father of her night-time secret life.'
- 'Beautiful Catherine, love of my life, how can I make you understand. This erotic subjection to lusty men hurts you more than you know. I just need you to quit the sex for money for good, as well as your ex, then our relationship can grow for real.'
- 'I wanted her to stop so that she would heal and love me without boundaries and pain. But she would never stop. It is like trying to stop a river's downward path in summertime with your bare hands. No, you must wait until winter when nature's freeze grips that sultry flow to stillness.'
- And most chilling of all: 'She wipes clean the shaft that slits her throat ...'

Paul argued in court that his diary entries were part of his song-writing and acting work, preparing him for parts. Most were written months and years before the murder: the one about the shaft was dated eight months earlier, and one entry read in court was ten years old, written by Paul when he was a teenager. But clearly some are very specific to his relationship with Catherine, and his deep distaste and resentment for her work.

A more recent piece of writing by him was a rap, 'The Killin' Machine', for which he wrote the lyrics just a month before Catherine's death, and which was also read out in court. Lines from the rap included: 'Get ya steel need, bleedin' on the killin' machine, eyes dilate, shakin' on the killin' machine.' He told the court these words should not be taken literally, but were meant 'to hold up a mirror to how most guys in today's society view sex.'

With more than fifty pages of Paul's diary submitted as evidence when the prosecution began in January 2007, they were confident they had enough good quality evidence to convict him. But they were surprised and unhappy when they found that for the first three days of his three-week trial Paul was not represented by a lawyer. It is a basic tenet of justice that an accused should have every chance to defend himself, and without legal representation it is very difficult, if not impossible, to claim it was a fair trial.

His two attorneys cited 'personal reasons' for not being there until the fourth day, by which time the jury had been sworn in. One of Paul's legal representatives, Laura Miranda, faxed a letter to the judge saying that she was in Puerto Rico with her sick mother, and the other, Dawn Florio, said she was at a funeral. It later turned out that Florio had actually been indicted for a crime, accused of smuggling drugs to one of her clients in prison. Allowing the trial to go ahead while Paul was not represented was controversial. Laura

Miranda was later fined $1000 for being in contempt of court.

Whether or not Paul was guilty of murdering Catherine, he deserved better treatment in court. The two lawyers produced a few character witnesses and then let Paul speak for himself. They said budget restraints did not allow them to employ forensic experts to assess the evidence put forward by the prosecution. And after the case, four forensic experts came forward to say that the handprint on the wall could have been there before the blood was sprayed over it, and was not the result of a bloodstained hand, but their testimony was not produced during the trial.

The chief prosecutor opened the case by describing Paul as a 'misogynist and narcissist who could not handle rejection'. The evidence against him came from phone records, the lies he told, the CCTV that showed him outside the apartment and the fingerprint. Friends said he did own a pair of boots similar to the one whose print was on the bedspread. The diary entries, which were not challenged by his lawyers as potentially inadmissible, probably sealed the case against him.

The defence did produce a video of Paul going into a shop earlier on the day of the murder wearing what he claimed were shoes, not boots. But when the jury scrutinized the blurred video while they were deliberating, they decided his footwear looked more like boots than shoes. These boots or shoes were not found when police searched Paul's home.

In his defence Paul maintained he was not making excessive calls and texts to Catherine, as she was replying to many of them. As for why he stopped phoning her after 6.30 p.m., one explanation is that he knew she was going to work and, after her shift started at 7 p.m., she was not allowed to use her phone. But that did not explain why he did not try to call her the next morning.

At the end of the three-week trial, the jury took a day and a half to come to a verdict of guilty, and Paul was sentenced to twenty-five years to life in prison. Catherine's family and her ex-lover David Haughn were in court to hear the verdict. David had moved back to Columbus, where he was living with his grandmother and working as a warehouseman.

The Court of Appeals heard Paul's appeal seven years later, in 2014, with the appeal based on the fact that he was not properly represented and the forensic evidence was not challenged. The Court agreed that his new lawyers had raised some substantial issues, for example that another defence team would have opposed the use of the diary material in court. But they said that the new forensic evidence about the fingerprints could not be heard, as it was not introduced at the original trial.

To the disappointment of Paul's many supporters, the Court of Appeals upheld his conviction. Since then, work has been continuing to help his case and he has an active online campaign group. Some of the supporters are not necessarily pledged to Paul's innocence, they simply believe that the case should be heard again to remove any possible doubts.

However, it looks like Paul is in jail for the duration because in 2017 the Supreme Court ruled against another hearing. His new lawyer argued that a CCTV video, recording the comings and goings at the apartment block, should have been produced at the original trial, but the prosecution argued that the date stamp on the video could have been doctored. The judge ruled that even if the date stamp was accurate, it was not enough to justify a retrial.

18

The Parachute 'Accidents'

ONE OF THE MOST INGENIOUS WAYS TO PLOT AND GET AWAY WITH a murder is to make it look like an accident. There may well be murderers in our midst who have managed this trick, but it doesn't always work, even if it may seem to have played out the way the killers wanted in the early days after the death.

Staging an 'accident' is much easier if the victim already takes part in a dangerous sport, where there is always a chance of disaster. That's what gave the potential killers of Els Van Doren and Victoria Cilliers a great advantage: both women were enthusiastic skydivers. While skydiving sounds risky it actually has a risk far lower than road traffic accidents, with an average of only one death for every 250,000 solo parachute jumps. However, it is easier to cut the cords of a parachute than stage a traffic death.

When their parachutes were sabotaged Els died but Victoria miraculously survived, with life-changing injuries. The two cases are not related, but they have one striking feature in common: the murder and attempted murder were carried out by someone who had access to their parachutes, someone who believed they could get away with it, and by killing them they would get rid of a woman who stood in the way of their romantic happiness.

The murder of thirty-eight-year-old Els happened in Belgium in 2006, and attracted headlines around the world the following year when her love rival, Els 'Babs' Clottemans, was arrested for her murder. The victim was a married woman, with two teenage children, who worked alongside her husband, Jan de Wilde, in his jewellery business.

Els van Doren led a double life. At weekends she was an enthusiastic member of the Zwartburg Club, having made 2300 jumps, and where she was heavily and romantically involved with Dutch instructor Marcel Somers. Marcel was also having a fling with Babs, a twenty-six-year-old schoolteacher, and it was this rivalry that led to murder. He was in the habit of seeing Babs on Fridays and Els most Saturdays, but after Els died he told a journalist he had been 'trying to shake off' Babs.

Els died when both her primary and reserve parachutes failed to open, and she dropped from a height of 2 miles, hurtling at 120 m.p.h. into a back garden in the north-eastern town of Opglabbeek. She died on impact, but her horrifying plummet was recorded on her helmet video camera. She was seen looking up and tugging frantically at her gear. It was a particularly awful death, although as she fell she would have no idea that she had been wilfully murdered. For the final half a mile of her plunge she screamed and screamed. 'She tried everything to save herself. She tried to open the reserve parachute, but it wouldn't open. That never happens,' said the pilot of the Cessna plane that dropped the skydivers.

It should have been, for a parachutist with her experience, a routine dive, a regular weekend event, postponed from Saturday to Sunday because of bad weather. Twelve skydivers from the club were taken up, and Els was one of the final four to jump, planning to link together in the sky with her lover Marcel, her rival Babs and another member of the club. They were aiming to freefall together, holding hands in a circle and carrying out aerial manoeuvres. But

Babs delayed a few seconds before she jumped from the plane, and did not join the other three in the planned manoeuvres. She must have been able to see that her murder plan was working when she watched from above as Els hurtled towards the ground. It was later described by a prosecution lawyer in court 'as if you had pushed her from Mont Blanc'.

Babs had sabotaged her rival's parachute two days earlier, when both women stayed the night at Somers' flat in the Dutch town of Eindhoven. Els, his main love, shared his bed, while Babs, his casual fling, was consigned to the sofa. Smarting and bitter, she made two crucial cuts to Els' parachute, which was stored in a cupboard at the flat, that experts testified would have taken no more than thirty seconds.

The police investigation into the death was not initially a murder inquiry, and it was not until Babs tried to commit suicide shortly before she was due to talk to the police for a second time that they began to look at her as a possible suspect. They discovered she had sent anonymous letters about Els' love life to mutual friends and to her husband, and had bombarded Els with anonymous phone calls. Expert inspection of the parachute revealed the sabotage.

The evidence against her was circumstantial, but there was enough to arrest her two months after Els died. She was initially held in custody but then released on bail. While she was on bail she completed her teacher-training course and began teaching in a primary school in the Brussels district of Anderlecht.

Investigating detectives were unable to find out whether Els knew that her lover was also involved with Babs, but Babs certainly knew about his affair with Els. The two women were friends, and because they shared the same name Els suggested that her friend be known as Babs to avoid confusion. 'I always knew that I was number two for Marcel and that Els was number one,' Babs told the Belgian media before her arrest. She said she accepted this situation because she had a very low self-image and 'could only ever imagine being number two'.

She finally came before the court in the east Belgian town of Tongeren almost four years after the fatal jump. Plump and bespectacled, she sat feet away from the mud-caked parachute bag and helmet that Els wore on the day of her death.

Media interest in the trial was so large that a room next to the courthouse was equipped with a video relay for journalists. Babs' defence lawyers maintained that there was no forensic evidence, and tried to suggest both Marcel and Els' husband, Jan, were possible suspects. But Marcel told the court that Els was 'the love of my life' and that he bitterly regretted his fling with Babs, and Jan maintained that he did not know about his wife's affair until after her death, and therefore had no motive for murdering her.

Babs' main defence was that there was no forensic evidence against her, no DNA or fingerprints on the parachute gear, and that circumstantial evidence alone was not enough. 'I see no guilt,' her lawyer said of the sixty-eight-page indictment. 'We will not deny that Ms Clottemans has had some problems, but she is certainly not a psychopath.' This contradicted the report of the court-appointed psychiatrist, who found her to be narcissistic, manipulative and psychopathic.

'Els Clottemans carries an unspeakable anger within her,' said the lawyer for the victim's family in his final argument to the court. 'It has led to the most horrible type of attack: murder. She is totally intensive and feels no empathy.' He added: 'The first question a family normally asks is whether the victim suffered, whether she knew what happened. We don't have to ask. It was filmed. Try to deal with that as a family.'

In her final appeal to the jury Babs said: 'I'm really innocent and can only keep repeating it. For four years I have been accused of something I did not do. That does something to you … They questioned me [saying] "It's you, it's you." But it is not me.'

In October 2010, the jury of seven men and five women heard evidence from 170 witnesses over four weeks, and then took only four hours to find her guilty of premeditated murder, accepting that as an accomplished skydiver she knew how to disable a parachute. As the verdict came in, she remained ashen-faced. Her victim's husband and two teenage children hugged each other. The following day she was sentenced to thirty years in jail, bursting into tears as the judge said he was taking her 'feeble psychological condition' into account as an extenuating circumstance, and was not sentencing her to life imprisonment without parole. Prison authorities immediately put her on suicide watch.

Under Belgian law she can apply for conditional release after serving a third of her sentence. Six months after her conviction, Babs appealed against her sentence, saying that she had not been accompanied by a lawyer when the police interviewed her. Her appeal failed.

Was Emile Cilliers aware of Babs' case, which was dubbed The Parachute Murder when it figured all over the international media, including extensive coverage in the UK? It would be unlikely that he could have missed it, being so immersed in the world of skydiving. But even though this story should have told him that sabotaging a parachute could result in a lengthy prison sentence, the thirty-eight-year-old army sergeant in the Royal Army Physical Training Corps was determined to get rid of his wife, Victoria, so that he could pursue another affair. And death by parachute seemed a good way to murder the mother of two of his children.

It wasn't his first attempt to kill her, nor was she the first woman to be rejected by the charismatic South African who was described by several people who knew him as 'sex-obsessed'.

On Easter Sunday, 5 April 2015, Victoria, forty-two, leapt from the plane at Netheravon Airfield in Wiltshire. She was a fit, very experienced skydiver-cum-instructor, a physiotherapist and former army captain who had given birth to her second child just five weeks earlier.

When Emile invited Victoria to join him at the airfield that weekend, so that she could make her first jump since the birth of the baby, Victoria was delighted. For some months their marriage had been in trouble, but at last he seemed to want to do something with her and his family. He told her it was a treat to celebrate the birth. She really felt hopeful that he had changed his ways and was making an effort to save their marriage.

She was due to jump on the Saturday, but bad weather postponed it to the following day. Rather than return her parachute kit to the storeroom, Emile put it in their locker, later saying that this was to save time the next morning. Victoria, who had introduced her husband to parachute jumping, was unsure about this because it was against the rules. But it was nothing to start a row about, especially as Emile suddenly seemed to be so attentive to her, and he argued that it would be quicker for her the next day than having to get a parachute from the store.

In fact his reason for not returning the parachute to the store was much more sinister: he had already sabotaged the parachute in the toilet, and he had to keep it separate to make sure she was the victim, not another skydiver. The weather was still not great the next morning, Easter Sunday, and Victoria texted Emile that she was tempted 'to go home and eat my choc egg'. He persuaded her to stay, saying conditions would improve, which they did by 4 p.m., enough for a low-altitude jump where parachutes had to be opened within seconds of getting out of the plane, known as a 'hop and drop'.

Emile willingly took care of the children while she went up in the plane, happy and excited to be back doing a hobby she loved, fist-bumping the other skydivers who were boarding the plane with her. She later said she had a sixth sense that she should not be jumping – 'a premonition of something terrible about to happen' – but she showed no sign of nerves. She jumped last then quickly pulled the cord. Exhilaration turned to desperation as she realized something was wrong. 'It just didn't feel right. The lines were twisted. I was spinning.'

Her training kicked in and she cut away the main chute, then tried her emergency chute. It did not work and she blacked out, remembering nothing more. Horrified ground staff described her 'spiralling to the ground like a rag doll'. Racing to the place where she hit the ground, they took a body bag as they were sure she could not have survived the impact. Her astonishing escape from death was later put down to her light weight, and the fact that she landed on a field which had been freshly ploughed and was soft.

James Ranken, who parachuted with her said: 'She had no control of the parachute whatsoever. She was above and then she fell straight past me. My first thought was that she was probably dead. She was drifting in and out of consciousness.'

One of the first people to reach her was Mark Bayada, chief instructor and head of the Army Parachute Association, who immediately noticed that there was something very odd about her kit. As she was lifted on to a stretcher one of the paramedics asked him to check that no lines were still attached to her. 'That's the first time I looked at the equipment properly,' he said later in an interview. 'I could see the two ends of the risers on the reserve parachute were unattached.'

Victoria was rushed to intensive care. When her husband turned up at her bedside, he did not tell her he loved her or express any concern. Instead, he produced a critical injury insurance form to be signed by the doctor. 'He was counting up my fractures,' said Victoria. 'You get one thousand pounds for each break, and he was there totting them up.' He was even texting his latest lover as he sat at Victoria's bedside, saying: 'I can't imagine anything like that happening to you. All I can think of is you.'

In the meantime Mark was checking and rechecking the kit for signs of mechanical failing, but could find no loose stitching or other accidental damage. 'Phoning the police wasn't something I took lightly. But I absolutely wanted to know,' he said.

The police went to Victoria's bedside as soon as she was in a fit state to talk, and they were still half expecting to hear that there had been a mistake and that the kit would turn out to be faulty. But an independent investigation confirmed what Mark Bayada had seen: the kit had been sabotaged. Then they got a phone call from one of Vicky's friends, who said the relationship between Emile and Victoria was toxic, and that's when they started investigating Emile in depth.

They discovered that he was far from being a devoted family man: his two children with Victoria were the youngest of six he had fathered altogether, and he had split from two other families in the past. What's more, at the time of Victoria's parachute jump he not only had a girlfriend but was having regular sex with his ex-wife, *and* he was contacting prostitutes and adult websites. What's more, he was deep in debt ... An accident inquiry turned into an attempted murder.

Emile grew up in Ermelo, a small town east of Johannesburg in South Africa, and started working for his father's construction company, rising to be a foreman. His first serious girlfriend, Nicolene Shepherd, gave birth to his first child, a daughter Cilene, when she was just sixteen. She met him when she was thirteen and he was sixteen, and she found him 'charismatic and charming'. She was pregnant with her second child, Trevor, when Emile left them behind and travelled to the UK in 2000, telling Nicolene he was going on a working holiday and would come back and settle down.

He had cheated on her 'time after time, and I always took him back,' she said later. Her best friend was one of his conquests. She also learned early about his profligate spending, because when she was struggling to pay for nappies, he bought himself an expensive pair of golf shoes.

'He loved me so much, at least I thought so,' said Cilene. 'He was so attentive. I really didn't understand … I thought I was their world, I was their favourite person, [then he] just disappeared. Probably the most selfish thing he has done is not being able to at least apologize for leaving us all behind in his trail of dust.'

In the UK on a temporary work visa, Emile found work in a bar in Oxford where he met Carly Taylor, and married her a couple of years later. She also had two children by him. The couple moved to Ipswich, where he was assistant manager of a nightclub, and where, on a whim, he walked into an army recruiting office and signed on. He was posted to Plymouth, where he and Carly split up. After parting they remained on amicable terms – so amicable that Emile popped in and out of her life, and her bedroom, even after he married Victoria. She and her children lived less than 2 miles from the home he shared with Victoria, and the two families shared childcare.

The girl he left behind in South Africa, Nicolene, had to learn from Emile's mother that he'd married another woman. She and her two children moved to Britain to make a fresh start, but she had no intention of contacting him until Cilene started asking about her father. Nicolene did make contact with him through his mother, and he seemed keen to meet up, taking her and the children on a family outing to a water park. (This contradicted what he later said in court, when he asserted he had not been in contact with his two oldest children since leaving South Africa.)

Meeting Nicolene again, they soon resumed a sexual relationship. This was before he and Carly decided to divorce, but he told Nicolene that they were separated and going through a divorce. After one assignation with Nicolene he accidentally left his phone behind, and when it rang she answered it and found herself talking to Carly. The two women compared notes and agreed to meet at Carly's home. When Emile walked in to be confronted by both, he spoke to Nicolene in Afrikaans, asking what the hell she was doing there. She said: 'He looked from one of us to the other, as if trying to decide "Who wants me most." I knew I had to walk away.'

He first met Victoria when, as an army physiotherapist, she treated him for a skiing injury. He had recently separated from Carly, and Victoria was divorced from his first husband, an army captain with an impressive military record, but whose frequent overseas tours had destroyed the marriage, leaving her feeling insecure.

She and Emile married four years before the murder attempt, in a ceremony attended by forty guests in an exclusive venue in Cape Town, when Victoria was in the early weeks of pregnancy. She had already suffered an early miscarriage, and they were both, she said, thrilled with the new pregnancy. At first they lived in her home in Bulford, Wiltshire, and as soon as his military training was complete, they bought a house in Amesbury, in Victoria's name.

He had never parachuted before he met her, but he was fast-tracked through the early part of the training because Victoria was an instructor. She maintains that they were happy for more than three years, and that the cracks in the marriage did not start to appear until her second pregnancy.

While she lay in hospital, and slowly learned to walk again wearing a body brace, the investigation started, but it was a month before the police had enough evidence to charge Emile. Before his arrest, his mother Zaan flew in from South Africa to stay with him and look after the children. When asked whether he could have tried to murder his wife she said: 'I believe in my son, I love him, he is our child and we know him. I don't feel affected by these allegations as I know there is no truth in it.' His brother Dirk agreed: 'I know my brother, he comes from a good family and a good home. There's no way he could have done the things they said he has done.'

Nonetheless, the police believed they had enough evidence to charge him with attempted murder, maintaining that he had sabotaged the parachute in the ten minutes when he had gone to the toilet. Detective Constable Maddie Hennah went to the barracks to arrest Emile who was calm and cooperative and did not want a solicitor to sit through his interview. It was a lengthy six-hour process, and he stayed unruffled, answering all the questions, and even volunteering information about his girlfriend, Stefanie Goller. He had met her on the dating site Tinder when he was skiing with the army in Austria, while Victoria was heavily pregnant, and he told them that he wanted to end his marriage to Victoria. Stefanie was a qualified skydiving instructor and shared his passion for skiing and outdoor pursuits. He also owned up to his debts, obviously aware that the police knew or would find out this information anyway.

'He was very clever: he covered all the points he knew we would discover. He assumed we were going to accept what he was saying, and that he'd never see us again,' said Hennah. The only time he showed any emotion was when he broke down in tears because Stefanie had ended their relationship. At the end of the interview he told the detective: 'The worst part of today was that you arrested me in front of my subordinates.'

Realizing they were dealing with a clever, devious man, the investigating team took advice on how to interview him. 'He's like a politician,' Hennah said. 'You'd ask a question and he would not give you a direct answer. He'd lead off somewhere else.'

Emile showed no concern for Victoria, but in the second of his three police interviews, when he turned up at the police station in a T-shirt, shorts and flipflops, he broke down in tears when he said Stefanie, 'the love of his life', had finished with him. He pulled a blanket around him and appeared to sob, but the police believe it was an act, to show he was a man of feeling.

He quickly seemed to accept that Stefanie had gone from his life, later describing her as 'just an affair' and, in his third interview, claimed his tears were really for Victoria, until police pointed out that they had a video of the interviews. By the time he came to trial he said he had just been 'stringing Stef along'.

Stefanie was living in Innsbruck when they first met, and he told her he was separated from his wife, who was carrying another man's child. Even after the baby was born he continued to say the baby was not his, and falsely told Stefanie that he had undergone a DNA test to prove this; he even came up with names of men he said Victoria could have been having an affair with. He told Stefanie: 'I held the baby and felt no connection.'

When police told Victoria about her husband's affair and about his visits to prostitutes, she was shocked by the extent of his infidelity, and told them that she suspected he had tried to trigger a gas leak when she and the children were in the house. The gas pipe was sent off for forensic tests, and the report said it had been tampered with and a valve had been opened. Blood found around the valve was identified by DNA testing as Emile's, and pliers he owned matched the marks on the valve.

After tampering with the gas valve he had coldly and calculatingly left his wife, toddler daughter and newborn son in the house in Amesbury and made his way to visit his ex-wife Carly. After making love to her, he sent a couple of saucy texts to his girlfriend Stefanie, checked an adult website 'for thrills' and then drove to his barracks in Aldershot, where he found an excuse to stay the night, not wanting to be in the house when the gas explosion occurred.

The following morning, Victoria woke and went to the kitchen to warm some milk for her toddler. She smelled gas. She texted her husband because she found the blood around the faulty valve in the kitchen. 'Are you trying to bump me off?' she joked. He was. But it took another attempt on her life for her to realize it.

Victoria knew he was not faithful because she had seen the messages and emails. She also knew that he had money problems, as he borrowed from her, from friends and from payday loan companies. He now owed Victoria £19,000, which he was supposed to be repaying with a standing order, but often the payment did not come. He had also helped himself to £6000 from her savings, and when she discovered the loss he claimed her account had been hacked, but the bank traced the transaction back to their home computer. The police later traced another £22,000 worth of debt, but suspected there was much more. He was adept at moving money around from lender to lender, often on a daily basis.

The money went on prostitutes, casual flings, his affair with his ex-wife and holidays abroad with Stefanie, which he told Victoria were work trips. He splashed out on skiing equipment, golf clubs and the latest gadgets. Even when he was not with another woman, he would stay overnight at the barracks, complaining of the forty-five-minute commute to his wife and children, and seeking casual sex on websites. When Victoria was pregnant with their second child, he volunteered for residential training camps abroad.

Fearing she was losing him, Victoria had clung on tightly as the marriage was fracturing, sending loving texts and emails whenever he was away. 'I feel like a failure as a wife,' she texted him, when confronting him about the state of their marriage. While he was skiing in Austria he emailed Victoria: 'I need to decide whether I want to be in this marriage. I think we may have got married too soon.' Pregnant with their second baby, Victoria 'cried so hard I thought I might damage the baby'.

Divorce was not a solution for Emile because it would add to his financial problems. Murder would not.

When the detectives trawled through his Whats App account they uncovered 32,000 messages between him and Stefanie, in which he hinted that he would be freer to pursue their relationship in April, the month of the murder attempt. He said he could 'do random and spontaneous from April'. He later said this referred to when he would leave Victoria, and had nothing to do with his attempt to kill her. He also sent Stefanie over 700 texts in one day.

He and Stefanie had talked about marriage, he had looked on the internet for a house in Wiltshire, which he said he would buy for her, and planned holidays they would take. He took her to Germany and to the Czech Republic, siphoning money for these holidays from Victoria's accounts, and she travelled to England to spend time with him on at least four occasions. Stefanie even stayed with him at their barracks in Aldershot, where his fellow soldiers assumed he had split from Victoria. One text, sent the day after Victoria's crash, read: 'Will you be my cleaner? I only like nude house cleaners. I pay with hugs and kisses.'

The trawl also discovered that he contacted escorts, on one occasion offering £100 for 'bareback' sex, a term that means unprotected sex, on condition he could film it. He claimed in court that contacting prostitutes gave him 'a thrill', but he never actually met any. He was clearly able to compartmentalize his sex life because, shortly after offering the £100, he texted his ex-wife Carly arranging to have sex in his new car – which actually belonged to Victoria.

Detectives realized that he was hoping to cash the £120,000 life insurance policy covering Victoria's life. But unknown to him, she had changed her will to make sure her assets went to her children because she knew better than to trust her husband with money. Just a week before Christmas 2014 she sent him a text: 'U promised before we married not to use loan sharks and now I get a big guy turning up to door try to intimidate a pregnant woman with a visibly upset toddler. Both of us shaken.' He texted a reply: 'Why are you worried? They can't do anything.'

Poignantly, later the same month Victoria sent him a Whatsapp message: 'I entered into this marriage with my eyes open. I have loved u more each year. Feels like you keep trying to push me away until I jump ship. But I can't. I love you too much. It feels just now that you would be happier without me.'

While he was on bail for attempted murder and Victoria was struggling to overcome her massive injuries, he applied for a number of credit cards in her name and spent thousands in a shopping spree. He bought computer games, a Playstation and an iPhone, later claiming he needed 'a distraction' as he was unable to live at the family home and was living in a room in the barracks.

It was two years before the trial began. A small police team had spent nine months wading through tens of thousands of pages of data from his phone. But when they finally got him into court there was a sensational development. The jury had to be dismissed and a retrial ordered after two members developed stress-related illnesses, soon after the judge had said he would accept a majority verdict. Emile was remanded on bail pending a second trial.

And the police were still uncovering evidence. They discovered that even when Victoria was in intensive care he was searching for prostitutes online, and even researched a wet nurse for their five-week-old baby, as if he did not expect Victoria to be around. They also found videos of Emile singing love songs to Victoria, which they believed was part of his effort to manipulate her into not giving evidence against him in court.

The second trial lasted six weeks. Emile was confident and held himself with straight-backed military bearing. He wore a suit, often with a waistcoat, gold cufflinks and tiepin. When he heard someone say that a gentleman should wear a waistcoat with the bottom button undone, he took it on board and, from then on, his lowest button was open.

He answered calmly, deflecting questions with 'it's not up to me to prove that' and 'that's your perception'. Calm anger was a facet of his personality commented on by others who'd had dealings with him: Victoria told the police that when she asked him not to smoke in the car he didn't rant but his face 'went blank with fury'. Through-out his trial his emotions were kept tightly in check.

He was described by the prosecution as 'a pathological liar who is completely devoid of empathy', and whose behaviour was 'learnt', not genuine. He proclaimed his innocence all through the trial.

When asked by the prosecution if he was saying that a random stranger tampered with the gas pipe and sabotaged the parachute, he agreed. It was certainly not him, he asserted. He even suggested that Victoria may have tampered with her own parachute in order to kill herself.

Giving evidence, Victoria, who walked into court unaided and stood in the witness box, said she had changed her will to exclude him in favour of their children in 2014. 'I'm an intelligent person who knew what was going on. I was starting to feel insecure in the marriage. I knew he was having an affair. I wanted to get it done sooner rather than later.'

She said that after paying off his debts she found him extra work, packing parachutes, to make him some money. Discovering that he spent New Year's Eve with his lover Stefanie in Berlin, she said that was 'the final straw' and she began to feel suicidal. She mentally set a time limit of their wedding anniversary in September 2015 for him to 'shape up or ship out', but he tried to kill her six months before the date.

Yet despite everything that had happened and the overwhelming evidence against him, Victoria tried to protect him in court, saying that in her interview with the police she had exaggerated the time he was in the toilet with her parachute because she wanted 'to get her own back'. She said she 'despised' him and was 'out for blood'. 'I was humiliated, I wanted him to suffer. I got to the point where his lies and deceit had been disclosed to me and I wanted to get my own back to a certain extent.'

Speaking in his own defence, Emile said that Victoria was unaware of his debts when he first lived with her, but she helped him. He was still in financial difficulties: 'All my money would go on loans and by the end of the month I would take out another one to try to hide it.

I was embarrassed. I was afraid Victoria would be ashamed of me. I wanted to tell her but was scared of the consequences. I was scared she might leave me … I was constantly bailed out by Victoria.'

His defence barrister, Elizabeth Marsh QC, emphasized that 'he did not change in any way' after Victoria plunged to the ground. 'He was not stressed or sweaty, he didn't start to act panicked or guilty in any way.' But the jury agreed that he *was* guilty of two counts of attempted murder.

In a pre-sentence report on Emile, he was assessed as posing a high risk to adults, particularly partners, and as a medium risk to children. Victoria was sitting in the courtroom, but requested that her victim impact statement was not read out. It is believed that she tried to get him a lighter sentence.

Sentencing him to life with a minimum of eighteen years, the judge, Mr Justice Sweeney, said:

> This was wicked offending of extreme gravity. Your two attempts to murder your wife were planned and carried out in cold blood for your own selfish purposes. That your wife recovered at all was miraculous, she undoubtedly suffered severe physical harm and she must have suffered psychological harm in the terror of the fall and after. She appears to have recovered from the physical harm but not, having seen her in the witness box at length, from the psychological harm.

Emile was promptly discharged from the army as soon as the sentence was passed. The senior investigating officer, Detective Inspector Paul Franklin, said:

> From the outset Emile Cilliers showed no remorse for what

he has done. He lied all the way through two trials, but in the end justice won out with the guilty verdicts and now a long sentence. Emile Cilliers is dangerous; he's a cold, callous selfish man who cares only about money and his sexual conquests. Today's sentencing means that society is a little safer with him locked away.

It was three years to the day after the murder attempts that Emile went to jail, and during that time Victoria told her children that their father was away, for work. She revealed that it was still very hard for her to think of him as a killer, but later she told them he had 'done a bad thing'.

She said in a television interview:

I have been through every emotion under the sun. I've had plenty of time to think about things, which is probably why I am not overtly angry, partly because I'm still in shock, slightly stunned about the whole thing. Also, I've got two young children. I'm the sole carer for them. I can't be angry, bitter, really emotional. I need to keep an even keel for them.

Despite the welter of evidence against him, she seemed unsure about his guilt. She described him in a newspaper interview as a 'passionate, intense alpha male,' and accepted he was a sex addict. 'I have to go with, I suppose, the verdict. It's too big to get my head round … I'll always care for the father of my children, and I loved him and thought I was going to spend the rest of my life with him … I have seen him in court but not spoken to him in three years.' Of the full scale of his deception and his ongoing sexual relationship with Carly she said: 'I feel betrayed. Carly and I used to share childcare duties … I saw her probably on a weekly basis.'

Nicolene, his first love, said after the court case that she was not surprised to learn what he had done, describing him as able to cast 'a spell' over women. 'I feel like I've dodged a bullet,' she added. She thought he managed to manipulate Victoria and put her back under his spell before the court case. She explained: 'He always puts in a great amount of effort when he's in the moment with you. You're the best thing in the world. You're the only person in the world. But I think that's part of his charm. You forgive the bad things because you remember the good things, and the good things are so good that you forgive the bad.'

Stefanie, too, was devastated when she learned the truth about her ardent lover, and broke off contact with him after his arrest. At the time of his trial she went abroad to hide from the massive media interest. A friend said: 'She feels ashamed – ashamed and stupid that she fell for such a creature … She wanted children with Cilliers, and now she hates herself for that.'

Three and a half years after the parachute jump that was meant to kill her, Victoria took to the skies again and made a tandem sky-dive to raise money for the air ambulance service she credits with saving her life, with her six-year-old daughter and three-year-old son cheering her on. Agreeing to do the jump brought back painful memories. 'Putting the date in my diary made the memories of my fall come rushing back, more vividly than before. There have been many nights when I couldn't sleep or when I would wake with my heart racing. Climbing on board and preparing for take-off was an emotionally all-encompassing experience. It took me right back.'

After she and her skydiving partner successfully landed she said: 'I felt the most incredible sense of relief and release.'

19

Killed by the Dog She Loved

IT WAS A HIDEOUS WAY TO DIE. DOLLY KAPLAN'S LAST MOMENTS were filled with terror and appalling pain, inflicted on her by the pet dog who usually cuddled up to her on the sofa, his big head resting in her lap, his tongue gently licking her.

What turned Mack into a vicious killer? That was the question faced by police offcer Michaelene Taliano and her colleague Sam Reese when they were confronted by the bloody scene at Dolly's home in 1992.

True, Mack was a Pit Bull Terrier, a breed that is banned in the UK under the Dangerous Dogs Act. In the USA some states ban the breed, but in Cleveland, Ohio, where twenty-eight-year-old Dolly lived, Pit Bulls are classified as 'vicious' but not banned. Outside Dolly's home was a sign that read 'Beware of the dog', and Mack's presence alone was enough to put off unwanted visitors. But, according to Dolly, appearances were deceptive, and Mack was a big softie.

Dolly, whose real name was Angela, was a tiny woman with, her friends said, a big heart. She had loved animals all her life, enjoyed horse riding, as a child had bred rabbits and she now had a good relationship with Mack, telling friends and family that the dog was always gentle with her and her partner, Jeffrey Mann, and Dolly's two young daughters.

She and Jeffrey bought Mack five years earlier, when their relationship first started, and when Mack was already a year old. Dolly had no qualms about letting her daughters play with him. She taught him tricks so he lay down on her command, and when she walked him he loved fetching sticks for her to throw, his stumpy tail wagging madly. But in the early hours of 2 September something happened that triggered the worst in Mack, and his huge teeth ripped into Dolly's flesh, biting her more than 170 times until her naked body lay in a pool of blood.

It puzzled Detective Taliano, who, with Detective Reese, responded to an emergency call at 4 a.m. from thirty-six-year-old Jeffrey. He said his partner had been brutally mauled by a dog and was near to death. When the detectives arrived, they found Dolly's body on a blood-soaked couch in the living room. She had seventy-five bite marks on the inside of her arms, from which blood had poured, and another hundred bite marks on her arms, where the dog's teeth had not punctured the skin. Strangely, they thought, there were no bite marks on her hands. Surely she would have fought to stave off the berserk dog? Her hands should have been shredded.

Jeffrey had a cut on his forehead, and two halves of a drinking glass were found in two different rooms. He seemed to be dazed, and not simply because of the brutal killing of his partner. His answers to questions were full of odd contradictions. The police thought he was either high on drugs or had been drinking.

'He told me that Dolly had gone for a walk and was apparently attacked by a dog which was walking down the street. And she came crawling home, and that's when he brought her into the house,' said Taliano. 'I said to him: "Time out. There's no blood on the front porch and none on the sidewalk. I'm sorry, I'm not going to buy that." Then Jeffrey said that maybe someone broke in and did the attack. I said: "With a Pit Bull in the house, I don't think so." Then he said: "Maybe my dog did it.'"

Reese said: 'When I asked a direct question about the dog he wouldn't answer it. Either he didn't know or he didn't understand. He was never clear about how the glass broke, either. He could not answer our inquiries about that glass or other inquiries we put to him.' But the unemployed welder did ask the detective one question: he wanted to know if Mack would be destroyed as a result of the attack. When Reese asked if he was more concerned about the dog than his dead partner he replied: 'Is it wrong to cover for your dog?'

The officers made one arrest that night: Mack, the 70 lb Pit Bull. He was taken to the Cleveland city kennel. Normally, a dog involved in a vicious attack where someone was killed would be destroyed immediately. But the detectives asked for a stay of execution because they sensed there was something wrong, and the dog could be a crucial part of the case.

Jeffrey later told them that he was asleep at 2 a.m., when he suddenly woke up and saw Mack in the bedroom attacking Dolly. He managed to get the dog off her and lock him in another bedroom. He said Dolly refused to go to hospital and lay down on the living-room couch. He called the police when she turned blue at 4 a.m.

Although they knew that Pit Bulls can be dangerous, the police also knew that they are generally very loyal to their owners. There are well-documented cases of Pit Bulls rescuing their owners from danger, even standing in front of their owners and being shot by intruders or the police. Moreover, they have worked very successfully as police dogs. The really vicious ones are usually bred for illegal dog fighting, and even then are far more likely to attack other dogs than humans. Also, the police noticed that Dolly's injuries were not typical of a Pit Bull attack. The dogs are terriers, and their natural form of attack is to use their strong jaws to clamp in a bite, then to hold on and shake their victim. Dolly was covered in scores of separate bites, definitely not typical behaviour.

The police called in animal expert Karen Arnoff to see if she could discover why a loved and loving pet like Mack had turned viciously on the person he most enjoyed cuddling up with. Karen, who was the director of a behavioural training centre for dogs, was convinced that Mack would not have mauled Dolly without being commanded to attack.

She looked at other fatal dog attacks and found that owners are never victims, and that attacks rarely happen in front of owners unless the dog has been brutalized for dog fighting. Most victims of fatal dog attacks are children under five or adults over seventy-five – in other words, the vulnerable. Also, the areas of the body attacked in fatalities are critical areas like the head, neck or spinal cord, and the majority of deaths caused by dog attacks involve bites to the neck or throat, not to the arms.

Arnoff then trained Mack using the clicker method (a method used by many dog trainers where the click is the immediate signal to the dog that he has done the right thing), and tested him to see if he was trained to attack and if, during an attack, he would stop and attack again when commanded. She also experimented to see if he would attack without provocation. The conclusion was unambiguous. 'From the results, I believe the dog was instigated and re-instigated to attack,' she said.

While Mack's behaviour was being assessed, the detectives were making inquiries into Dolly and Jeffrey's relationship, and they quickly discovered it was volatile – he had been violent to her on more than one occasion. It was enough to believe they had a case against him, and he was charged with first-degree murder, the first time in American history, or probably anywhere else in the world, that a dog was classified as a murder weapon. The fact that Dolly had no bite marks on her hands was a major plank of the prosecution case.

Witnesses were called to testify to the regular beatings that Dolly had suffered from Jeffrey. Her babysitter, Patricia Tipple, who looked after her children, said Dolly confided in her about the brutal treatment she suffered. 'Dolly was just in tears,' she said, describing a day when Dolly returned home with a red, swollen face. 'She was very upset. She just said she was tired of this, tired of being beaten up.'

On the night of the attack, Dolly's daughters, aged eleven and seven, were staying with their father. A friend of Dolly's, whose children were in the same school as hers, testified that Dolly was having problems with Jeffrey. She said: 'I told her to leave him but she said she did not know what he would do. She said she was afraid. She didn't know what would happen.' This friend, and another mum from the school, told the court they had seen Dolly with a black eye in the spring of 1992, five months before her death. 'She acted strange. She wouldn't elaborate on what had happened.'

The jury was shown a photograph of Dolly holding Mack on her lap, and the caption 'Me and the head of security catching a nap.' The picture, the prosecution claimed, showed that Mack would not have attacked Dolly without provocation.

Karen's testimony was crucial, and she maintained that in her opinion Jeffrey had set the dog on Dolly. The jury was shown a video of Mack attacking the padded sleeve of another dog trainer, Ben McPeek, who was also called to give evidence. 'There is no doubt in my mind that Mack was trained to attack,' he told the court, although he admitted he had not found the verbal or hand signal that prompted an attack. Later the experts speculated that Mann either used a command in a foreign language or even invented his own word.

In defence, Jeffrey's lawyer stated in court that at the time Mack attacked Dolly, he was so groggy from a combination of prescribed medication and drink that he was slow to react and struggled to pull the dog away. He did not call the police or ambulance straightaway because, he claimed, Dolly did not want any problems with the law as she was in the middle of a bitter custody battle with her ex-husband over her two young children. Mann also claimed, through his lawyer, that Dolly had an epileptic fit, which must have startled and unnerved the dog because she was thrashing about on the floor, so Mack acted in self-defence, believing he was being attacked.

But, although Dolly had been diagnosed with epilepsy earlier that year, the medical examination of her body after death (called an autopsy in the US, a postmortem in the UK) showed no symptoms of her having had an epileptic fit prior to her death. There were no signs of tongue-biting or loss of bladder control, two of the most common symptoms. It was highly unlikely that she had had a seizure, the coroner had concluded.

The court heard that both Dolly and her partner had recently received minor injuries in a car crash, and they had both regularly been prescribed with painkillers, muscle relaxants and anti-depressants, which the defence team meant they were both heavily sedated when the attack happened and didn't react promptly. The defence also produced a neighbour who testified that he'd seen Mack attack a tree stump ferociously, and that a door-to-door political campaigner had been scared off by the Pit Bull. Jeffrey did not take the stand to testify in his own defence, and after the case one of his lawyers said he did not have a good answer to what happened that night because 'he was pretty much out of it'.

Summing up, Assistant County Prosecutor Ed Walsh gave a detailed description of what the police believed happened on the night that Dolly died. A neighbour saw her arriving home at 1.45 a.m, walking unsteadily to the side door. Jeffrey was mad at her for coming home late and he started to beat her in the bedroom; she grabbed a drinking glass that broke when she hit him on the head, causing a cut to his forehead. His blood was found on the glass. Then he grabbed her arms and gave Mack the order to attack. Afterwards he cut off her clothes and moved her to the sofa, covering her with a blanket. He cleaned the blood off Mack and put him in an upstairs bedroom.

He said: 'Put yourself in her shoes for one hundred and eighty seconds of being torn apart by this animal before she blacked out. She must have been crying out to him. What that must have sounded like ... There's another bite, and another bite ... Count to seventy or seventy-five bites. That's what this woman went through.' The biting pattern was described as 'the work of a rational mind, not a crazy dog that went berserk. The marks also fit the theory that Mann pulled Dolly's arms open.'

Prosecutor Peter Gauthier said: 'Why didn't she use her hands to get the dog off? If you're being attacked by a dog, are you going to open up and show the interior of your arms and say, "Here doggie, doggie, come and get me?"'

The final word went to the defence team for Jeffrey, and his lawyer, Gordon Friedman, told the court: 'This dog was both a loving pet and a vicious beast. This dog was, in fact, Dr Jekyll and Mr Hyde. An epileptic seizure is a startling event. The dog may have been startled and caused it to go for somebody he knew. Can I prove it? No. But it is as likely as any theory posed in this courtroom.'

The jury took nine hours to agree, unanimously, that Jeffrey was guilty of second-degree murder, and he was sentenced to between fifteen years and life and ordered to pay $5000 dollars to her two young daughters. Mack was destroyed as soon as the case was over. Second-degree murder means the attack was not premeditated or planned in advance, although by teaching his dog to attack, Mann had taken steps to prepare for the murder, but the court agreed he had not necessarily intended to commit the crime that night.

Detective Taliano was delighted and relieved, especially as she had taken a lot of ribbing from colleagues about the idea that a dog was capable of being trained as a murder weapon. 'It was a very tough case,' she said. 'I had only one witness, a dog. And I don't speak dogese. I've taken a lot of abuse from my own kind. I'd get phone calls from mystery callers barking *Woof, woof.*'

Twenty-five years later in 2018, now retired, Detective Taliano once again became involved with the case, teaming up with Dolly's mother, Joyce Ragels, to help block Mann's appeal for parole. She produced her scrapbook from the case, which included crime scene photographs of Dolly's mauled body. She said: 'I think he should spend the rest of his life in the penitentiary. This was an exceptionally cruel murder. It was the first case in the history of the world where somebody was charged with using an animal as a murder weapon and successfully prosecuted.'

Joyce said: 'I don't believe you can fix whatever is broken in him. And I do believe something is very broken in him.' She praised Detective Taliano highly, but also added that she wished they'd never had to meet over the death of her daughter.

Parole was also opposed by the County Prosecutor. In his view: 'Mann has never taken responsibility and never shown any remorse. He has even refused to pay the five thousand dollars restitution to her two children that was ordered by the Judge at his trial. He's grossly unfit for parole.' The Parole Board listened: Jeffrey Mann was denied parole.

20

The Army Wife

MARIKA SPARFELDT WATCHED IN HORROR AS THE DARK BLUE SAAB careered across the stable yard, ramming into the back of another car. Frozen in horror and fear, she watched the driver reverse, swerve and head straight for her. The fit young woman did not have time to dive for cover, and although her lover grabbed her to pull her from the path of the Saab, he was too late and she was thrown up and over the bonnet. Her massive internal injuries included a ruptured spleen, pancreas, liver and kidneys. She died in the shelter of one of the stables, cradled in the arms of her lover, Tony Dryland, a major in the British army stationed in Germany.

Her killer was his wife, Christine, a woman driven over the edge by her husband's infidelity. As she revved up around the yard, smashing into the back of his white Mercedes, both he and Marika tugged at the car doors, imploring her to stop. But in a demented rage she swerved and hit the accelerator. Later, she claimed she wanted to kill herself by driving into the wall, and that she had no memory of the moment when she saw Marika and turned all her fury, and the two-ton weight of the car, on her rival and enemy, the woman she believed had ruined her life.

Climbing out of the wreckage of the Saab, she did not wait to see how badly she had injured Marika. She knew her rival was dead, and when she ran home she blurted out to her fifteen-year-old son,

Robert, what she had done. She said Marika deserved to die. Robert told her nobody deserved to die, and ran to the stables to see if she was telling the truth. He found his father, blood pouring down his face, cradling Marika in his arms. He ran back home to be with his mother to wait for the police to arrive and arrest her.

Christine, unexpectedly calm and collected, rang the babysitter who had been booked to cover her evening out with Tony to celebrate his forty-sixth birthday. Realizing that her life was in tatters, she then rang her family in Australia to tell them what had happened and waited for the police to arrive at the army house where the family lived in Soltau, in the Luneburg area of Germany, where the British army had a base.

When the police came to arrest her, she was composed and offered them a cup of tea, every inch the army officer's wife. Perhaps she felt some relief: at last the agony of her husband's affair was over, even if it had ended in a violent and devastating way. She had been wretchedly miserable for the past eight months since she became aware of his affair, and seeing the lovers together in the stable yard was the final realization that, whatever he promised, he was not going to turn his back on Marika and become a dutiful husband again.

Sixteen years earlier, Tony had had another affair with the wife of an army colleague, and in despair Christine had attempted suicide by taking an overdose. She was found in time and saved, but those who treated her believed it was a serious attempt, not simply a cry of help. She said she was just as serious about ending her own life when Tony now failed, despite promises, to break away from Marika.

She said in a statement to the police: 'I feel detached. It is so unreal. We have been living a nightmare for the past eight months. The awful thing is that I did not plan to do it. I just went up there and saw them together and just snapped.'

Christine and Tony married when she was only seventeen and he was twenty-one. She had been brought up in an army family because her father was an NCO, and she met Tony, who at the time was serving in the ranks, when he and her father were both posted to Berlin. Their life together started in Germany, and ended in Germany.

Tony, too, came from a military background, the son of a physical training instructor with the King's African Rifles, a colonial regiment that was disbanded when African countries gained independence in the 1960s. During his childhood in Africa, Tony learned to ride at an early age, and horses became a lifelong passion for him. He enlisted as an army apprentice at sixteen, and for twenty-two years worked his way up through the ranks of Royal Electrical and Mechanical Engineers Regiment, eventually being commissioned as an officer.

For Christine, his commission was not an easy time: suddenly she was expected to attend functions in the officers' mess, mixing with wives whose husbands had been commissioned when they first joined the army. There was always a feeling that LE (late entry) officers were not quite 'the real thing', and socially she may have felt out of her depth. Tony, too, perhaps felt that he never quite fitted in, although he was a dedicated career soldier, and in 1990 was promoted to major.

The couple struggled to have children but, despite a series of miscarriages, by the time of Marika's death they had fifteen-year-old Robert and six-year-old James. Her gynaecological problems had taken a toll, and she had to have a hysterectomy in the 1980s, which brought on an early menopause. She was treated with hormone replacement therapy which, in the years since then, has been refined and improved, but for Christine it was later discovered to have been inappropriate. It should have been monitored much more than it was.

When he was first commissioned, as a lieutenant and then captain, Tony was serving in Paderborn, another army base in Germany. Robert, like many army children, was in boarding school in England, flying out to join his family for holidays, and James lived with his parents, Christine being a full-time mother and housewife. On promotion to major, Tony was transferred to Soltau, about 125 miles away, but for the first four months of his posting Christine and James stayed in Paderborn, sorting out their army house and arranging their next move.

While the family were still based in Paderborn Tony was able to indulge his love of horses, buying two black Hanoverians, elegant and strong horses that are favourites for showjumping competitions. They were an expensive hobby: stabling alone cost him £150 a week (more than £300 now). He loved competing at local events, and although Christine did not share his interest, she loyally turned up to watch him with the children.

On moving to Soltau, Tony was pleased to find stables close to his home, and he soon found himself immersed in the life of the local horsey fraternity, preferring it to socializing in the officers' mess. He was a flirt, and all the young women at the riding club and the stable hands were soon buzzing around him. And that's where he met the attractive thirty-four-year-old Marika, who shared his love of horses and riding. She lived with her boyfriend, Joachim, whose brother-in-law, Rolf Sander, owned the stables. Joachim ran a local meat factory, and Marika worked there as a secretary, having previously worked for the British forces. She supplemented her earnings by freelance journalism, supplying reports of local equestrian events to magazines and newspapers, and was always willing to lend a helping hand at the stables. She was well liked, with a good sense of humour.

She and Tony, who was 6 ft 3 in tall and good-looking, soon fell for each other, and those around them could not fail to notice how infatuated they both were. They took every opportunity to ride off across the heath together, and gossip about their relationship spread throughout the local horse-riding world and around the army base, so that when Christine arrived it was not long before she picked up on her husband's affair. She had endured this before, but this time it struck when she was particularly low, struggling to find a role among the other officers' wives and battling with her health problems. She was naturally shy, and all her life had taken refuge in her devout Roman Catholic religion, and soon immersed herself in the activities of St Martin's church on the base, going to Bible study classes and social events, as well as being a regular at mass.

She could not escape the gossip and the knowing looks. She tried her best to recapture her husband's attention: she went on a diet, bought new clothes, had her hair cut more fashionably, but nothing diverted him from his fascination with Marika.

On Boxing Day 1990, soon after Christine and the children arrived in Soltau, they joined him at the riding club for a 'fun ride'. It was difficult for her. Not only was Tony the centre of attention for many of the young women there, it was clear that he and Marika were an item, and the others accepted this. He was attached to Marika's side, his arm around her, drinking from her glass. Christine realized that it was more than just a passing flirtation; Tony was deeply involved. She did not know that he had already discussed with Marika his plans to divorce his wife and then marry his new love.

Tired of watching him make a fool of her, Christine eventually interrupted the lovebirds to tell Tony it was time for the children to go home. He refused to go with her, but said he would be back within the hour. She and the children waited, but in the end they had the usual Boxing Day meal of cold meats. She put a plate aside for Tony.

Four hours passed and, unable to stand it any longer, she drove back to the stables where she found the party had dispersed and only Tony and Marika were left, sitting together, their knees touching, gazing into each other's eyes. When Tony realized she was there he said: 'Be quiet, my wife is here.'

'You could see it was very intimate. You could see something in their body language. If you see two people like that you know it,' Christine said later. She stayed calm. 'I didn't shout. I wasn't angry. I told him the children wanted him to come home.'

She said later that Robert had persuaded her to fetch Tony, worrying that he had had a lot to drink and might be doing something silly. On the way home she reminded Tony of his previous affair and its devastating consequences and, she later claimed, he said: 'You must be mad if you think I would do that again.' He then, she said, told her that the other woman in that affair had taken a fatal overdose when it ended. Christine dubbed it 'another cruel lie'.

The couple tried to put on a show of unity for their children for the rest of Christmas but on New Year's Eve, after promising to spend it with his family, Tony abruptly left home at 11.30 p.m. to join a party of his German friends, knowing that Marika was there. Christine was distraught. Within a few hours Tony was leaving for the Gulf War, for a two-and-a-half-month tour supervising the repair of tanks.

All army families find the time immediately before a tour difficult to deal with, especially when they are embarking for a dangerous destination. The fact that he wanted to spend his last hours with his mistress was deeply distressing for Christine. She could see the writing on the wall for their marriage, but as a devout Catholic she was fundamentally opposed to divorce; she loved her husband, and she wanted to give her children a stable and happy upbringing. She was clinging to the wreckage of her marriage, yet she genuinely thought that the enforced break would give him time to reflect, and time apart from Marika might break the spell Christine felt he was under.

Christine, an experienced army wife, knew that contact with home was important, and she wrote to him every day, sometimes twice a day, sending him parcels of treats that break up the monotony of service food. Tony wrote back ten times, which was a perfectly normal effort for someone kept busy with his duties, but he also found time to write forty-seven letters to Marika, swearing his love for her, remembering their happy times together and pledging to make his future with her. Astonishingly, even though he was in the throes of this great passion, he also wrote to two other women throughout the time he was away. They were only penpals, women who volunteer to write to lonely servicemen and whose correspondence with him ended as soon as he returned home, but the content of the letters he sent them was suggestive and flirty. Of course, neither Christine nor Marika knew about this: and Marika never found out because the penpals only came forward after the news of her brutal death was covered in the British press.

At this time Christine also took on another family duty: Tony's mother, who was dying of cancer, gave up her home in Kent and moved into the house in Soltau. Christine and the old lady got on well, and characteristically Christine took on the task of looking after her willingly and tenderly.

Christine's hopes that distance would extinguish his feelings for Marika were dashed as soon as he was back in Germany. After greeting his family he virtually went straight to the stables, ostensibly to see his horses, but in reality to reaffirm his love for Marika. He later said: 'The war changed a lot of my attitudes. I saw how cheap life was. You think, "I'm only going to get one crack at this." I decided to change my life when I got back and marry this girl.'

It may sound like a clear resolution, but Tony was still vacillating between his two futures – or, at least, he was not yet prepared to stand by the decision he said he had made. When Christine confided in the wife of Tony's commanding officer about her husband's affair and the distress it was causing, an army chaplain was sent to chat to Tony and he brazenly denied the affair. Christine's anguish had also pushed her to see Rolf Sander, the owner of the stables, to ask if he knew anything about the affair. At the time Rolf could truthfully assert that he did not know, but after Tony's return from the Gulf the lovers became more open about their involvement, and had Christine asked the same question just a few weeks later, Rolf would have had to give a different answer.

It was at this time that Tony told both women he had decided on a divorce. For Christine, although the writing had been on the wall for some time, the cold reality was hard to take. The family had planned to live in Australia, where both Tony and Christine had relatives, when his army career ended; the dream lay in tatters. Tony, who spoke fluent German, now announced he planned to make his new life in Germany, with Marika.

Marika, sure of her new future, split from her fiancé, Joachim, and started to look for a new flat to share with Tony. Christine was on the verge of a complete breakdown. Many nights were spent neurotically cleaning the house because she could not sleep. She stopped eating. Unable to contain herself, she turned up at the riding club at times when she knew they would be there, and she slapped Marika's cheek on one occasion.

To get away, she took the children to Australia for a holiday, and when she returned Tony told her he had changed his mind and would stay with her. The relief was short-lived, however, because his promise turned out to be empty and cruel: he could not break away from Marika. That was the situation that came to its tragic end on Tony's birthday. Elated that he wanted to come back to the family, Christine booked a babysitter so that she could share a quiet meal with him to celebrate. But she quickly realized that he was at the stables again, and not to exercise his horses. She was sure that he was with Marika because he had showered and changed his clothes.

Christine set off to drive after him with no clear idea of what she intended to do. She said later that she half intended to kill herself. But when she saw the two of them together, she later told the investigators, 'a flood of grief' came over her and she got out of the car and started shouting and swearing.

> I saw them. They were ready to go riding and her whole manner towards my husband was as though he was still seeing her and was having an affair with her. I was so shocked. Things had been better between us for the past week or ten days. He had actually made love to me once or twice that week, the only time since before Christmas. I realized he had been lying, which was so cold and cruel. I just felt I was going to pieces. I was so hurt and felt destroyed. It was just unbearable.

Tony grabbed her by the arm, but she broke free and ran back to her car.

> I thought there is only one way out of this. I have got to do it this time. I have got to kill myself. I could not see how I could cope any more with anything. I could not see any way out of the nightmare and the sheer torment of it all … I felt utterly destroyed. All the grief we had been through and how hard

I'd tried to make our marriage work. I wasn't thinking about the children or my husband specifically. I felt I had to get out of the pain. I was going to kill myself.

She described driving towards the stable wall, and then found she was pointing straight at her husband's Mercedes, the car she had bought him. She decided she would die by symbolically crashing into it. She slammed into it at speed yet realized she was not even injured. She reversed. Tony and Marika tried to open the car doors and drag her out, but she had centrally locked them. The sight of the two of them together was too much, and she steered the car directly at Marika, who was thrown over the bonnet and then crushed beneath the wheels. Tony, who tried to drag the woman he loved clear, was also hit but only had minor injuries.

Later, when he talked to the police, Tony claimed that Christine drove the car at Marika several times, but her injuries showed it was just one catastrophic collision. Marika was still alive when she arrived at hospital, but died soon afterwards while Tony was being treated for his injuries down the corridor.

The German police handed the case over to the British Military Police, which was standard procedure for relatives and dependents of services personnel stationed there. But the German press and local commentators were outraged because it was a German citizen who had been killed. Marika's parents were dead and she had no close family, but she was well known in the area and popular, and many of her friends were furious that Christine was not standing trial in their judicial system.

Marika's funeral was well attended, but Tony was not among the mourners, with friends claiming the strain was too great for him. He also knew that press photographers would be there to capture his grief. But he visited her grave, leaving flowers, small toy ponies and love letters written in German. During the build-up to the trial he was on sick leave, and he filled his hours riding his black horse on the routes through the forest that he and Marika loved.

Christine came up before a court martial seven months after Marika's death, a terrible time for her whole family. The boys were initially cared for by friends, and then Robert returned to boarding school, with James staying with Tony. The case came up at Verden in northern Germany, another British military base. The court building is now part of the town's own administrative offices. The panel of judges was four women and three men, in compliance with procedure, which dictates that if the defendant is a woman the balance of the judging panel should be towards her gender.

The court accepted Christine's plea of guilty to manslaughter on the grounds of diminished responsibility, and the prosecutor told the hearing that one reason for this was that a contested murder charge would involve her son, Robert, having to give evidence against his mother. 'This would have a severe and detrimental effect on the young man. The ordeal of giving evidence against his mother and inevitably being cross-examined would be out of proportion to the gravity of the offence,' he said.

The main thrust of the trial concerned Christine's mental state at the time she killed Marika. She did not dispute the events. Two psychiatrists who had spent time with her gave evidence. Army psychiatrist John Coogan said she told him about her intent to kill herself and described her as being in a 'state of utter desperation … She retained just enough control to avoid colliding with her husband, who stood between her car and the wall.'

Home Office psychiatrist Paul Bowden gave evidence that her first suicide attempt, after Tony's previous affair, was genuine, and he testified that her responsibility for her actions were substantially impaired when she ran down Marika. He cited the inappropriate hormone therapy as a contributing factor to her imbalance. Accepting her mental imbalance, the court sentenced Christine to a one-year probation order, to be spent in a London psychiatric hospital.

Tony wanted to go back to work, but the controversial and very public case meant that ten months after the court martial the Army Board gave him a month to resign his commission. An MoD spokesman refused to give details of the reasons he had to leave, but Tony later said he had been told that if the court case 'wasn't excessively messy and unpleasant' he would have been able to resume his career. But it was highly publicized and, despite his bid to salvage his twenty-eight-year career, he had to leave.

He was bitter about the decision, believing he was being punished for what his wife had done. His relationship with Marika was, he maintained, a situation that many couples, including service personnel, find themselves in all the time, without suffering any consequences. He said: 'I think I have been treated shabbily. If I had been stealing or fiddling the books I could have understood it … My relationship with this girl was not based on illicit sex. I was in love with her and wanted to marry her. She was a lovely person to be with. We shared a love of horses and countryside.'

He claimed that he had been blackened in court, his behaviour accentuated to help Christine's case for lenient treatment. Despite this, he did not wish her any more severe punishment as a prison sentence would not have helped his sons, who were collateral damage in the whole, messy affair. She was held in liberal conditions in a flat supplied by the army, and her sons were able to visit her. She and Tony were divorced while she was serving her probation, and Tony was given custody of both boys.

21

Kinky Sex and a Brutal Murder

WHEN YOUR DAY JOB IS SELLING KINKY, SADISTIC SEX TO MEN with bizarre tastes, it can be hard to have a normal relationship with a member of the opposite sex. That's why many prostitutes whose services cover the wilder shores of sexual perversions find their deepest emotional attachments are with other women. Men are for business; women for loving.

That's how Christie Offord and Margi Dunbar felt. They met because they both made a living pandering to clients who wanted to be whipped, abused, insulted and debased. Both had had other female lovers, but Christie, as soon as she met pretty, blonde Margi, was sure she was *the* one, and she persuaded Margi to move in with her. At home the two women were a devoted couple, sharing their comfortable house in a quiet road in Hounslow, Middlesex, with Christie's two teenage children and the baby that the couple had together, finding a sperm donor through a gay women's group. Christie felt a baby together would cement their love, and that when Margi experienced motherhood she would be happy to settle down. The sperm donor, they were told, was a fair-haired medical student: Christie had insisted on fair hair because both the women were blonde.

Christie, who was well educated and from a middle-class background, had been in a conventional marriage to a wealthy businessman and had her two children. When they divorced she looked around for a means to fund her expensive tastes and support her family, and that's when she stumbled on her true calling, which was dishing out pain and humiliation to men who were prepared to pay her well for it. She left home every morning perhaps looking a bit butch with her cropped hair and masculine jackets, but otherwise blending in with all the other commuters, and made the twenty-five-minute tube journey to a rented flat in Queen's Gate, South Kensington.

Once behind the closed front door of the flat she transformed herself completely, only her tattoos – a spider's web on her shoulder and a snake coiled around her foot – remained of the respectable commuter. She changed into a tight leather outfit and pulled on a long wig, ready for her first client. Men paid £100 an hour (£300 today) to be whipped, spanked, chained up, gagged and were some-times made to perform menial jobs like polishing the floor while Christie stood over them barking orders. Her nickname, Miss Whiplash, was not on her black-and-gold embossed cards, where she described herself as a 'masseuse'.

It paid well, with the first two clients of the week covering all the costs of the flat. At home in Hounslow they had a swimming pool, and Christie showered her lover Margi with expensive jewellery and exotic holidays. When their son was born, Christie was at the bedside, holding Margi's hand and behaving like a doting father. Neighbours commented that she spoke about her son 'like any ordinary father'.

At first, after the birth, Margi stayed at home playing the perfect housewife. She came from a working-class Liverpool background, and had gravitated to London to earn more as a sex worker, in the same line of dominatrix business at Margi. Both were already lesbi-ans and had other female lovers, and when they met they fell in love and moved in together.

But by 1984, after eight years together, their relationship was rocky. Margi was not really cut out to be a stay-at-home wife. She had nothing in common with the other women at the school gates, and perversely she missed the excitement of her job. But the main problem was that Christie was becoming increasingly butch, dressing like a man all the time when she wasn't working, never wearing make-up, even buying Y-fronts from Marks & Spencer. She started to drink pints and smoke cigars, and began talking about wanting a full sex-change operation. Margi said it started to happen after the baby was born, as if Christie somehow really did think she was the father, and wanted to make the role a reality.

Margi was alarmed and sexually turned off, especially when Christie started demanding that she wear sexier clothes, see-through nighties, suspender belts and sheer stockings. 'When we made love she expected me to react to her as if she really was a man,' she said. 'But it was a right turn-off for me. I began to find it all very distasteful. I'm a gay girl and I wanted to make love to another woman, not someone who was becoming more and more like a man.'

The announcement that Christie wanted a full sex change tipped the relationship into violence, something both women, through their working lives, knew about. Margi had very expensively capped teeth, paid for by Christie, who in anger hit her lover so hard that the caps were knocked out and had to be refitted. On another occasion Margi tried to stab Christie, who retaliated by throwing a television set at her.

Fed up and angry, Margi announced that she was going back to work and did not want to live with Christie anymore. Christie was furious: she had grown desperately possessive about Margi, and the thought of her sharing her body with a procession of clients horrified her, even though that was how the two of them had originally met. She reacted like an angry husband, demanding that Margi stay at home to look after the children. 'She became even more jealous and possessive. She considered herself the man of the house, and the breadwinner. She said it was my job to look after the baby. She wouldn't hear of me working and we had some dreadful rows about it,' Margi said.

Undeterred, Margi took her small son and moved out, renting a flat close to Christie's workplace, and deliberately turning it into an even more elaborate torture chamber than Christie's. She had leather harnesses, rubber suits, chains, handcuffs, gags and other medieval-looking torture equipment like a rack, and also an electric hot-air paint stripper, which she said cost clients extra. Scrawled on the walls were messages for her clients – 'Lick my Boots, Dog', 'Worthless Slave' and 'Your life is nothing'. She also ran a transvestite room, where men could come and fulfil their desires to dress as women.

For a year the two women, Margi and Christie, competed with each other for customers, and carried on a bitter running battle over the custody of their young son. Margi wanted him to live with her, but as her home was now her workplace, Christie, who legally had no right to him, claimed that Margi was not fit to care for him. Their battle ended with the violent murder of thirty-five-year-old Christie.

Her landlord and a friend found her half-naked body in the bath. She was wearing bondage gear, was tied at her wrist and ankles with shackles she used for clients, and a rope was looped around her neck. But she had died before being put in the bath: her throat had been crushed against a wall by a heavy instrument and she had died in agonizing pain from being unable to breathe. The murder weapon, an iron bar, was nearby.

The flat had been ransacked, so the obvious conclusion was that one of Christie's clients had killed and then robbed her. That was the first line of inquiry followed by the police: they appealed for her clients to come forward, offering them anonymity. More than thirty men did so voluntarily, and another twenty were tracked down from Christie's little black book of contacts. They told bizarre tales of their own weird obsessions, but they were systematically eliminated from the inquiry when their alibis checked out.

Initially, Margi's involvement with Christie was ignored because it seemed as if the relationship had ended completely twelve months earlier. But as the police became aware of the ongoing acrimonious relationship between the two women, Margi was brought in for questioning. She had illegal drugs in her possession when she was picked up, and her behaviour in the interview room was later described by one of the detectives as 'right off the wall'. But after holding her for the maximum amount of time allowed, she was released. She was under suspicion, but nothing had emerged that tied her to the crime, apart from the fact that she had talked of 'getting even' with Christie and of arranging to have her ex-lover hurt or killed. She had an alibi – a client – for the time of Christie's death.

Prostitutes like Christie and Margi, particularly in their kinky and clearly dangerous line of work, usually employ 'maids', women who help run their flats, keep the premises clean, change sheets and towels, greet and entertain clients if they have to wait, keep a log of who comes and goes, more or less like a receptionist, and make sure that nothing untoward happens. Maids are usually women but can be male, working as minders as well as running the place. It's a precaution that helps keep vulnerable prostitutes safe.

Christie, however, worked alone, probably because she was powerfully built and physically strong, able to handle herself. Margi, on the other hand, had a male maid, a gay man called Tony who was imposing in size if gentle by nature. It was from Tony that Detective

Constable Peter Bleksley extracted the key bits of information that helped unlock the case. Tony talked about two of Margi's clients, naming them only as Barry and Bob, and said he had heard them mention the town of Littlehampton, in West Sussex. It was a good bet that two people had been involved at the murder scene because Christie could probably have handled one man on her own.

DC Bleksley contacted the local police station in Littlehampton, and asked a detective there if they had a couple of likely lads by the names of Bob and Barry who might be the ones he was looking for. He had an incredibly lucky break: the local CID detectives were able to point him to Robert Causabon-Vincent, a forty-two-year-old petty thief who first met Margi as a paying customer, and his friend Barry Parsons, forty-five, who lived in nearby Worthing, and who had also come under Margi's spell. They fitted the descriptions Tony had given, and also of two men who had been seen near Christie's flat. The murder weapon, the iron bar, was traced back to Margi.

All three were charged with murder. When the case came to trial at the Old Bailey in April 1986, Margi argued that she had only asked the two men to hurt Christie, not kill her. She sobbed as she said she still loved her and never wanted her dead, and was horrified when she heard that Christie had been killed. The threats she had made, she claimed, were when she was high on drink and drugs. She described how the relationship had broken up because Christie was becoming too masculine for her.

But her version of events was undermined when the husband of a former maid of hers, John Holmes, gave evidence that Margi had rung him in the middle of the night and asked him to visit her. When he got there she answered the door naked, and told him she had a client in the bedroom. They sat together on the sofa and she made him an astonishing offer: £1000 a week for the rest of his life if he murdered Christie. He said she was drinking red wine and was clearly tipsy. He told the court he knew that the couple had fallen out and were at loggerheads, and that on one occasion Margi had tried to stab Christie before Margi left the Hounslow home. Now Margi reclined on the sofa and said: 'I want to kill her.' She insisted she was not kidding and that she would pay him the money faithfully. 'I said don't be so stupid,' Holmes told the court. 'I told her I didn't want to listen to any more of this nonsense.'

The public gallery at the Old Bailey was packed with prostitutes: both Christie and Margi were well known, both popular with the other girls. At the end of the trial the two men were found guilty of murder, but Margi's conviction was lessened to manslaughter, and she was given seven years in prison. Two years later she was freed on appeal, but the appeal court judges said they did so reluctantly – the judge at her trial had been wrong to allow the jury to return the lesser verdict of manslaughter. Altogether Margi had served three years in Holloway, one awaiting trial and two since the trial. With good behaviour she would only have had another six months to serve, even if her appeal had failed.

During her time in prison her little boy, who was made a ward of court, had been cared for in Liverpool by her mother, and had been brought to visit her every month. After her release they were joyfully reunited.

22

So Much for Rehabilitation

'RACHEL, IF YOU COME IN WHEN NOBODY ELSE IS IN, PLEASE SIGN below. Because you have vanished we are beginning to wonder where you are! So is John, who says Hi!'

The students who shared the terraced house in Argyle Road, Oxford, were all worried. Rachel McLean, who lived with them, wasn't the sort of girl who vanished without trace. She was a second-year English student at the then all-female St Hilda's College who took her work seriously. She wasn't just a bookworm, though, and liked going to rock concerts, especially to see her favourite band Guns n' Roses, and her friends tried to persuade themselves that she'd simply taken off, perhaps with an exciting new boyfriend. But in their hearts they knew this was unlikely.

Rachel had missed an examination that week, something she would never normally do. She had worked hard to get to Oxford. She was the oldest of three children, brought up in Blackpool where her mother taught French and German and her father was an engineer with British Aerospace.

As for a boyfriend, she already had one, and she never let her love life interfere with her college work. She was a pretty, popular student involved in the life of the university, helping run the Junior Common Room, and in her spare time volunteered for the Samaritans and Christian Aid. She was a vegetarian and a feminist, but there was nothing militant about her. She cared about keeping women safe, and even gave up a part-time job in a burger bar because the management refused to pay for her taxi home after a late shift.

John Tanner, her boyfriend, was very possessive, and the other girls felt uneasy around him. They knew that Rachel was thinking about breaking off with him because in their late-night chats over mugs of hot chocolate she had said so, and they all shared her feeling that it would not be easy. He was on the phone several times a week, sent her letters and came to visit at weekends.

At twenty-two, he was three years older than Rachel. He was born in Hampshire, but his parents emigrated to Whanganui, a small city on the North Island of New Zealand, about 270 miles from Auckland, when he was six. His father, Bill, was a prison officer and his mother, Jan, a bank clerk. John went to Whanganui Collegiate School, and was a pupil when Prince Edward spent two years teaching there, and John was in his drama class. He was offered a place at university in Wellington, but decided to travel back to Britain and settled on studying classics at Nottingham University. He was popular with the other students, presenting a twice-weekly chat show on University Radio Nottingham called *The Fast Show*, played football on the university team and was student union rep.

John and Rachel met when he spent the summer months in Blackpool with another Nottingham student, an old friend of Rachel's. He found work at the popular Adam and Eve bar, and had a few flings with girls who were looking for fun. One evening his friend took him to another club and introduced him to Rachel.

There was an instant attraction. Despite his long hair and pimples, to Rachel he seemed worldly and well travelled; he was witty, good company and shared her taste in music. She invited him to her nineteenth-birthday party and they became an item, spending every available minute together during the rest of the long summer vacation. When they went their separate ways back to university, John kept closely in touch with Rachel, and the girls she lived with grew worried that he was too possessive about her because he cross-questioned them about her whereabouts if she was not in when he called. He travelled to Oxford most weekends, and the couple kept away from her friends, wrapped up in each other.

At first, like many victims of obsessive, controlling love, Rachel was flattered and enjoyed his attention. By the end of the first term they were still very much a couple, and he spent Christmas with her family. Her mum and dad liked him, but they didn't like the intensity of the relationship because Rachel was still very young. They simply hoped the affair would run its course which, had John had a different personality, it would have done.

Back in Oxford after Christmas Rachel was having doubts. She was moving on from John, but because his love for her was so overwhelming, she found it very hard to break free. Mentioning once that she felt they ought to cool it a bit, he countered by saying he had cancer of the groin, and that splitting from her would worsen his health. She promised not to break up, but she was not taken in by him, recording in her diary: 'What is really cancerous is the self-pity he allows to gnaw away at him and the vampire-like way he leeches my affection.'

On some level Rachel either still liked the attention he gave her or, more likely, was afraid of the consequences of cooling the relationship, so she fed his feelings by answering his love letters with equally romantic cards and letters. But for her it was just an exercise. On Valentine's Day, 14 February 1991, she sent him a card that read:

To my one and only John, the one who is with me through all the wondrous moments of my life, the one who holds me totally through the tears and shares my smiles, the one who prizes me above all others. To the man who has made me feel like a woman once more, who lights my fire and burns with me, and takes me to places of which I had only dreamed. To my John, the fulfilment of the heart and mind's desire, to the man of all I had hoped for, to the length of our days together, to the sweetness of the time and place that is ours and only ours.

Yet in her diary she wrote:

What a joke! I just wrote John's Valentine card, full of sweet pure words. Words that I shovelled from a fountain inside me, a fountain that has dried and cracked. Somehow I don't think he would have appreciated sweet nothings along the lines of 'you sick, childish bastard, you are so busy generating self-pity that you can't see how you slice me to pieces. I hope your romance (with yourself) lasts for ever and ever ...' Where does my venom come from? I was never so deeply in love with him. I loved the laughter, the tenderness. Where did they go? ... How sad it is to love a man only to discover that all men are children if allowed.

She wrote reams about John's possessiveness. After his proposal she wrote: 'Will I marry him? Will I get engaged to him? Will I let it roll on simply because I cannot be bothered to make the effort to stop him? The wolves are coming. I don't want to find myself. I want to lose myself.'

At the end of the term, at Easter, back in Blackpool, Rachel told her mum that she was going to split from John, and they discussed how difficult it would be. Her mother, Joan, drove her back to university on Saturday, 13 April. They spent the day together, and Joan left to drive home about 4.30 p.m. It was the last time she would see her daughter.

At 7.30 p.m. John arrived. They had the house to themselves as the other girls were not rushing back: Rachel had returned early because she wanted time to revise for her exam in peace. The next day she studied in her bedroom while John watched football on television. At 4.30 p.m. they were seen together outside the house, arguing. This was the last time Rachel was seen alive.

John gave his own self-serving version of what happened at his trial, but friends and family of Rachel's have challenged it. He said that Rachel talked about being unfaithful to him with other men, and told him she wanted to be free.

> She said she had deviated twice from our relationship. I was most taken aback and deeply offended, and to my deepest regret I called her a tart. She tried to strike me and instantaneously I flew into a rage and placed my hands round her neck. I feel I must have lost control because I have only a vague recollection of what happened after ... It was as if something snapped in my mind.

It was not only the word of those who knew Rachel that contradicted him: forensic evidence showed up his lies. He did not strangle her with his hands, he did it with a ligature, from behind while she was lying down. She had desperately and futilely pulled out her own hair to lessen the pressure around her neck. He countered this by saying he had no memory of the act, despite previously describing it.

After murdering Rachel, he claimed her body lay on the bed overnight. Despite his later protestations that he was deranged by passion, his actions the next morning were cool and calculated. At no point did he summon help or alert anyone to what had happened. He went to a cupboard under the stairs, where there was an 18 in gap in the floorboards, below which was an empty space. Forcing her body through the gap, he calculated which was the coolest spot, where decomposition would take the longest. It was more or less directly under Rachel's room.

He cleaned up all evidence of the attack, and left the house how the other girls would expect to find it when they got back. Then he boarded a bus to the railway station, and before catching a train back to Nottingham sat in the station buffet and wrote a letter to Rachel, saying he was writing it on the train. It is the handiwork of someone who was in no way distraught at the loss of his girlfriend, but was coldly building himself an alibi:

My dearest, lovely Rachel, thank you for such a wonderful weekend. Please excuse my handwriting. I am now on the train wending my way away from your smiling face. How can I leave you on the platform? I am sorry I had to go early but your meetings do take precedence and I appreciate how much work you have to do. You cannot read Dante's *Inferno* with a gorgeous teacher like me around – that's supposed to be a joke. I hope they give me another year because I do not think I will be ready for my exams. God, I will be thirty by the time I get out of university. I love you Rachel, can you believe that? Still, you will not be lonely – fancy seeing that friend of yours at the station. It was nice of him to give you a lift. But I hate him because he has longer hair than me – ha, ha! It is nice to know you will not be alone for the next few days. I worry for you being in the house on your own. God, this train is bumpy. Still, I had better go or I will get misty-eyed and sad. I love you now and forever. Big hug. Your devoted, John.

Rachel was not officially reported missing until the following Saturday, the day after she failed to turn up for her exam. Her flatmates had already been making enquiries, asking the college porters if they had seen her, checking if she had visited the library and they left the note asking her to sign in if she came back when they were out.

The exam invigilator was so surprised by her non-attendance for the crucial exam that she rang the house in Argyle Road, wondering if Rachel had got the date wrong, even though this would have been completely out of character. The college principal was told she was missing, and that evening one of the college staff rang Rachel's parents. They were used to Rachel calling them once a week, so they had not been concerned until they heard she had not been seen all week. The college, too, sensed it was serious. Plenty of university students are capable of dropping out for a week and turning up unharmed: they knew Rachel was not one of them.

Thames Valley Police were informed of her disappearance on Saturday morning, and at first they did not regard it as an emergency as they, too, knew of students who 'disappeared' and then reappeared at their digs later. But by Monday, with no news, the case was handed over to the CID. After detectives talked to the college staff, the girls she shared a house with and Rachel's parents, the report that landed on the desk of Detective Superintendent John Bound made it clear that this was a very serious case. Rachel was simply not the kind of girl to take off without telling her tutor, friends or family.

The house at Argyle Road was searched for clues. The first time was a quick check, the second search more detailed. John had written to her again, and he wrote about ringing when she wasn't in, and said he assumed she was in the library. Tellingly, the other girls were aware that his phone calls were not as frequent as they usually were, but he did ring a couple of times. He said in the letter that he was staying at his university and was looking for a job. The police read both the letters he sent, and they also read Rachel's diary, which spelled out her ambivalent feelings about her boyfriend.

Detectives went to Nottingham to speak to John: by his own admission, he was the last person to see her alive and was therefore crucial to the enquiry. He repeated the story that Rachel had accompanied him to the station and had then left with a male friend. He described the clothes she had been wearing, a black bomber jacket and high boots, but these were found in her room at Argyle Road, so if John was telling the truth she had gone home, changed and gone out again. Her purse and all her money were still in the room.

John was immediately a suspect. Inspector Bound found him strangely calm for someone who, by all accounts, had been a jealous and possessive lover. He didn't ask many questions about the search for her. The description he gave of the man she left the station with was remarkably like himself, and he probably deliberately wanted to introduce the possibility of this lookalike for previous encounters. The young man, he said, was scruffily dressed, with long hair, and aged between eighteen and twenty-two. A photofit was made and widely publicized because by now the media were alert to the mysterious disappearance of an attractive, popular student. But nobody came forward saying they had seen Rachel with this young man.

A fortnight after her disappearance, the police staged a reconstruction of what John claimed was Rachel's last journey with him, to the station. He strolled hand-in-hand with a young policewoman of the same height and build as Rachel, while a barrage of press photographers recorded them walking between the bus station and the train station buffet. Afterwards, John gave a press conference appeal for help in finding Rachel, and film of this event has since been used by body-language experts to demonstrate when someone is lying.

While the reconstruction and press conference brought no new witnesses to John and Rachel's trip to the station, it provided other vital evidence. A passenger on the bus remembered John on his own, particularly recalling the tassels on his cowboy boots. Another woman saw him in the station buffet on his own, writing a letter. Irrefutably, the computerized ticket system for Oxford buses showed that only one ticket had been bought from the stop near Rachel's home in Argyle Road.

Police also discovered that John had given a different account of his last journey with Rachel to his mother. She spoke to a local newspaper in New Zealand and said that he had seen Rachel climbing into a car with the mysterious long-haired young man, and that the car tooted to him as they drove off. Yet he had told police his last glimpse of Rachel was on the platform as the train pulled out of the station. Tellingly, for such a possessive lover, he seemed unconcerned about her going off with another man, even if he was just a friend.

Evidence against John was building up, but there was still no body. Gardens, woodland and scrub areas near the house in Argyle Road were searched, local residents were asked to check their outhouses and garages and police divers went into the chilly waters of the two Oxford rivers, the Isis and Cherwell. Eventually, a more thorough search of the house was carried out, and this time the cupboard was moved and the hole in the floorboards was discovered. A slim, young policeman was able to wriggle into the hole and almost immediately saw an arm. The body of Rachel McLean had been found, well preserved because of the cold void underneath the Edwardian house.

John was arrested while drinking in a pub in Nottingham. Under questioning he soon gave up his story about Rachel's disappearance and admitted killing her, breaking down in tears in the interview. There was criticism of the police for their failure to find the body earlier, and the girls who shared the house were understandably upset that, for seventeen days, her body had lain under the floorboards while they lived there.

In December 1991, John Tanner appeared in court in Birmingham, pleading not guilty to murder in the hope that he would get a manslaughter verdict. To do this, he needed to prove that Rachel provoked him and that the killing was a spur of the moment reaction to her behaviour, which is why he claimed she told him she had been unfaithful. It was a vicious lie.

He claimed that after her death he lived in a state of 'pseudo-reality', but anyone who had dealings with him during that time remembers a very cool, collected individual who was intent on throwing suspicion away from himself, and this was underlined by the video of his press conference played in court. He expected the jury to believe that the phone calls he made and letters he wrote were because he did not accept that she was dead. But they did not accept his defence. He was found guilty of murder and sentenced to life imprisonment.

Rachel's parents sat through the court case, and were strong enough Christians to afterwards express forgiveness and pity for his family. 'I think you have to forgive, otherwise it eats into your life and the lives of those around you,' said Joan. 'We feel as we have always felt: that it is a tragedy for him in his life as well, and that it was not just Rachel's life. It was him and his future and his family and his friends.'

It was magnanimous of them to forgive, but some would argue that their generous feelings were misplaced, and that the ensuing years in John Tanner's life have demonstrated this.

He spent eleven years in prison, and within days of his incarceration had established a penpal relationship with a seventeen-year-old girl. His arrogance remained intact, as illustrated by a letter he wrote to a friend: 'It [prison] gives me a great chance to sit back and watch the crazy world outside destroy itself by its own folly. It is rather like having a box seat at the theatre of social Armageddon … My chance to observe human nature without having the problems of normal interaction.'

After he was released in 2003, he was deported back to New Zealand. At first he carried on with his aborted university studies at the University of Victoria in Wellington. Then he worked as a personal trainer at a gym in Wellington, but by 2010 he was back in Whanganui, working as a baker and playing football for the Whanganui Collegiate Old Boys team.

By the time he was forty-nine, in September 2018, John was back in prison for a series of assaults on a girlfriend that have chilling similarities to his attack on Rachel. On a number of occasions over six months he had assaulted his partner, culminating in his arrest after one particularly violent attack.

The couple were living at his address in a rural area of Whanganui when they had a row. She was in the bathroom brushing her teeth when he walked up behind her and dragged her out of the bathroom and threw her on to the bed. He straddled her, slapping and punching her in the head and putting both hands round her neck. His partner, who cannot be named by order of the court, escaped and checked into a motel in the centre of town. She sent him a text telling him the relationship was over. John stormed to the motel, ripped off her clothes, demanded sex and hit her several times on the head.

In court the prosecutor Michele Wilkinson-Smith said there were similarities between this new offence and the murder of Rachel McLean, citing 'the loss of control and restriction of breathing, and the similar sort of domestic relationship.' Acknowledging that the girlfriend did not want to see him prosecuted on some of the charges, the prosecutor said: 'While I will always consider the views of a victim, the role of the Crown is to prosecute on behalf of the community. I have to lay the appropriate charges on the evidence that I have, bearing in mind public interest in prosecution and bearing in mind issues of safety for the community.' The defence lawyer countered by claiming that John had been 'dumped' back in New Zealand in 2003 without any support apart from his family.

At the end of the trial the judge, in summing up, said that during a different argument when his partner said she was leaving, John threatened to kill her if she tried. She did not take the threat seriously, said the judge. In yet another row he grabbed her wrists and when she was crying on the floor said: 'Look what you have made me do.' The judge commented on 'a tendency or a potential in certain circumstances to lose control'.

His partner said in a victim impact statement that she knew of his previous conviction for murder, that she was standing by him and did not want some of the charges to have been brought against him.

In sentencing him to two years and nine months behind bars, the judge said: 'Mr Tanner, it is not, of course, and never has been, acceptable for violence within a family context. You have one significant aggravating factor: a previous conviction for murder.'

John Tanner was eligible for parole in February 2019, but the Parole Board turned down his application, on the grounds that he had yet to address the factors that led to his violence against intimate partners. Speaking in front of the board, he said he accepted the need for 'a cautious approach to the resumption of his relationship with the victim.' He complained that he had only recently been approached about seeing a psychologist, and then his appointment to discuss treatment had been cancelled. He argued that it was 'unfair' and a 'burden' to have to remain in prison, while he could undergo counselling on parole.

The Board argued that, although he presented as highly intelligent and very articulate, he could not explain why he offended or how he could overcome that. 'It is clear to us that, notwithstanding his high intellectual level of understanding, there is still a worrying concern about how and why in the heat of the moment he reacts to a tense situation of the type that occurred in this case.'

The Parole Board recommended that he undergo counselling with a psychologist while in prison 'to target the specific factors which predispose him to perpetrate intimate partner violence.' Until and unless this happened, they said, he was a risk to his present victim and any other person he formed an intimate relationship with in future.

23

A Vengeful Suicide

DID SHE KILL HERSELF OR WAS SHE BRUTALLY MURDERED, WITH her children in the next room? If she killed herself, it was a clever and bitter final payback for the husband she was squaring up to in an unpleasant divorce. She left him facing a charge of murder, a charge that would rip her family apart and cause months of terrible unhappiness for everyone.

Recovering from the death of their mother was difficult enough. Monica's children also had to come to terms with the knowledge that it was their dad who had taken Mum away from them: and they heard the shot that killed her. But who pulled the trigger?

Paul and Monica Dunn lived in Farmington, New Mexico, where Paul was a police officer, a motorcycle cop. Monica was a local girl and her parents were well established and well liked, her father, Nestor Sanchez (known as Torry), running a successful electrical contracting business. They were pillars of the local Roman Catholic church, and they idolized their beautiful daughter, Monica, who was so close to them that she visited them every day. She had a baby when she was fifteen, and later married the father, Patrick Cortez, her childhood sweetheart. They were divorced a few years later, and then Patrick was tragically killed by a drunk driver, a death that deeply affected Monica.

Paul grew up a couple of hundred miles away in Santa Fe. He was only sixteen when he decided he wanted to join the police, and after high school took a law enforcement course and then joined up. He, too, had been married before: at twenty he married Juliet, and they too had a daughter, April.

Paul loved being a cop, and was meticulous about keeping himself, his uniform and police motorbike in perfect condition. He was a perfectionist, which irritated some of his colleagues, who found him arrogant and in some ways overbearing. It was no good a driver appealing to him for mercy over a minor traffic violation because Paul would hand out the ticket whatever the circumstances. He was not clubbable, not a cop who liked to socialize with other cops.

On the plus side he was good-looking, going to the gym to stay in good shape. He took courses, and did extra training in firearms, becoming an expert in accident investigation. He was also a popular speaker in the local high school, he gave talks to learner drivers and he joined the 'adopt-a-cop' scheme for younger children, visiting schools in his own time.

He met Monica at Farmington Police Station where she worked as a court clerk. She was a stunner, nicknamed the Hispanic Marilyn Monroe by the staff at the station. When they first met Paul was still married and Monica was dating a police sergeant, but within months they were seeing each other, and Paul split from his wife when April, his daughter, was only four.

They married on Valentine's Day 1986, when Monica was twenty-two and Paul twenty-five. They looked like the perfect couple and were blissfully happy. Monica's family were not keen on her choice though, referring to him as The Gringo because he did not share their Spanish heritage, and her brothers and sisters always spoke Spanish around him so that he was unable to join in the conversation. But her parents, Torry and Dora, welcomed him and he had a good relationship with them.

Although Monica came from a large family (being one of five), she was used to being treated as a princess, and Paul soon had to take on extra work as a security contractor to help pay the bills. Monica loved clothes, and was always 'dressed to the nines' according to the wives of other police officers, even if she was going to a baseball game. It cost money to keep her looking so good.

The couple had two daughters, Diane and Racquel, born very close together, which made Monica despair: she hated pregnancy, hated being fat, and didn't like the stretch marks or Caesarean scars. She found two babies hard to cope with and Paul, despite having two jobs, helped with the night feeds, nappy changing and housework.

Breast implants, paid for with $3000 from the boss of the bail bonds company where she was working, soothed Monica's self-esteem, and at the time Paul did not question how she 'earned' the bonus. Her new look made her happier with her own body, but not with her husband, and the marriage started to deteriorate amid Monica's accusations that Paul was having affairs. The bad feeling between them escalated and there were, Paul admitted, occasions when they were both violent. He later claimed she was always the one who started it, but it's clear it was a toxic relationship.

Eventually, after living with Monica's moods and jealousy for years, Paul did start an affair with a woman he met while working as a security guard, when she rode her horse across the land he was patrolling. Anita was the opposite of Monica, never wearing makeup, always in jeans and T-shirts. Discovering a letter that he wrote to Anita, but never sent, precipitated the end of the marriage. In the letter he swore his love for Anita, but accepted that their relationship could not go on.

Monica was not going to take his declaration of love for another woman lying down, she was used to having the upper hand in the marriage and if Paul was no longer hers, she was determined to make sure he was not going to be anybody else's. She made a scene at the bank where Anita worked, and then went to the police station (with Rick, her sister's boyfriend) and asked to see 'Dusty' Downs, another police officer she knew. She showed him a bruise on her face. He said: 'It was common knowledge throughout the building that she and Paul were having marital difficulties. It was an assumption on my part that the bruise may have been something partially related to that.' He took photographs, noted her concerns about the physical violence and gave her a domestic violence pack.

The couple were now living apart, although Paul had not moved in full time with Anita. He was still devoted to the children and spent a lot of time back at the marital home looking after them, including for a weekend when Monica went to Las Vegas. According to Monica's friends, he was still very possessive about her, constantly monitoring her movements, and her work colleagues later said she was often in tears at work. She filed for divorce.

Monica lost weight and genuinely seemed distraught. When Paul appeared at the house, there were acrimonious rows and on more than one occasion physical violence. Monica saw Dusty for lunch, and again he got the impression she was deeply unhappy. Then on Easter Sunday 1994 she paged him while he was in church, and when he rang her she told him there had been an incident the previous day. He arranged to meet her at the police station, and again she came with Rick, her sister's boyfriend, and discussed how to file charges against Paul for domestic violence. She also told Dusty that Paul was taking steroids as part of his body-building programme.

She may have genuinely been trying to protect herself from a violent ex-partner. Or she could have been making devastating accusations that she knew would cost Paul his career as a policeman, and she knew how much this mattered to him. She asked Dusty to call her the next morning, but instead he found himself at the scene of a violent death, and the corpse was Monica.

There are two versions of what happened at the Dunn home that morning, and nine months later a jury had to decide which one to believe. Was Paul a murderer? Or did Monica engineer her own death, making sure he would be blamed for it, so ruining his life?

When Paul arrived at the house early that morning he found Monica reversing in the car, with the children in the back. He didn't understand: he had arranged with her that he would come over, give the children breakfast, take care of them and do some jobs around the house, as he normally did on his days off. He even had the breakfast cereal and milk with him. They all followed him back into the house, and while he poured out the cereal for the children, Monica quietly told him that she was filing battery charges against him later that day.

Paul was devastated. Although their marriage had deteriorated and he accepted they would divorce, he never imagined her bitterness would cost him so much. She walked away and locked herself in the bedroom. He pounded on the door and she opened it. The next thing the children heard was a shotgun blast.

Amanda, aged fifteen, rushed in and demanded: 'What have you done to my mom?'

'Nothing,' Paul shouted. 'She just shot herself. Dial 911 and don't let the babies in here.'

Diane, aged five, was already calling the emergency number, having been taught in kindergarten how to do it. Amanda took over the call. Paul, not wanting to wait for an ambulance, half-carried and half-dragged Monica through the house, aiming to get her to hospital faster in his van. But by the time he reached the garage he realized he didn't have time and started CPR. When the ambulance arrived, the crew took over and tried to stem her bleeding but, by the time they got her to hospital, Monica was dead.

When the police turned up it soon became clear that they regarded Paul as the suspect in a murder case. They would not let him follow the ambulance to the hospital, and they would not let him wash his hands, which were covered in Monica's blood. He co-operated, telling them in his statement how she was sitting on the bed with the shotgun against her stomach, and when he came in she pulled the trigger.

Paul gave a urine sample to prove he was not on steroids and offered to take a lie detector test; he also gave a blood test for alcohol and drug readings. All the time he could sense that Dusty and the other officers at the scene did not believe him. He heard them talking among themselves: 'Monica would never kill herself'; 'She's too tiny to reach the trigger'; 'You can't kill yourself with a shotgun'; 'Paul always kept loaded guns in the house.'

Logic was on their side, to some extent. She was a beautiful woman with three lovely daughters, a loving family and even though she was going through a divorce, she had a lot to live for. As a good Catholic, suicide was a sin. And shooting is an unusual way for a woman to commit suicide. Also, Dusty had evidence of their abusive marriage. And why had Paul, an experienced police officer, moved the body, when he must have known that this would later be construed as interfering with a crime scene?

One of the policemen at the scene confirmed Paul's fears that he was under suspicion when he advised him to get himself a lawyer. Paul's choice of lawyer was inspired: he rang a friend, Victor Titus, who was only a couple of years older than he was. Victor had never been involved in a murder case but he was clever, determined and prepared to go the extra mile for his client because he did not believe that Paul was capable of murder. When he took on the case, though, he did not know that Paul was having an affair and Monica had filed for divorce.

Paul's family, his father, stepmother, mother and sister, all agreed that Paul could not possibly have killed his wife. But Monica's family all immediately decided he *was* guilty of murder. The two sides would remain entrenched throughout the investigation and the court case. The community fell in behind the Sanchez family, and at her funeral people wore yellow ribbons, interpreted as support for the murder theory. Paul was not at the funeral, which was mobbed by press cameramen. Soon afterwards a flag in Monica's memory was hoisted at the local domestic abuse centre. To the local people in Farmington, it was an open-and-shut case.

But not to Victor Titus. One thing that surprised him, and led to a massive breakthrough, was the fact that he was asked to be a pall-bearer at Monica's funeral. Why had her family chosen him? Especially as he now represented Paul, who they believed had killed her? It made him suspect that Monica herself had named her pall-bearers, and that the family were simply following her instructions. This meant she must have left a letter or a document concerning her death, unusual in a woman of only thirty-one. He knew he needed to see that letter.

In the meantime, the District Attorney, Alan Whitehead, was running with the murder theory. A first postmortem on Monica's body suggested that the shotgun was pressed against her abdomen, but a second autopsy found that it must have been held from 1 to 3 ft away from her body, making it impossible for Monica's arms to have reached the trigger. With the evidence of domestic abuse, he felt he had a strong case to arrest Paul and charge him with murder, two weeks after Monica died. Ballistics evidence from the scene seemed to make it an open-and-shut case. Paul was held in custody, with demonstrators outside the jail opposing his bail.

His main worry was the children, who had been moved to live with Monica's parents on the day of their mother's death. But to Paul's dismay, Diane and Racquel had been separated, Diane living with her grandparents and Racquel living with Monica's sister, Teresa, and now husband, Rick, and being told to call them Mummy and Daddy.

Victor assembled a good defence team. He persuaded Paul to take on a more experienced attorney, Gary Mitchell, and a private investigator, Dave Pfeffer, an ex-cop who had a longstanding working relationship with Mitchell. Paul's father and stepmother gave him their life savings, surrendering their retirement pot of $400,000 to fund the team.

First, they got an independent ballistics expert to examine the bedroom where Monica died, and a forensic expert on wounds to assess from the damage to Monica's body where the gun had been held. Their reports immediately reassured the team that Paul was telling the truth, and that the police crime scene investigation had been hurried and inadequate, clearly because they believed they had Paul in the frame. The defence team were convinced Paul was innocent when they saw the video of a lie detector test he took, after which the expert conducting the test said: 'I'm sorry for what you have been through. I would stake my professional reputation that you are telling the truth.' It was his second lie detector test because he took one for the benefit of the prosecution, and passed that, too.

But what of Monica's letter? Victor remained convinced that it must exist, but it had not been produced in evidence by the prosecution. On his instruction, Dave Pfeffer visited Monica's parents, where he wasn't invited inside, but he managed to have a conversation with her father both in the hallway and outside by his car.

Torry admitted he had liked Paul, and did not know anything about the alleged domestic abuse until after the couple split. He said his daughter was hysterical after finding Paul's letter declaring his love for Anita. He confirmed that he believed, deeply, that Monica would never have killed herself, and that she was now in heaven (her religion would not permit a person who committed suicide to enter heaven). At the last minute, as he turned to climb into his car, Dave threw in one last question, about the letter Monica wrote. He made it a casual, throwaway question, and Torry clearly believed from the way he asked it that he knew all about the letter.

He replied that the letter was addressed to Rick, Teresa's husband, that it was private and that he had decided not to show it to anyone. The defence team knew they had to see it, but they had to get a court order to have it released. It was a bombshell, written just days after Monica found the letter Paul wrote to Anita, which was a month before her death. It was handed to Rick the day before she died. She wrote:

My friend Rick, I am writing you this letter because I know I can trust you. First of all, thank you for all your kind words, friendship and your ear for listening to all my depressing words. I now realize life isn't fair, most of the time it seems very cruel. I have yet to understand why some people can be so mean. Whatever happened to kindness, honesty and caring? ... It's all very inexpensive, anyone can afford it, yet it is so rare.

The girls, please tell them that I love them very much. All

I ever wanted was what is best for them. I do understand they will grieve, it is a process everyone must go through, but they're young, and they will learn to go on and live long, happy, healthy lives, God willing.

Paul is not to get custody of the girls. He not only can't support them, plus I know he condones drugs. Dad has the proof! He doesn't have it in him to care about anyone else but himself. He is honest with no-one, so how can he even try to take care of them? He is a compulsive liar, not to mention an alcoholic, which he has admitted … The girls need stability in their lives, he has none. He's lost himself.

The letter then included details about her property, and the details for her funeral, including dressing her in a jumpsuit: 'I used to look good in them when I was a whole person. I am now a nothing. Paul managed to strip me of me.' The list of pall-bearers included Victor Titus' name, and also Sgt Dusty Downs. She was adamant that no money, not even from the sale of their home, should go to Paul, but should be held in trust for the girls. She added: 'He has hurt so many people in his life that I don't want him around the girls without supervision so he won't hurt them also. He can be very violent … When I am gone, the bruises on me will show.'

The concluding part of the letter said:

Help everyone get through this and remember, I will never be totally gone, through my beautiful girls. I am really sorry about this. I just don't have any more strength or power to go on. I'm tired.

I was fighting so hard and struggling so hard for something that I know was never there or never would be there. But during the time I fought I had no idea I was dead for him. If I had been told the truth, maybe, I would have some strength left and an ounce of dignity.

I look in the mirror and I see nothing. I lost myself to someone who doesn't even care. I was led to believe he loved me in the same manner I loved him. How can a human lead another one for years and years to believe a lie. I don't understand. I have thought and tried to remember where I screwed up. I must have been so blind or lost, really stupid.

I know I must do what needs to be done.

Don't mislead my girls. I could do that and be so dumb, never even realize it.

It was an astonishing letter, which more than anything read as a suicide note. But there were lots of ambiguities. How did she know she would have bruises a month later, when she died? When she said she knew what she had to do, did it mean, as her supporters suggested, that she knew she needed treatment for depression?

Her vitriol aimed at Paul makes it clear she believed she was going to die. But there was no way she could have known she would be murdered. Yet if she was intending suicide, as the letter implies, she certainly went out of her way to blacken Paul's name. And in the manner of her death she made sure he would pay, in the most savage way possible, by being accused of her murder.

The trial caused a sensation in the local community, and Monica's family packed out the spectators' area of the courtroom. Paul had been held in solitary confinement for the eight and a half months leading up to it because he was refused bail, and because cops in prison get a very rough ride from the other inmates. But it had been a soul-destroying time.

Meanwhile, there were more sensational discoveries. The private investigator followed a tip that Monica had been having an affair, and discovered that she had to have an abortion. As Paul had had a vasectomy after Racquel's birth, it was clear the baby was not his. Although the doctor who carried out the medical procedure confirmed this, the judge ruled the information irrelevant and refused to allow the defence to present it at the trial.

So, the prosecution argued that Monica had not been intending to kill herself as she was dressed for work, her face carefully made up, and when Paul arrived she had been backing her car out of the drive. Furthermore, there was a whole parade of police officers willing to testify against Paul. But there were certain areas of evidence that both sides agreed on: there was gunshot residue on Monica's hands, yet inconclusive tests for residue on Paul's hands, the tests being done before he was allowed to wash them after Monica died.

Astonishingly, Paul's five-year-old daughter, Diane, was brought in to court to testify. She no longer referred to Paul as 'Daddy' but, chillingly, called him Paul. She said she had heard 'bad words and stuff' on the morning her mother died, and then a loud sound, which she thought was a piece of furniture falling over. When Paul's lawyer asked her where she was staying, she said with 'Mommy and Daddy', who she explained were her Aunt Teresa and Uncle Rick. She admitted, in a whisper, that her new parents did not allow her to see Paul.

There were more emotional moments in court when Paul's fifteen-year-old stepdaughter, Amanda, admitted she had confided to a friend that her mother had killed herself. She denied telling Paul that she knew he didn't do it, but admitted telling him she still loved him, and she admitted she had never seen him threaten or be violent towards her mother.

But although all this testimony was riveting, it was the techie detail that undoubtedly made the case for Paul, and showed up the police investigation as shoddy and rushed. Ballistics and forensic experts picked over the details of the angle at which Monica was shot, the closeness of the gun to her body, the blood spatter, the tissue from her body that was displaced by the shot and the imprint of the gun muzzle on her wound. The second postmortem report was shredded by the defence, and a great deal was made of the attempt to have the first postmortem report shredded, which was highly unorthodox procedure.

In his defence Paul's first wife, Juliet, the mother of his daughter, April, gave evidence that she had never known him be violent and that when they rowed he simply walked away. She told the court April was made to feel unwelcome by Monica, and April herself gave evidence confirming that Monica was mean to her.

Paul himself gave evidence, emotionally reliving the events of his wife's death. He explained that he had moved her body in panic, trying to get her to medical help faster. In answer to the prosecution lawyer he said: 'I think we're all victims in this. I'd never seen anything so horrible in my life. If I see it again, I'll start crying. This will be with me for the rest of my life.' In the summing up, Gary Mitchell proved he was worth every dollar Paul's family had raised to hire him. He was masterful.

The jury was out for less than an hour, and came back with a unanimous verdict: Not Guilty. According to one of the jurors who spoke later, they came to their verdict within a minute or two of reaching the jury room, but had to wait because the judge had left the building. They spent the rest of their time chatting among themselves, not one of them raising any concerns. They all believed him innocent.

Paul's assessment that 'we're all victims in this' was true. He lost the job he loved, agreeing to be reinstated as long as he resigned immediately. He was paid $30,000 by the City of Farmington. Victor Titus, his lawyer, tried to sue various officials for their mishandling of the case, and although he failed in most, he was given permission to sue some of the experts, including the medical officer who carried out the postmortems. But in the end, the prospect of more years of legal wrangling made Paul walk away.

One theory that has gained some traction and is believed by the private investigator in the case is that Monica did kill herself, but that she only intended to scare Paul when he walked into the bedroom and saw her with the gun pressed against her stomach.

Most important to Paul after the case was his fight to get his children back. What would have seemed to be automatic on his acquittal turned out to be a long-drawn-out nightmare. Although the trial ended on 12 December 1994, he did not see his children over Christmas. On Valentine's Day, the anniversary of his wedding to Monica, the determined Victor called a press conference to alert the world to the injustice. But it was not until May, when Paul found himself back in court, this time fighting Monica's family for custody of his children, that he finally got to live with them full time. By then he was allowed to see the children every other weekend and on Wednesdays, but the Sanchez family still had temporary custody.

The result of the trial reversed the situation: Paul had custody but the children saw their grandparents every other weekend and on Wednesdays. It involved a trip: Paul moved to Albuquerque, a three-hour drive, to get away from the poisonous atmosphere in Farmington where many residents still refused to accept the verdict.

His relationship with Anita continued, albeit cautiously, and they did not commit to each other full time in the early years after the trial, which had rocked both their lives. Eventually he returned to Farmington, when Diane was eleven and Racquel ten. Six years after the trial, he and the girls set up home with Anita and her son, and became a family unit.